Can This Elephant Curtsy on Cue?

LIFE LESSONS
Learned on a Film Set
FOR WOMEN IN BUSINESS

DANIELLE WEINSTOCK

SMITH AND KRAUS
HANOVER, NEW HAMPSHIRE

This book is dedicated to my father

in appreciation of his support, motivation,

and creative contribution.

A Smith and Kraus Book
Published by Smith and Kraus, Inc.
177 Lyme Road, Hanover, NH 03755
www.SmithandKraus.com

First Edition: February 2008
Manufactured in the United States of America
9 8 7 6 5 4 3 2 1

Book production by Julia Gignoux, Freedom Hill Design
Text design and format by Kate Mueller, Electric Dragon Productions

ISBN 978-1-57525-568-2
Library of Congress Control Number: 2007939328

Contents

1

Why I Wrote This Book

Backstory

We All Need Strong Power Tools

Do you own a toolbox? A bright, shiny, red carrying case filled with hammers and drills and pliers and bits and maybe even a few items that whir and grind when you plug them in? In my opinion, a toolbox is a must around the house. Even if you do not use its contents very often, just having it available instills a sense of confidence you are good to go.

Many years ago I decided to build a closet in my mother's house. I gave little thought to the chasm between the requirements of the job and my skill set. Surely, if thousands of carpenters could do it, I could too with proper guidance. Since my mother was fortuitously in a long-term relationship with a building contractor, I was able to obtain the support and direction I needed. OK, he helped a tad in the construction, too.

What I found striking about the experience was not so much the difficulty in obtaining necessary information or developing certain skills to execute the project, it was that the job could not be properly completed without the right tools. Tasks that might take hours could be executed in a quarter of the time with the right implements. I just needed the right bale breakers, bradawls, dibbles, flails, grapnels, hawks, krenging hooks, bushwhackers, and trepans. I learned that being armed with the right weapons can make all the difference in the world in achieving one's goals.

With that revelation in mind, I decided to write this book. It is an account of my personal experiences as a producer in the film business, the lessons I learned along the way, and the tools I used to achieve success. By sharing these lessons and tools, I hope to provide you with fresh ideas that can help you on your own career journey.

As you read on, you will find I have placed considerable emphasis on stories that highlight conflict and setbacks. I do this not only to provide an entertaining backdrop for learning opportunities, but because in film we always start with conflict in order to find resolution. No one is particularly riveted by a story about a genuinely happy person whose life is perfect in every way. It is through struggle and sacrifice that character and people grow. It is through struggle and sacrifice that you and I will grow. That has been my experience both personally and professionally, and to make my points, I will share some of my most vulnerable moments with you.

You may wonder how a book about the filmmaking process will translate into your own personal experience. It is because filmmaking encompasses all aspects of the basic business enterprise including human resources, marketing, finance, management, legal affairs, safety, accounting, quality control, manufacturing and product development, to name a few. Then it compresses standard business time lines tenfold creating pressures and fissures that temper executives in the fire. What is accomplished in the real world at leisure is accomplished in filmmaking at a gallop.

Mix in work in every conceivable setting and at every conceivable location, interactions with incredibly difficult but talented people, oceans of cash, glamour, substantial safety hazards, artistic genius, the latest in fashion, repeated unemployment, and relentlessly long hours, and you begin to see why filmmaking is a practical microcosm of the business world at large. It is a useful crucible in which to hone skills and learn from mistakes.

I write this book to share stories. I write this book to encourage and motivate women in their business and personal lives. Perhaps I can spare women some of the frustration, pain, and suffering I have known. Perhaps together we can find humor and comfort in the similarity of our experiences.

I have learned to think fast on my feet; to become adaptive; to know when to concede and when to fight; to sharpen my intellect; to perfect my team-building skills; to maintain my confidence; to admit to and fix my mistakes; to take on or let go of personal responsibility; to accept my limitations; to preserve my integrity; and to praise and criticize myself, when necessary. So can you.

In this book, we will discuss personal development and how to manage others. We will address sexual discrimination, male/female relationships, responsibility without authority, and working with difficult people. We will analyze how to obtain what you want, how to balance work and family, and how to execute an exit strategy. And most importantly, we will discuss being true to yourself in all that you do.

We all share similar experiences. We all struggle, fail, learn, and eventually succeed. All it takes is determination and the right power tools.

ALL THAT GLITTERS

While this book is designed to help women in any kind of business, and perhaps offer useful advice to women in general, the stories I share are based on my experience as a filmmaker. Because some of the material may be unfamiliar to readers, I would like to briefly explain various aspects of the business so that my stories are more understandable in context.

Throughout this book I use the word *film* to include both feature films and television shows. Since filmmaking first began, these shows were photographed on 35mm or 16mm film. Thus, the name became a catchall phrase used by the industry. Over time, as technology changed, so did the film format. Today, numerous television shows and certain features are moving to the use of high-definition digital tape stock, yet the designation "film" remains.

Additionally, there are two styles of photography. The first, which we discuss most often in this book, is called single-camera, and the second is called multicamera. For years, sitcoms such as *Friends* and *Will and Grace* were shot multicamera while dramas such as *Law and Order* were shot single-camera. The difference is that a single-camera show will film each scene independently by moving the camera from place to place to capture different perspectives of each performance. Traditionally, single-camera coverage will include masters (complete coverage of the scene from wide angles), and then various close-ups of each character in the scene. Although the format is referred to as single-camera, it is not uncommon for more than one camera to be used. The important point is that the camera moves around. The completion of this process can take five to eight days for a television show and months for a feature film.

In the multicamera format, which is cheaper than the single-camera format, numerous cameras are set up in stationary positions to capture the show in its entirety; much like photographing a play. The show will normally be rehearsed for a number of days prior to filming, and then the entire episode will be shot in one evening. In the past few years, multicamera sitcoms have become less common as newer comedies such as *Scrubs* have moved to the single-camera format. As audiences become more sophisticated, they demand the cinematic look that the single-camera format provides. That said; let me describe, in general terms, the basic business model of film

Each show begins with a script. In features, a script may be written on spec. This means the writer creates the script without pay and then tries to sell it to whoever will produce it. Sometimes the writer will pitch (orally sell) his idea for a film to a studio, which will then pay him to write it. Only a handful of scripts go into production and make it to the big screen.

In television, the process is much the same. A writer will meet with a number of networks and pitch an idea for a show. If a network likes the idea, it will pay for a complete script to be written. Once written, it may decide to produce a pilot (introductory episode) to see if the show will have broad appeal. Once the pilot is complete, the network will decide if the show, among many available, will be picked up for a series. Once a network decides to invest in a series, its initial order will usually be for eight to twelve episodes. If the show performs well, or the network has high hopes for it, the network might agree to produce additional episodes.

Once a script has been given a green light (approved) to go into production, and the financing has been arranged, things begin to move very quickly. The network or the studio will hire a director and producer. Together, they will decide where the show will be shot. Depending on the demands of the script, the show might be shot on location or in a film hub like Los Angeles or New York. Either way, the producer and director will decide which sets will be permanent (built on a soundstage) or practical (actual location).

Next, the producer and director will hire a production manager, and the three of them will hire necessary staff. This will include a production designer, costume designer, cinematographer, first assistant director, editor, composer, stunt coordinator, hair and makeup stylists, and transportation coordinator. All these department heads will then hire their own staffs with the approval of the production manager.

All employment deals will be based on guidelines set by each employee's union. If a union agreement is not in place, one will have to be negotiated to include, among other things, salary rates;

pension, health and welfare contributions; working hours; meal penalties; and rest periods.

Next, the producer, production manager, and first assistant director will meet to create and adopt a shooting schedule that will determine the order in which the show's scenes will be shot, how long the entire shoot will take, and what elements will be required to effectuate it.

From the schedule, a budget will be created to determine the overall cost of the show. Usually, script changes will have to be made to bring costs in line with the dollars the network or studio has agreed to spend.

While all this is happening, sets will be built, wardrobes created (and/or purchased), props selected, stunts choreographed, soundstages prerigged (for grip and electric), locations scouted, equipment obtained, and actors cast. Numerous meetings will be held to ensure everyone is moving forward on a coordinated basis.

Eventually, preproduction will end and filming will begin. The day-to-day filming will be managed by both the production manager and the line producer to ensure that all necessary work is complete, all production elements are available when required, all spending is in line with the budget, and all personnel are properly informed about what is to happen next.

A daily call sheet will be prepared, which is essentially a work order for the next day's tasks. The call sheet will let each person know what time he or she needs to be at work. It will notify both the cast and crew when filming is to begin. And it will provide information on how many extras are needed; how many meals should be served; what additional equipment is required; and what props, special effects, stunts, set dressing, makeup effects, emergency personnel, and animals are needed.

Each day usually begins with the transportation department parking and setting up as many as twenty trucks to support the shooting crew. This will include work trucks for each department along with trailers for the cast. Most days start with a "prerig" for the grip, electric, camera, and sound departments. This gives them time to get their equipment off the trucks and onto the set. For example, the electric department will lay miles of cable to provide power for all the lights that will be needed. Separately, the caterers will set up and be ready to serve breakfast at the arrival of the cast and crew.

Next, the director and the actors will rehearse the scene. They will talk through the dialogue and settle blocking (where each actor will stand or move within the scene). Once this is decided, the rest of the shooting crew will be brought in to observe the rehearsal, lay down marks (tape the floor so actors remember where to stand), and light the set. Actors will be sent back to hair, makeup, and wardrobe to complete the look of their characters. Then filming will begin and will continue for six straight hours at which time lunch is called, and everyone sits down to a hearty meal. The cast and crew are given a half hour to eat and rest before they are due back on set for another six to seven hours of filming. Normally, a shooting crew will only work Monday through Friday; although on some feature films, the shooting crew will work a sixth day.

While all this is happening, the set dressing crew stays one step ahead of production by preparing the sets that will play the next day. On television shows, where numerous episodes are filmed consecutively, an additional director and assistant director, along with the producer, will be preparing for the next episode to be filmed.

The post-production department will edit footage as it comes in. Once the show is completely cut (edited), the director will make his changes, the producers will make their changes, and the network or studio will make its changes. Once everyone agrees, the show is locked. If the show features visual effects, cut footage (edited and locked footage) is given to the effects house (an outside technical vendor), and the necessary computer generated images are created, approved, and cut into the show.

In addition, once the show is locked, music is composed and/or existing music purchased and cut in. Sound is enhanced through looping (replacing inaudible dialogue with freshly recorded dialogue). Foley (sound effects) is added, such as birds chirping, sirens blaring, doors slamming, and footsteps ringing. When music, dialogue, and sound effects are all perfected, a final mix is made to properly integrate all the sound for good. Then the show is color-corrected (a fine-tuning of the film's color and contrast). Once all this is complete, the show is delivered to the studio or network and ends up on your television set or in your local theater.

While this process is underway, the producers must see to it that hundreds of people are paid, safety is maintained, unforeseen problems are resolved, cost reports are prepared, difficult personalities are appeased, failing employees are replaced, harassment or discrimination claims are addressed, creative differences are reconciled, impossible deadlines are met, and, most important of all, the story is supported in every possible respect.

There is more—so much more—as is the case with any business model. Entire books have been written to describe in detail what I have covered in just a few short paragraphs. But, hopefully, I have given you enough insight to realize that Hollywood's glitter rests on hard work, not gold, and to assess for yourself whether my stories and the lessons derived from them have merit for you and others.

FALLING OFF THE CORPORATE LADDER

Have you ever assembled one of those thousand-piece puzzles? You know, the kind you labor over for hours on end with little food, insufficient sleep, and infrequent potty breaks just to be rewarded in the end with a picture of Monet's haystacks and that feeling of complete satisfaction when you finally see how each piece fits together and serves the picture as a whole. Assembling a career is much like that. You cannot see the significance of each step without the final picture, and you cannot know if the puzzle will satisfy until you reach the end. Here are my steps so far:

My working life began at the ripe old age of thirteen when I was hired to clean my father's apartment for a pittance in order to "build my character," "develop a strong work ethic," and "become self-sufficient." I waited in vain for these benefits to uplift me as, once a week, I whipped out the old mop and bucket and got down to business. Lamentably, they remained beyond the grasp of my tender mind, and I was consigned to lonely contemplation of life's unfairness.

My career took off in my late teens when I was offered a plum position waitressing at a local home-style coffee shop that catered to the discerning "early bird special" crowd. Each night, I thanked my lucky stars that I was the recipient of not inconsiderable tips that might place me in a higher tax bracket. I became a generous tipper myself as a result of that experience.

During my early college days, I was enriched by the sales experience. Think high risk; think uncertainty; think commission only; think kneeling at the feet of others. Of course, I was selling the next hot thing in elegant footwear to the stylish. If you can do that, you can do just about anything.

The rest of my college days were spent doing a variety of odd jobs: running a small law office, scheduling temporary health-care workers for local hospitals, and teaching English as a second language to low-income high school students. It was while standing in front of a class of ninth graders knowing that few of them could grasp what I was saying that I realized striving for clarity would be a key requirement for career success.

Upon graduation, I went to work for a midsized accounting firm in order to gain the two years experience I needed for a CPA certificate. While there, I construed tax returns, prepared financial statements, conducted audits, filed my nails, became one with the clock, and centered and recentered my "wa."

After that, I dipped my toe into the wonderful world of entertainment. As a business manager to the elite, I catered to the rich and famous and sometimes financially careless. I helped purchase their assets, write their checks, manage their investments, monitor their insurance, and hold their hands if they inadvertently spent more than they earned.

Finally, I began my journey in movies and television and set forth below my résumé of pilots and shows. You might well ask, "Can't this gal hold a job?! Thirty shows in eighteen years!" I answer simply: Fits and starts. Fits and starts. That is the nature of freelance production work in the film business.

SHOW TITLE	TYPE	YEAR	CREDIT
She Knows Too Much	TV Movie	1989	Production Accountant
Hollywood Detective	TV Movie	1989	Production Auditor
China Lake Murders	TV Movie	1990	Production Auditor
Child in the Night	TV Movie	1990	Production Accountant
Working Trash	TV Movie	1990	Production Auditor
Seeds of Tragedy	TV Movie	1991	Production Executive
Carolina Skeleton	TV Movie	1991	Production Accountant
Burden of Proof	Mini-Series	1992	Production Executive
Criminal Behavior	TV Movie	1992	Production Manager
Woman Who Loves Elvis	TV Movie	1993	Production Accountant
Complex of Fear	TV Movie	1993	Production Manager
Harts of the West	TV Pilot	1993	Production Manager
White Fang	Feature Film	1993/4	Associate Producer
VR Troopers	TV Series	1994	Writer/Associate Producer
No Ordinary Love	Feature Film	1994	Line Producer
Midnight Edition	Feature Film	1994	Line Producer
Second Noah	TV Series	1995/6	Production Manager
Automatic Avenue	TV Pilot	1997	Production Manager
Love's Deadly Triangle	TV Movie	1997	Production Manager
Fantasy Island	TV Series	1998	Production Manager
Disciples	TV Pilot	2000	Production Manager
Freakylinks	TV Series	2000	Line Producer
Crossing Jordan	TV Pilot	2001	Co-Producer
The Agency	TV Series	2001	Production Manager
Hidden Hills	TV Series	2002	Co-Producer

"24"	TV Series	2003	Co-Producer
Cracking Up	TV Series	2004	Co-Producer
A Song's Best Friend:			
John Denver Remembered	Documentary	2005	Writer
Weeds	TV Series	2005/6	Co-Producer
Minor Accomplishments of			
Jackie Woodman	TV series	2007	Producer

While I have not yet completed assembling my career puzzle, with each new challenge and each new experience, I move forward piece by piece and take pride in the progress I have made and the lessons I have learned—lessons derived from my stories—not on the basis of one lesson per story per show but sometimes multiple lessons and stories per show, as you will see.

Won't you join me as I fill in the picture?

2
Getting the Job You Want

THE JOB SEARCH

SEE IT, SMELL IT, TASTE IT

What is the perfect job? If you could create the ultimate position for yourself, what would it be? Whether you have to work, or choose to work, time at the office will represent a considerable portion of your time on earth. Indeed, the average person will spend a whopping 110,000 hours—over six and a half million minutes—making a living! Minutes that cannot be recovered. But, please, not as a lawyer or hairdresser.

Unfortunately, we all too often allow circumstances to determine our lives. We graduate from high school or college and take the first position offered. We labor for years in a career that does not utilize our skills or challenge us. We rationalize where we are and what we are doing. We justify our situation by insisting we are content. After all, the money is good. Why change now? What if nothing better is out there?

From time to time, I am asked to mentor young people starting out in the film business. Too often, they rely on external factors to help them choose a career. They look only at jobs that are currently available or that will net the most financial gain or that have been easily navigated by others. They fail to look inward and ascertain what is right for them.

Indeed, the same is true for seasoned professionals: A career that was once fulfilling is now empty; an industry downsizes and people are cut adrift; new career passions start to surface.

I learned this lesson on my own a few years into my first career. I was a certified public accountant and business manager but realized over time it was not for me. At first, the more disillusioned I became, the more I fought it. I kept telling myself that my chosen career had many advantages. I was utilizing my education. I was on a fast track to becoming a partner. There was tremendous job security. I could practice anywhere in the country. The work provided the lifestyle I wanted. I even tried convincing myself that I had it better than most. But regardless of the dialogue in my head, the suspicion grew that this path was not right for me. I was dispassionate. I felt a constant drain on my energy. I was unwilling to extend myself or strive toward goals necessary for success. I finally had to make a change but what should it be and where should I look?

I joined a business management firm. The more promotions I received, the more depressed I became. I was disappointed rather than thrilled at the offer of a junior partnership. Ennui followed languor, which begat inquietude. I was ready, again, for something new and began to explore my options.

First, I looked into career placement counseling. I was advised to become either a hairdresser or a lawyer. Hmmm! Second, I tried using a headhunter. I interviewed for many jobs consistent with my level of experience but nothing inspired or excited me. Third, I tried reading the want ads. (Monster.com had not yet been invented.) Lastly, I considered going back to school.

As time went by, I became more and more discouraged by my poor prospects and lack of direction. Then, I decided to change my perspective. Instead of looking at what was out there, I decided to look inside. And I began asking the hard questions.

Did I want a career that was analytical or creative? I decided both. My education and experience were business related, but I felt I had a lot to offer creatively. Did I want the security of being employed by a company or did I want something more entrepreneurial? I decided I would not be happy with nine to five and two weeks vacation a year and preferred something less structured. Did I want to work for others or start my own business? I decided freelance work would be best. Did I want to provide a service or a product? I knew that I was a people person and decided service offered a more rewarding path. Did I want to manage others or be on my own? I knew I derived a great deal of satisfaction from working with others and felt management was one of my greatest strengths. I also knew that I needed a great deal of challenge and variety to keep me interested and engaged. I decided management was for me.

By asking these and many other questions, I was able to construct a template in my mind of the manner in which I wanted to work. But how to turn this into a specific job? I decided to start talking to some of my friends and clients to see if they had any worthwhile advice. I wish I could say they were all supportive and willing to help. Sadly, that was not always true. But overall, it helped.

The first person I contacted was a very high-powered studio executive whose personal accounting I had done for years. We had a good relationship, and I was certain she would be happy to provide me with sound advice based on her own career path. Much to my surprise, she was annoyed that I was leaving the firm and that she would have to work with a new accountant. Not only was she unwilling to help, she "encouraged" me further by assuring me I could not do better. Damned by faint praise, I decided to disregard her hurtful advice.

The next executive I contacted was far more helpful. He spent a great deal of time talking with me about my strengths, my interests, and my weaknesses. He told me that producing films and television might be the perfect job for me. I knew we were onto something because I immediately became excited about my future. Here was an opportunity to work in an industry that combined both business and art. It allowed me to work project to project. I could travel, meet new people, experience new challenges. How great would that be!? Only one problem. How would I succeed in such a competitive business? Thousands of people want to work in the entertainment industry but never succeed. What made me think I could?

Then, I received the definitive advice from another client. He assured me I would not fail. When asked how that could be, he simply said, "The easiest way to succeed, is don't give up until you do!"

Ahhh! That was how I would do it. I would not give up: end of story. (And in eighteen years in film, I have not.) Many of those years have been hard. I have had to struggle with personal failure, financial insecurity, fear, and self-doubt. But I have created the job that suits me best. A job that meets my personal criteria, utilizes my skills, relies on my education, and continues to challenge me. And I am happier for it.

I wish I could assure you that I have never wavered in my conviction. The truth is, like many of you, I have. I have questioned it and considered changing it. But in the end, I come back to it because it serves a purpose, my purpose. I enjoy the work each and every day, and if I have to spend 110,000 hours doing it, what the hell—in for a penny, in for a pound.

Starting out on a new career path can be scary. There is so much to consider, so much from which to choose. Take the time you need to know yourself. Determine what your strengths and weaknesses are, what your passion is, and how you want to spend your working hours. Look inward for the answers so that you will pick the job that is right for you. See it, smell it, taste it. Then you will know you are headed in the right direction.

> To find the perfect job, you must first look inside
> yourself. By understanding who you are and what you
> want, you will be able to visualize what is right for you,
> then gain perspective by talking to those you respect,
> then be indomitable in pursuit.

KINSEY MILLHONE HAS NOTHING ON ME

I always thought that if filmmaking did not pan out, I would love to work as a private detective like Kinsey Millhone, Stephanie Plum, or Kay Scarpetta. I admire their unflappable determination. Through intuition, relentless investigation, information gathering, and interpretation of clues, they always seem to find success. Just as a Supreme Court justice might.

A couple of years ago, I had the opportunity to hear Sandra Day O'Connor speak about the start of her legal career. Having graduated top in her class from an Ivy League law school, she sought employment with a leading law firm. Unfortunately, no one there was willing to interview a woman much less hire one as an attorney. Finally, a classmate and close friend talked his father's law firm into meeting with her. Despite her credentials, the firm offered her a secretarial position only. Unwilling to compromise, she turned down what to that point was her only offer.

Through extensive research, she found one attorney located in California who had hired a female associate. She journeyed to California to meet him and convince him to hire her. Unfortunately, he was not looking to expand and had nothing to offer. Relentless in her determination, she offered to work for free. It was a generous offer but he declined it because he had no place to put her. Ever persistent, she set up a desk in the corner of his assistant's office and began working anyway: much to his bemusement. There she labored for free until a position became available.

Years later, she spoke at a function hosted by the firm that had offered her a secretarial position. She thanked them and joked,

"Instead of working with you in your practice of two hundred lawyers, I opted for a firm of just eleven." She was, of course, referring to, and was the first woman to serve on, the U.S. Supreme Court. Justice O'Connor's experience illustrates the point that a job worth taking is a job worth searching, striving and stretching for; and I can confirm it worked for me.

After five years in the film business, I decided to assess where I had been and where I was going. Based on my experience, I knew I wanted to be affiliated with the Director's Guild of America (DGA) as a production manager, and then to continue on to higher and higher producing positions. Having determined my goals, I needed to create a plan to achieve them. My first objective was to obtain membership in the DGA, a union that primarily represents directors and their support staff. Not an easy feat.

The most popular route into the directors guild is through the DGA training program. In order to be selected for the program, you must pass a comprehensive exam, which is only given once a year, and then successfully complete a series of interviews. Should you be one of the few selected, you would then work as a trainee for three years to gain full membership status.

Once work as a trainee is complete and membership obtained, there are still a number of steps that need to be taken before you can become a production manager. You must work as a second assistant director and must do so for two to three years. Then, you must move up to first assistant director and then to production manager. Each of these steps requires four hundred days of work experience. Of course, finding opportunities to complete the four hundred days at each level is a challenge. Not only do you have to find the work, you need to find someone at each new level who will take a chance on you despite your presumed lack of experience.

I realized that if I chose this path, it would take me approximately nine years to become a DGA production manger. I was not willing to wait that long.

My other option was to work as a nonunion production

manger. If I could complete four hundred days in this category, I could present supporting documentation to the DGA and be immediately eligible for membership at the production manager level. Unfortunately, the obstacles were enormous.

First, very few television shows worked nonunion (perhaps 10 percent of all shows produced). Since I had worked exclusively in network television, I had no contacts in the nonunion world. Second, most of the nonunion shows paid next to nothing. But I was not to be deterred. This was the path I would take, and I was determined to make it work.

I realized I needed to rethink my strategy for finding employment. I needed to dig like a detective. I began reading all the independent film magazines I could find in addition to the standards like *Variety* and *The Hollywood Reporter.* I visited film schools and scoured their billboards. I even talked my way into an interview with the insurance company that bonded most of the low-budget independent films, just to increase my contacts.

Eventually, my detective work paid off, and I was able to secure a production managing job on a very, very low-budget feature. Not only was I paid almost nothing (about $300 per week), I even had to perform as an actor; not my strongest talent, as I shall describe later.

I should mention that low-budget, nonunion features have their own unique set of problems often attributable to inexperienced personnel. I, along with the rest of the crew, became accustomed to eating erect in the street when equipment and vehicles were improvidently placed. Footage of entire scenes had to be scrapped when the actors enrobed themselves in the wrong costumes. And I found chatting with a complaining actor in a chintzy, one-eyed, nose-bobbing monster suit detrimental to guffaw suppression. Nevertheless, I persevered.

Once I had my foot in the door, I did everything I could to build relationships in the nonunion world and increase my list of contacts. I made a name for myself and was able to secure other projects. I worked on two more independent features then struck gold and found a full-time job on a children's television series. A few years later, I gained membership in the directors guild. By being creative and relentless in my pursuit, I was able to obtain my goal seven years ahead of schedule.

Once you determine your goals, be steadfast in pursuing them. The more creative your approach, the more detective-like your search, the more successful you will be.

> **Be creative in finding that perfect job. Look beyond conventional options and approaches, dig deep for information. Once you have determined your goals, persevere until you meet them.**

NETWORKING IS JUST AN E-MAIL AWAY

So, you are either ready for your first job, your current job has ended, or your job is mind numbing and it is time to go back into the marketplace to look for something new. What is the best course of action? Where do you begin your search? Who do you turn to for help? Maybe it is time to reach out and touch someone.

Over the years, I have watched many friends struggle with this problem. A friend of mine who teaches decided she wanted to switch gears and become a business writer. Another friend who worked in administration decided he wanted to become a development executive. And my sister decided to abandon eighteen-hour days as an assistant director in film to produce television commercials and promotions. All these people had similar obstacles to overcome. They were interested in careers they knew little about and for which they lacked the necessary experience. But the challenge did not stop them from attaining their goals. How did they begin? They started with who and what they knew and leveraged it.

How does this happen? The key is networking. By reaching out to the people you know, the people you have worked with, you gain access to information, additional contacts, and potential employment that otherwise would be outside your knowledge. Networking opens the doors to numerous possibilities you could not discover on your own.

For some, the idea of networking seems daunting. They are not comfortable selling themselves. They fear they might be rejected. They worry they will be inconveniencing others. They lack the confidence to put themselves out there. But here are some examples of those who overcame their fear:

There was a time when cold calling or person-to-person interaction was the only way to make contact. (This is no longer true in the technological age where the world is but a click away.) I remember a friend in college getting up at 4:30 A.M. each morning for months so that he could place calls to advertising agencies all over the country whose names were given to him by people he knew. By placing his calls before a secretary could intercept them, he was able to make contact with ambitious executives who worked around the clock. Once on the phone, he lost no time in pitching his ideas. His approach paid off, and he landed a job with a leading firm.

In my case, I secured one of the most important jobs of my career by networking. As I mentioned, I needed four hundred days of work as a unit production manager on a nonunion show so I could become a member of the director's guild. Most of the nonunion work occurred on low-budget, independent projects; something with which I had little experience. I decided to go to the Academy of Motion Picture Arts and Sciences Library to do some research. There, I spent hours looking over every independent film and television show I could find until I had compiled a list of people who worked on them that I knew. From there, I spent weeks contacting everyone on the list until I secured an interview with a friend of a friend and finally got a job.

Another friend of mine wanted to work for a particular restaurant, though she lacked the necessary experience. One of her friends gave her the name of the head chef. In what I consider a move of delicious hubris, she walked right into the kitchen, found the head chef, and told him in as few words as possible why he needed to hire her. He did.

Some people are also full-time networkers. I work with a freelance set decorator who continues to network even when gainfully employed. She knows that staying in constant contact with potential employers makes it a lot easier to find the next job. For her, the tactic works. She is continuously employed.

Another friend of mine who recently graduated with a PhD in psychology found that getting a job was harder than she thought. Although discouraged, she decided to make contact with three new people every day, Monday through Friday. If someone was willing, she would set up a face-to-face meeting. Even if they refused to meet with her, she asked them to provide her with the names of three additional people she might contact. She thus had ready access to more and more people and more and more information and eventually found a job that was perfect for her. It is true, of course, that informal contacts are easier to obtain than face-to-face meetings, but either way each connection can provide a new set of opportunities.

I am often willing to meet with or talk to someone who is looking for advice or direction. I know how hard it is to break into the film business and, but for a helping few, I would not have succeeded at it. I feel obligated to give back and am happy to do so. I keep that in mind when I, too, am reaching out to others for help. Not everyone will want to assist, but many will. That is why I recently joined the producer's guild; not just for the mentor and the contacts, but so I could be part of a community of professionals who assist each other.

The nice thing about the way networking has evolved is that a request for help now can be less intrusive. Instead of calling someone on the phone and possibly catching him or her at a bad time, you can use the Internet as a way to make contact with minimal interruption. The recipients of your e-mails can address your requests at times most convenient for them, making it more likely that they will cooperate. E-mails also provide a shield if they do not want to get personally involved but are willing to offer some advice. And on the off chance you get a curmudgeon, you can spare yourself the pain when he or she tells you to pound sand.

With new networking tools at your disposal, there is every reason to reach out and make contact with as many people as you can. The more you network, the more friends you have in support. There is potential in numbers. And you can never have too many friends!

> **Networking is a powerful tool when looking for a new job because it multiplies known assets. With the Internet at your disposal, you can now make contact with all those employers who need you but do not know you, or know you but do not know they need you.**

INTERVIEWING

YOU'RE NEVER TOO OLD FOR HOMEWORK

I can report with confidence that a college education, a CPA certificate, and twenty-two years of business experience has left me ill-equipped to tackle my daughter's third grade school assignments. Woe betide the day she brings home advanced trigonometry and asks for my help. The best I can do now is to give her the skills necessary to succeed: to instill in her the idea that when she does her homework she should not just memorize but truly understand; to convince her that she should never rush to complete her assignment but should take the time to do her best work; and to confirm that she should not shy away from that which is most difficult in her homework but tackle it head on. These are also good rules to follow when preparing for a job interview. Cleaning your room can wait.

In the freelance world of film, it is not uncommon to interview ten to fifteen times a year for the right job. Since I so often sit across the desk from a potential employer, I have learned the benefits of doing comprehensive homework in advance.

Fortunately, in this day and age, information is plentiful. We need no longer roam the dusty stacks of the local library looking for timely and useful information. Now, with a few clicks of the mouse, we can enter the world of the Internet where all the latest data is at our disposal. But as I tell my third grader, it is not enough to skim the surface; diligence, commitment, and time are the watchwords.

For example, when I am preparing for an interview, it is not enough for me to simply know about the company with whom I am dealing. It helps to know what is happening in movies and television as a whole. What direction are shows taking? What is succeeding and what is failing? Which companies are merging and contracting with whom? What directors, writers and actors are most in play? Of course, each industry is unique and special in its own way. And each requires a different approach to gathering useful information. But the key is to take the time and make the effort to understand your target company and its industry as a whole.

In preparation for one of my past interviews, my research concluded that certain states were offering lucrative tax incentives that could have a significant effect on the show's bottom line. By discussing these options in detail, I was able to show the interviewer that I had a strong knowledge of film finance and that I was conversant with the latest location alternatives. I believe both helped set me apart from the other candidates.

Now I admit the preparation required active suppression of my procrastination demons. As a kid, I cleaned my room to postpone homework. In college, my cramming occurred so late I was unaware the library had been renovated. Without Google, there would be too few research chestnuts pulled from the fire. But suppress the demons I did, and my paycheck is (and yours will be) better for it.

On another occasion, and with the roles reversed, I was interviewing a production accountant for a new pilot. I was immediately impressed by what she had to say. Not only had she taken the time to research our company (a multimedia conglomerate), she spoke directly with other accountants who had worked for us in the past. She was well prepared to discuss potential challenges and offer possible solutions. Her level of insight left me confident she was the right candidate.

Naturally, there is no way to know what direction an interview will take. Perhaps all your preparatory work will go unnoticed. But on the chance that a good opportunity to demonstrate your skills does arise, you can speak with knowledge, understanding, and confidence. By weaving informed sound bites into your responses, you will show the interviewer that you care enough to learn about the company, to learn where you might fit in, and to learn how you can make an important contribution. You also show that you are willing to invest the time and effort to make a good impression.

I am personally impressed when potential employees speak knowledgeably about subjects that are important to me. The more informed they are, the more confidence I have in their abilities, their work ethic, and their potential for success. And the more willing I am to hire them.

The candidate who brings the most insight to the table is rewarded in kind. If you are competing with twenty other equally qualified candidates, homework is what will set you apart. Preparing for an interview the way you might prepare for finals can give you the edge you need.

During an interview, you have one opportunity to make a good impression. The more you know, the better off you are. Come prepared. Do your homework. Wow the audience!

Prepare for an interview with diligent homework.
Be committed, do research, take time, be informed.
It will set you apart.

I THINK I CAN, I THINK I CAN

Positive thoughts; positive results. This idea of focusing positive thoughts to influence behavior has long been a tool used by highly successful people. Visualization and affirmation techniques to improve quality of life have become increasingly popular. Health professionals adopt these strategies to help patients heal. Star athletes use these techniques to improve performance. In all facets of life, channeling positive thoughts can yield significant advantages. So how can we alter our thoughts to enhance our ability to succeed? Perhaps a little chug uphill.

Last year, I was asked to meet with a potential employer for a new television pilot. The interviewers would include the president of the production company, the head writer, a development executive, and the assistant to the president. Normally this type of meeting would not faze me, but the president had been the head of a major network that he helped create. His success was legendary, and I was concerned I might not be seasoned enough to meet his expectations. As the interview approached, I began to doubt my chances.

Instead of focusing on my strengths and successes, I obsessed on ways I might fail. First, there was the physical: the soggy handshake, the twitchy eye, the unraveling panty hose, the dreaded mumble. Then, there was the mental: What if I forgot facts? What if I was inarticulate? What if I answered incorrectly? What if I contradicted myself? I had yet to be interviewed, and I was already supposing I would not get the job.

The day before the interview, I had lunch with a friend and previous employee. She was in need of advice and wanted my counsel. We talked about her problems and ways to resolve them. We talked about projects we worked on and experiences we shared. As I sat across from her, I was struck by my own demeanor. In this setting, I was confident, self-assured, and able to give advice. There was no fear or self-doubt. I realized I liked myself a whole lot better this way than as that wimp contemplating a difficult interview. So what changed?

My thoughts; my thoughts had changed. In the context of a familiar setting, I was the resolute person I had always been. If I could hold on to those thoughts about myself and my experiences, I could approach the upcoming interview with confidence. I decided to try.

The morning of the interview, I jotted down the past accomplishments of which I was most proud. I replayed in my mind how I had handled different problems and how I felt about myself as a result. As I replayed my experiences, I was able to build a sense of strength and confidence that had been lacking. Then, I role-played the interview in my mind. I visualized the beginning, middle, and end. I saw myself at my best: knowledgeable, engaging, at ease. In sum, I created a vision of the perfect interview with me as the star.

By the time I was called into the president's office, I felt strong and in charge. I had dispelled fear and doubt and was looking forward to meeting and engaging a legend. I was struck immediately by how personable he was and realized he was responding to my confident and positive deportment. Had I allowed thoughts of inadequacy to manifest themselves, the interview would have taken a very different turn. Instead, it was a success I helped create.

Your thoughts are your own, and only you can control them. They are a powerful tool to be used wisely. If you want to succeed at interviews, start by changing your thoughts and feelings to reflect a positive self-image and a successful outcome. This is a lesson we all learned long ago from *The Little Engine That Could*. By repeating, "I think I can, I think I can," the engine made it up that hill—and so can you.

How you see yourself is entirely between the ears.
It will govern how others respond to you.
So, alter your thinking, visualize yourself as confident
and determined, and interview success will be yours.

RELAX AND ENJOY THE RIDE

Adaptation: a change in structure, function or form that improves the chance of survival for an animal within a given environment; a change in behavior to conform to the prevailing cultural patterns.

Does this concept have value when preparing for an interview? Will it help us be more relaxed and confident? In my experience, it most assuredly will. If we relax and adapt to the forces in play at an interview, we can put our best foot forward and enjoy the experience. Especially if it is a celebration.

Recently, I was sent to interview for a new half-hour comedy that was being produced by a popular late-night political satirist. Now, having worked in the business for years, I am not normally susceptible to stargazing or celebrity worship. Performers are just like you and me: no better and no worse. But this was different; he was my idol. His comedic brilliance, enormous success, and significant contribution to both politics and entertainment awed me. I was thrilled to be interviewing for his new show.

To complicate matters, the interview was to be held the morning after the Emmys where his show was expected to receive numerous awards.

In addition, in the weeks leading up to the interview, the meeting details kept changing. Almost daily, my agent would receive a phone call from one of the show's representatives changing the place and time of the interview and the staffers who would participate. Initially, the interview was to be held at the production company's corporate headquarters, then at an upscale restaurant, then at a local hotel. Each change affected the type of people who would be present and the number who would attend. With each change, I reworked my approach to the interview: the dialogue, the dress, the tone, and the professional perspective. But with so many changes happening so quickly, my head began to spin.

So, on the morning of the interview, as fate would have it, I found myself driving to a trendy hotel in the heart of Hollywood with no clear idea of who or how many people I would be meeting. The chips would certainly fall where they may.

I arrived on time, confident, and appropriately dressed. My group had not yet arrived, so I positioned myself in the lobby where I could keep an eye on the restaurant entrance where the interview would take place. I waited patiently. Five minutes turned to ten; ten to fifteen. With each passing moment, I became more and more concerned that the interview had been relocated yet again, and I had not been notified. Finally, I made my way to the front desk to leave a message. The hotel clerk, on hearing my name, informed me that the "guys" wanted me to join them poolside for the interview. "Guys? What guys?" I thought. And who conducts an interview poolside? While I wasted an anxious fifteen minutes fearing I had made a mistake and gone to the wrong place at the wrong time, the "guys" were catching rays and hanging out by the pool. Harrumph!

I decided to take a minute to regroup. I knew I would look ridiculous conducting an interview poolside dressed the way I was. I raced to the car, swapped my briefcase for a casual purse, ditched the nylons (with all requisite embarrassment; ass and elbows akimbo), and traded my pumps for a pair of summer sandals.

I also decided to take a minute to change my attitude. Since this would not be the formal interview I anticipated, I had to let the interviewers take the lead and adapt to whatever tone they set. I had to relate to them in a way that would make them most comfortable and would allow me to best present myself. If I tried to make them conform to my idea of how an interview should be conducted, disaster was in the offing. They were in charge of this interview; I was a guest at their party and had damn well better fit in.

And what a party it was! When I arrived, I found myself seated in a cabaña with five underthirty writers, all in various stages of inebriation. They had been recognized at the Emmys for their hard work and had been partying ever since. My presence was a small hiccup in what would otherwise be a day of fun and sun. I knew in light of their state of mind that I needed to keep the interview light and fun. There would be no room for the serious discussions that normally accompany an interview. Whatever my message, I had to get it across quickly and with humor. After all, who was I to detract from the moment? Indeed, I felt like a house-mother at a fraternity party and wondered if I should be apportioning booze, encouraging naps, or chastising leers.

I also needed to hide my disappointment. For some reason, my idol, the very reason I had agreed to the interview, was nowhere in sight. I knew I had to refocus my attention on the interviewers and eliminate any previous expectations I might have had.

We talked for an hour about the shows I had worked on, the people we knew in common, and their script in particular. We shared ideas and strategy and laughed a lot. I must admit, it was one of the more unique and, yes, enjoyable interviews I ever had. But it could have easily been a disaster had I not been willing to adapt to the environment at hand. The success of the meeting, and it was a success, was attributable to my willingness to be flexible and adaptable and to allow the process to unfold in a natural way.

What makes interviewing so challenging is the very thing that makes it so frightening: the unknown. You never know what to expect. You never know what the interviewer will be like. Will the interviewer be personable and easy to talk to or an ill-mannered bore who takes his frustration out on you? Will you have anything in common? Will you know the proper questions to ask? Will you discern the best answers to give? Will you be qualified? Will you have a clue?!

The truth is that everyone is nervous in an interview. But by being flexible, by adapting to the situation, you can remove some of that fear. By expecting the unexpected, you gain freedom. Though you are a guest at the table, like any polite guest, you must take your cue from the host.

When interviewing, pay close attention to the interviewer. Listen to what he or she has to say and what is being asked of you. Get a sense of the interviewer's personality and style. Take note of the tone being set. By doing so, you can adapt successfully and respond appropriately. By being flexible, you can significantly improve your chances of success.

> **Be flexible and adaptable when interviewing.**
> **Expect the unexpected. Take your cues from the**
> **interviewer and subordinate all thoughts of**
> **how you think the interview should proceed.**

GETTING WHAT YOU'RE WORTH

CAN'T YOU READ MY MIND?

How often do we get into trouble with a loved one, a friend, even an employer because we assume they know what we are thinking? Your husband gives you a toaster for your birthday even though you crave fine jewelry. Your friend forgets to invite you to a fundraiser even though you have already purchased the perfect dress. Your boss fails to offer you the new account even though you are clearly the most qualified. If these things are happening to you, maybe it is time to stop internalizing and to speak up. Unless, of course, you work for the clairvoyant.

Many, many years ago, I learned this lesson the hard way. I had just started my fourth project as a production accountant with one of my favorite employers—a man I both admired and respected. He was the type who brought out the best in the people who worked for him. I so admired his work ethic and motivational skills that I worked tirelessly to surpass his expectations. I knew as long as I strived to improve, he would give me greater and greater responsibility. Whenever possible, I would offer to do extra work just to gain experience and demonstrate my capabilities.

On this particular show, we were working on a television movie in a large city in the south. The show centered around a young black boy who was executed for a crime he did not commit. Because of the show's content and the complexity of production, my boss decided he needed someone to take over some of his responsibilities as a producer so he could be more creatively involved.

I was thrilled. This presented the opportunity I had been looking for. To work as a production executive would not only provide greater opportunities for advancement in the future, it would provide an invaluable learning experience. I worked overtime to clear my desk of as much regular work as possible to make room for my presumed new responsibilities. I waited patiently for my boss to call me in to discuss the new plan of operation. Prudently, I declined to celebrate in advance though I desperately wanted to notify my friends and family, buy a new outfit, order drinks all around, and update my résumé.

Imagine my surprise and disappointment when our production coordinator, a very capable and experienced woman, changed her title to production executive and began working in that capacity for my boss. I was shocked! She had gotten my job! I had been so certain that I was the perfect candidate; I had worked so hard. I could not understand how he could take advantage of me like that. I was furious.

Improvidently, I stormed into his office to demand an explanation. Once before him, I discovered I was too angry to speak. How humiliating is that!? I must have looked ridiculous: apoplectic on the one hand; dumbstruck on the other. Seeing me in such a state, this lovely man became gravely concerned. He jumped up from his desk and rushed over to comfort me, obviously worried something terrible had happened.

"Yes, something terrible has happened!" I blurted out. "You gave my production executive job to somebody else!"

What was so obvious to me was entirely lost on him. He was baffled.

"All the work I have done for you and this is how you repay me!" I (may have) yelled.

I waited while he processed what I was saying and began to realize we were speaking two different languages: Talk about apples and oranges!

"Danielle," he finally said. "How was I supposed to know you wanted that job?"

"How could you not know!?" I exclaimed. "Why else would I be killing myself to prove myself to you?"

(At this juncture do allow me to point out it is hard to stay angry at someone who looks thoroughly bewildered and utterly wounded.)

He responded, "Had I known that was your goal, I would, of course, have considered you for the job. But you never expressed an interest in moving in that direction."

(Now listen up folks, because here comes the punch line.) He continued, "You can't assume people know what it is you want just because you're thinking it. I can't be expected to read your mind!"

Oh! Whoops. As much as I hated to admit it, he was right. I did not know whether to laugh or cry. I quickly realized that in all the time we had worked together, I had never shared my goals and aspirations. I just assumed he would figure it out on his own. By making such an erroneous assumption, I had done myself a disservice.

The next three months were incredibly difficult. I had to watch someone else do the job I wanted and do it well. But I came away with a better understanding of the need to communicate clearly. And because I finally spoke up and asked for what I wanted, I was given the promotion the very next show. Fortunately, my boss was a fair and reasonable man, willing to help me learn from my mistakes.

Do not let opportunities pass you by because you are afraid to speak up. Do not assume someone else will intuitively know what it is you want just because you are thinking it. People are not mind readers. They need to hear from you to fully understand what you are after.

Never assume someone else will know what you want. Speak up. In a busy world, quiet excellence is all too often recognized but unrewarded.

NEVER UP, NEVER IN

We have all experienced movies that resonate with us: films whose characters, story lines, and visual images remain in our memory years after we have seen them. One of those films for me is *Oliver*. It is the story of a young boy in an oppressive orphanage who is thrust into a harsh world and finds a better future. Most memorable is the scene in which Oliver returns to the food line at the orphanage for a second helping and asks, "Please, sir, may I have some more?" His ill-fated words cause him to be expelled from the orphanage because no one ever had the temerity to make such a request before. One could argue that Oliver showed either great courage or incredible naïveté. Either way, he stood up and asked for what he wanted. Go Oliver!

Now, it happens that I do not generally recognize male/female stereotypes. But in the eighteen years I have been in the film business, I have seen a difference time and again between men and women in their willingness to negotiate aggressively on their own behalf. Men are simply more willing to take risks and ask for what they believe they deserve. Women, not wanting to be confrontational and always wanting to please, tend to compromise their requirements.

To illustrate, let me share an experience with you that was a revelation to me. I had been asked to take over production of a television show in its third season. Because the cast and crew were well established, I did not need to find, interview, or hire new people. I did, however, have to renegotiate salaries for all the returning staffers. The show was very popular and had garnered a great deal of notoriety. I felt, as did others involved, that the success of the show should be shared; everyone should benefit in some way. All those who had been involved in the establishment of the show, whether they cooked meals, sewed costumes, or acted on-screen, had made significant contributions and deserved to be recognized. In considering raises, I tried to be fair not only to the returning employees but to the parent company as well, taking into account its fiscal policies and guidelines.

Most of the negotiations went well. We were able to strike a balance between the individual's performance and the company's requirements—with the exception of one particular employee. The gentlemen in question was the production designer on the show. He had been with the series since its inception and had done a beautiful job. No one disputed his value or contribution. Most everyone wanted him to return for another year. But when he made his request for a salary increase, word of it got out and a shock wave rippled through the company.

No one had ever made such an overblown request before. It was so far beyond anything production management considered reasonable that we were stunned. My first thought was that it was ridiculous. Yet, to my surprise, he stood firm in his demands.

What I found illuminating was my reaction to his request. I was deeply offended on a personal level. Who did he think he was? Could he possibly be that egotistical? I began to dislike him solely on his unwillingness to compromise. To me, he was arrogant and self-centered and completely unrealistic about his worth.

Conversely, I took pride in my own sense of worth and fair play knowing I would never do what he was doing.

I determined we could not possibly meet his compensation demands when others were getting so much less. And I was relieved when the company backed me. I was told to quickly look for a replacement, and I did. In fact, the phrase "strutting peacock" comes to mind when I recall my boasts to co-workers that I had single-handedly prevented a gross injustice.

But then the tide turned. As the actors, directors, and other producers got involved, it became clear they wanted the production designer to stay, at almost any cost. We debated for days until we were forced by senior management to acquiesce to his demands.

At first, I felt betrayed. I felt the company should have supported me and refused a disproportionate raise for one when others received so much less. While the rest of the crew received a 4 percent increase, the production designer received a whopping 50 percent gain.

As time passed, I was compelled to look at the situation somewhat differently. After all, business is business, and the purpose of business is to make money. No one faults a corporation for competitive business practices or hardball negotiations. Why should they fault an individual? Why should I fault an individual?

I had to accept that this employee's request was not a personal affront. He was merely asking for what he felt he deserved. It was up to us to agree or not. Ultimately, we had the right to refuse. In this case, the company chose to agree. And once that decision was made, it was my job to accept it and to create the best working environment possible.

Work is not a humanitarian effort; it is not a philanthropy for which we volunteer. We work for a variety of reasons, one of which is to earn as much as we possibly can. In the end, the production designer's firmness paid off, and I had to recognize that his success took courage and the willingness to take a huge risk.

I also had to admit that he had done something I was not yet able to do myself. Too frequently, I chose the path of least resistance. Too frequently, I agreed to a contract that was not always in my best interest. I planned to change that.

So why then do we, resolute women all, fail to speak up and ask for more? Whatever our reasons, we need to recognize our contribution, find our inner strength and make our voice heard. For heavens sake, *speak up*! Let people know you are a force to be reckoned with. Ask for what you deserve. The worst that can happen is they say no, and you are back where you started. But if they say yes, now that is an accomplishment.

> **Do not be afraid to ask for what you deserve;**
> **for what you are worth. Hold out for it if you can.**
> **Show how much you value yourself and**
> **open the door to fair compensation.**

TURNING DOWN THE WRONG JOB

IT'S JUST MONEY AND NICE RESTAURANTS

Many of us are slaves to our jobs. We work to pay the mortgage, the car payments, the ever-mounting pile of bills. We become responsible adults buried in debt. Living this way, paycheck to paycheck, robs us of the freedom to love the work we do. Instead, we simply work to live. All too often we find ourselves in situations where we can no longer bear the work we are doing or maintain the fiction we are fairly compensated. But we cannot walk away from a job that does not satisfy if we are obsessed with the money it provides. Unless, of course, we apply the lottery test.

I found myself facing this very kind of balancing dilemma not too long ago. I had been invited back to the second season of an edgy comedy series to work as a co-producer. Despite a somewhat extensive negotiation, we could not agree on the terms of my contract. As with others who have been in similar situations, I was deeply concerned about being out of work.

On the one hand, I felt I would be compromising my integrity by agreeing to a deal that did not compensate me fairly. On the other hand, I had grave concerns about turning down long-term employment that would provide a substantial source of income. I really had to struggle with my decision.

But if I did not stand up for what I felt I deserved, no one else would take me seriously. I owed it to myself to demand what I thought was fair given my level of experience and the contribution I had made in the past. Unfortunately, my potential employer could not or would not agree to my terms.

So I had to ask myself: How important was the job and the money it would provide? If I accepted it as offered, would I regret my decision? Would I feel taken advantage of? Would it affect my approach to work?

After careful consideration, the answer was yes on all counts. I had to take the risk and turn the job down because it was not right for me. I wish I could tell you that the money did not matter, but it did. But I also knew that with some significant lifestyle changes, I could make ends meet for a while and that was good enough for me. I decided to embrace curly mac and cheese and coupon cutting.

I turned down the job because I knew exactly what would have happened had I absolutely needed that paycheck to pay the next month's mortgage. I would have gone to work each day feeling unappreciated. I would not have given 125 percent when I was being compensated at 75 percent. I would have felt my reputation as a hard-nosed negotiator had been severely compromised.

The fact that I had enough of a nest egg to get by made it possible for me to have choices and ultimately to make the right work decision for me. In retrospect, I feel confident I did what was best given the circumstances. But there were even larger social pressures I had to overcome because of their debilitating effect on me.

We have become a society that feeds on conspicuous consumption. Our homes keep getting bigger, our cars more expensive, our toys more plentiful. But these assets do not provide a level of happiness that exceeds the sense of security and freedom a little savings can provide. Love affairs with new purchases are short lived: the car stops smelling new, the boat spends more time on a trailer than in the water—but the payments keep coming. Damn it, I wanted these things! Advertisers told me I needed these things.

Yet, I finally learned that being able to say "so long" to an unfulfilling job is a bigger pleasure that lasts and a more satisfying philosophy that works.

So good-bye for a while to the luxuries—nice restaurants, expensive vacations, days at the spa—all the yummies. Sometimes, you just have to be willing to forgo a few of life's pleasures to reach higher goals.

A good way to understand how money affects people's work lives is to ask what they would do if they won the lottery. Those that work to live will change everything about their present situation, including most certainly their jobs. Those that live to work will probably buy a few things and give the rest to family and the needy.

So set yourself up to make work decisions that are right for you. Give yourself enough of a nest egg to walk away from any employment situation that is not satisfying and fulfilling. You deserve to be in a job that supports you, fairly compensates you, and provides you with fulfillment. Otherwise, you are simply clocking in and possibly watching your life unspool purposelessly.

Money alone is the root of a bad job choice.
Live to work. It is more satisfying than toys.
Have the wisdom to maintain a nest egg and the
integrity to decline unfulfilling employment.

BE BRAVE, LITTLE BUCKAROO

What happens when we decide our present job is not satisfying or we are offered a position that does not meet our requirements? We talked of nest eggs and integrity. But what else is required to subordinate the need for security and take a risk? How do we stare down our fears and jump into the void? A leap of faith, perhaps?

In the last decade, we have seen a huge increase in the number of people leaving the conventional workforce to start their own businesses. No longer content to see someone else benefit from their labor, they want to profit from their own ability. Even those who choose to work for others are frequently changing jobs in search of something better. No longer are people willing to make a lifetime commitment to one organization. A gold watch in exchange for years of service is not enough.

I remember struggling with this issue. I had been asked to return for another season of a show I had production managed. The first season was terribly unpleasant, and I promised myself I would not go back under any circumstances. But three months of unemployment made me reconsider. When the call came asking me to return, I debated doing so. I used every rationalization I could think of to convince myself that taking the job was the right choice. But the truth was, I was simply afraid I would not get anything better. Instead of seeing the glass half full, I had become the kind of person who saw it half empty. Trite but true. I let fear and my personal insecurity lead me toward compromise.

As I was about to accept the offer, a friend and co-worker called. I told her what was going on; that in light of my present situation, I needed to accept the offer or risk having no job at all.

She asked me a few questions. First, she asked, "How long have you worked in this business?"

"Thirteen years," I responded.

"And in all that time, have you ever gone without work for an extended period of time?"

I thought about that for a while and realized that I had lost sight of the big picture. Sure, like most freelancers, I had my dry spells. Yes, I had gone months without work. But work always came. I had always been able to make a good living.

She then asked, "How will you feel if you take this job and a better one comes along tomorrow?"

Absolutely awful, I thought. I knew I needed to trust myself, my reputation, and my experience. This was not going to be the last job I was offered. There would be many more.

I gathered my courage, trusted my future, and turned the job down because it was not right for me. In doing so, I gave up forty-five weeks of employment. But they would have been forty-five stressful, unfulfilling weeks. I deserved better.

Whenever I have to take a risk, I take comfort from looking at well-known entrepreneurs who have met far greater challenges. Fred Smith, the founder of Fed Ex, created the idea for his company while writing a term paper as a graduate student at Yale. The paper earned him a C. Yet despite the negative feedback and the odds he faced, he created one of the most successful companies in the world.

David Neeleman, founder of Jet Blue, watched his first travel agency go bust, was ousted when his company merged with Southwest Airlines, and was forced to "stand by" for five years as a result of a noncompete agreement. Yet, Jet Blue is one of the more profitable airlines flying today.

Finally, let us not forget Milton Hershey. It took two failed attempts at starting candy companies before he got it right. Now Hershey Chocolate is one of the most widely sold products in the United States.

When you look at the risks these leaders of industry have taken, somehow walking away from a job that is not right does not seem so intimidating. Sometimes the most difficult decisions prove to be the most successful. It takes risk to earn reward.

Looking back at my situation, the risk paid off. Shortly after turning down the show, I was called to produce a new series. The credit and financial compensation were far better then what I had been offered. The job responsibilities were more interesting. The people were fantastic. All in all, it turned out to be a truly rewarding experience.

It is clear people who succeed in life are the ones willing to take risks. They are unwavering in their confidence in themselves and the belief that something better is out there. Do not let fear deter you from doing what is right for you.

Sometimes we must buttress our resolve, stare down our fear, and take a risk. Turning down the wrong job may be one of the hardest things you do, but it frees you for something better.

SUMMARY OF RULES

THE JOB SEARCH

RULE 1 To find the perfect job, you must first look inside yourself. By understanding who you are and what you want, you will be able to visualize what is right for you, then gain perspective by talking to those you respect, then be indomitable in pursuit.

RULE 2 Be creative in finding that perfect job. Look beyond conventional options and approaches, dig deep for information. Once you have determined your goals, persevere until you meet them.

RULE 3 Networking is a powerful tool when looking for a new job because it multiplies known assets. With the Internet at your disposal, you can now make contact with all those employers who need you but do not know you, or know you but do not know they need you.

INTERVIEWING

RULE 1 Prepare for an interview with diligent homework. Be committed, do research, take time, be informed. It will set you apart.

RULE 2 How you see yourself is entirely between the ears. It will govern how others respond to you. So, alter your thinking, visualize yourself as confident and determined, and interview success will be yours.

RULE 3 Be flexible and adaptable when interviewing. Expect the unexpected. Take your cues from the interviewer and subordinate all thoughts of how you think the interview should proceed.

GETTING WHAT YOU'RE WORTH

RULE 1   Never assume someone else will know what you want. Speak up. In a busy world, quiet excellence is all too often recognized but unrewarded.

RULE 2   Do not be afraid to ask for what you deserve; for what you are worth. Hold out for it if you can. Show how much you value yourself and open the door to fair compensation.

TURNING DOWN THE WRONG JOB

RULE 1   Money alone is the root of a bad job choice. Live to work. It is more satisfying than toys. Have the wisdom to maintain a nest egg and the integrity to decline unfulfilling employment.

RULE 2   Sometimes we must buttress our resolve, stare down our fear, and take a risk. Turning down the wrong job may be one of the hardest things you do, but it frees you for something better.

3

Personal Development

FOLLOWING YOUR PASSION

MONEY FOLLOWS FUN AROUND

What if money had a conscience? What if we lived in a world where all work was compensated fairly? What if failed executives were denied multimillion-dollar severance packages and teachers were paid enough to make a decent living? Would we take a different career path? Would we try something more alluring? Hmmm . . . Perhaps the Joffrey has room for a middle-aged, somewhat out-of-shape prima ballerina.

Forty-some-odd years ago, in a small town in Arizona, a young boy began making films. Equipped with a store-bought video camera and the assistance of family and friends, he began his journey as a filmmaker. He made movies from the heart and has been quoted as saying, "The only time I'm totally happy is when I'm watching films or making them." Many years and many films later, he has been recognized as one of the most successful American filmmakers of all time. Films like *Indiana Jones, ET, Jaws, Shindler's List*, and *Saving Private Ryan* exemplify the vision of one man who followed his dream. I am, of course, talking about Steven Spielberg.

Most people do not approach their life's work with such certainty. For many of us, the path is less well defined and often the promise of high pay trumps job satisfaction.

I was no exception. While attending college I had only one goal in mind: a degree in business despite the fact that I was uninspired by business courses. I pushed forward so I could readily find a job. It never occurred to me to pursue a degree in art history or anthropology or ballet—I loved ballet. And I was concerned for those who did because they seemed destined for a life of financial struggle. I forced myself to attend classes that did not challenge me, graduated as planned, found a high-paying job as a certified public accountant, and cursed my good fortune. Only after a few years in my career did it occur to me to broaden my perspective.

Of course, accounting did have its moments: My professors were chagrined that I was not the accounting equal of my mother who preceded me in the same college classes by only a few years as she pursued a postdivorce profession. During my excruciatingly boring audit of a savings and loan, I was left with only a chair and table (and a genuine sense of relief) when the Feds raided the joint and seized every pen, pencil, paper, paper clip, computer, phone, and filing cabinet within and without my temporary but humble office, and as I conducted an inventory count for a client from the bottom of an ocean of prosthetic arms, legs, and breasts, I knew without doubt that, to paraphrase a famous British statesman, "This was something up with which I could no longer put."

Having thus stumbled down the wrong road, and the years having passed, I often like to ask my contemporaries how they ended up in the film business as I did. Few say, "Oh, I just love the financial insecurity and want to be on my feet fourteen hours a day." Instead, most talk about their love of films, their need to perform, their lifelong passion as a storyteller, or their journey from an amateur photographer to a seasoned cinematographer.

Perhaps that is what I love best about the film business. People do not commit to it unless they are passionate about what they are doing. Indeed, there are few other businesses in our economy that set a better example of fortitude, commitment, and dedication in the face of uncertainty, and it should be heralded as such.

But, sadly, the risks really are high. A few years ago, for example, I received a call from a distant relative asking if we could meet. He and his wife were moving to California from the East Coast so he could pursue his aspiration of becoming a filmmaker.

Prior to the move he was a computer programmer, and she was a schoolteacher. They lived an upper-middle-class life with all its comforts and conveniences. But he wanted to leave all that behind in pursuit of his dream. His wife was strongly opposed to the move and expressed her dissatisfaction openly. She had no interest in living in Los Angeles; she was concerned about a substantial reduction in their income; her desire to have children was put on hold; and she knew she would miss her family terribly.

But her husband realized it was now or never, and he needed to take his shot. Heretofore, he had always made practical choices: going to the right school; picking the right major; taking a secure position with a reputable company; and marrying (and loving) a girl anyone would be proud to take home to mother. By society's standards, he had made all the right choices. But he still felt stuck in his current situation. Hence, the move. I worried about him and wondered how long he would last.

After a year in Hollywood, he was gone, returning to a job he found unsatisfying. Upon hearing the news, I was saddened by his setback and wondered what his life would be like from now on. Had he stuck it out, I believe he would have found success, but he was unable to sacrifice long enough to give success a chance. Other factors and influences took precedence.

I often wonder how much creative talent is lost because people fail to follow their passion or give up too soon. I often wonder how much creative talent is lost because people put money before passion. Is there another Spielberg out there who will never be known or appreciated because he chose another path?

The truth is success can be found in any career as long as success is not defined solely by the accumulation of wealth. Consider the minister Rick Warren. His book, *The Purpose Driven Life*, has sold over 25 million copies worldwide. I doubt he became a minister to assure his financial security. Just the opposite. Despite being one of the most successful evangelical ministers in the United States, he donates 90 percent of his income to charity.

The point is: Wealth often follows success, but it is a side effect, not a raison d'etre.

We should learn from these examples. Choose a career that not only satisfies but also inspires you with financial considerations being a secondary factor. The more you enjoy your work, the harder you will try, and the more successful you will become. In time, the money will follow.

> **In choosing a career, visualize it from finish to start by asking yourself the following questions: Will I have no regrets? Will I have pursued my dream? Will I have had fun? If the answer is yes, you will know what choice to make now, and money will likely follow.**

FEAR ISN'T WELCOME HERE

When I was a child, I had high ambitions. I was going to be either a trampoline star or a fire-truck driver, possibly both. I had no doubt I was capable of accomplishing grand tasks and would eventually show the world my estimable talents. I knew I was destined for success if not greatness! Were your childhood dreams as lofty? Did you reach for the gold?

My daughter recently took up gymnastics and in a very short

time went from a tumbling toddler to participating on a competitive team. She is eight years old. As the proud mama, I do everything I can to support her dreams and encourage her participation. While attending a recent meet, she surprised all of us by announcing her intention to become an Olympic athlete.

Do not get me wrong. I would be thrilled to see her accomplish such a towering goal. But for some reason, alarm bells went off in my head, and I began to internalize all the reasons she would not or could not succeed. After all, only a handful of girls ever achieve that level of success. Here was a child who anguishes over the smallest scratch. How would she endure the constant pain and strain attendant on an athlete's body? Did she have the discipline, the perseverance, the competitive spirit she would need? I was concerned she did not.

My initial instinct, of course, was to protect her from the likely disappointment to come. I wanted to ground her in reality so that she would focus on more attainable objectives and reap associated rewards. But, as often happens, she caught me by surprise:

"You don't think I can make it, do you?" she asked, obviously reading my mind.

"Yes, I do!" I reassured her, despite my concerns.

"No, you don't. I can see it in your face. Why don't you think I can make it?" Her question was innocent but not without resentment.

My lack of support concerned her and she became visibly upset. Here was a child who had no doubt she could achieve great things yet her foremost ally was letting her down.

"*What is wrong with me*?!" I reflected angrily. I was doing the very thing I abhor—letting fear control me. After all, she had as much chance as anyone else. If she put her mind to it, it was entirely possible she could reach her goal. So what if she fell short? Even if she decided a week from now to focus on something different, why impose artificial limitations on her from the outset?

I realized I could learn a great deal from my own child. She had the youthful innocence that makes all things possible and many things happen. The question for me was: Where did my "Olympic dreams" go? I was an equestrian high jumper during middle school; an aquatic high diver during high school; and a deranged skydiver in college. What had dampened my ardor?

A recent UCLA survey referenced on the Internet found that the average one-year-old hears the word *no* up to four hundred times a day. That seems high to me but the number of no's per day per child must surely be inordinate. It is no wonder people give up or lose confidence. The journey from childhood to adulthood teaches us to limit our ambitions, to be cautious, to hold back. We have been told in numerous obvious or subtle ways from the very outset that we should not try, and naturally, we do not.

But despite these universal negative cues, there are many who refuse to give up at any cost. In the film business, that means actors. One of the most inspiring aspects of the business to me is watching these professionals persevere. Time and again, I see the same faces auditioning for a part in a show, waiting for that one big break. Most spend a lifetime trying and never give up. Some break through.

A story circulates in the business that Barbara Streisand so wanted to be noticed in her early career that she deliberately began an audition chewing gum both rudely and loudly. When the director asked her to dispose of it before singing, she made a great display of removing it from her mouth and sticking it under the stool on which she was seated. When her audition was finished and she left the stage, the director brusquely ordered a stagehand to dispose of the stool. When the stagehand lifted it up to carry it away, he was surprised to see that Ms. Streisand had mimicked the entire performance and no gum was left behind. She managed to get noticed—and not just noticed, remembered.

But just imagine the long-term fear and uncertainty that actors must endure: ten, fifteen, twenty years spent pursuing one ambition, one goal, one calling. Many of them struggle in menial jobs just to pay the bills. Many have to live in substandard housing. Many know the bitterness of repeated rejection. It takes enormous courage to be so dedicated and so devoted, and I admire them tremendously for it.

But there are other good examples of courage in the film business and techniques for achieving success. When a young, thirty-two-year-old female executive was hired to run a major network several years ago, she confided to those close to her that she planned to approach the job as if it was her last year on earth. She believed this would liberate her from making decisions based on fear of failure, and it did.

Some say live each day as if it were your last. I say do whatever it takes to regain your childhood optimism; an optimism that will allow you to replace fear and doubt with courage and hope. I look forward to the day I sit in an Olympic stadium and cheer for my child. She deserves nothing less and so do you.

> **Do not let fear stand in the way of following your passion. Strive to preserve your childhood confidence that all things are possible. Perseverance, courage, and hope will get you where you want to go.**

KNOWING WHO YOU ARE AND WHAT YOU WANT

PLEASE DON'T GIVE ME WHAT I'M ASKING FOR

Growing up I thought the only career choices available to me were doctor, lawyer, or certified public accountant. (Indian chief was no longer de rigueur, much less politically correct.) It was not until later in life that I realized it took all sorts of people doing all kinds of things for life to be rich and varied. Yet society has a way of telling us how our life should be lived. It tells us what success should look like; how much money is enough; which homes and cars to purchase; and how we should spend our time. We are barraged with information that manipulates and persuades us to hew to the societal line. If we fall short of these standards, we are deemed to have failed. Through all this noise, it is difficult, perhaps impossible, to hear that authentic voice inside our head trying to be heard. Instead, we accept the moon.

Before I entered the film business, and after my stint as a CPA, I had a short career as a business manager for various clients in the broader entertainment business. Actors, directors, producers, and other participants would pay 10 percent of their gross income for our firm to manage their affairs. Not only did we provide standard accounting services such as tax planning and basic bookkeeping, we also made investments, paid bills, managed insurance needs, purchased assets, obtained necessary financing, and prepared monthly financial statements. We basically did whatever our clients needed us to do within reason and the law.

Servicing such customers was not always easy. We had one extremely wealthy client who preferred to keep his money liquid and would only let us buy short-term CDs. Since banks will only federally insure up to $100,000 per account, and he wanted the insurance coverage, we literally ran out of banks in which to invest his money.

Another very successful female development executive at a major studio was getting married, so we invited the executive and her shy and retiring fiancé to a meeting to discuss maximizing, protecting, and securing her assets. We made a big fuss about her need for a prenuptial agreement. The effort proved ludicrous and offensive—as we later learned—because he was a multimillionaire many times over and had about one hundred fifty times her net worth.

Another client had a habit of accepting and using every credit card that was offered to him regardless of the applicable service charge or interest rate. He had fifty-some credit cards that he used regularly. At one point, he purchased a condo in Palm Springs for his mother using credit cards only for financing. At least he was racking up frequent flyer miles.

Then there was the client who was one card shy of a full deck. She was a famous actress who was too lazy to go to the doctor to submit a urine sample needed for an insurance policy. Instead, she collected her own sample and mailed it directly to us for "processing." *Yuck!*

While famous and infamous clients made the job interesting, I suspected early on that I had made a serious mistake in my choice of career. This was not the job for me nor was it a good use of my talents. I wanted to participate in the work of my clients, not handle their business and financial affairs.

Accepting this fully was difficult at first. I had no idea what to do. Four years of college, months of studying and finally passing the CPA exam, two years of focused work experience—all for nothing? I kept rationalizing that mine was a solid career that would provide security, money, a nice home, and exciting vacations. But no matter how hard I tried to rationalize my situation, it became harder and harder to get out of bed in the morning.

Then it was time for my annual review. One of the senior partners scheduled an appointment with me to discuss my future at the firm. I stayed up all night trying to assess my commitment, my happiness, and my enthusiasm. Clearly, I needed a way out. The morning came too quickly and I found myself seated in a large corner office wearing my new designer suit, sensible pumps, tasteful but understated jewelry, and a forced smile as I sat opposite the firm's only female partner.

Then, I had an epiphany. I would simply ask for the moon: a doubling of salary, an assistant of my own, a bigger office and three weeks paid vacation a year. If the partner agreed, which was highly unlikely, I would undoubtedly be happy with the windfall. If she turned me down, I had the out I was looking for. I could walk away from a career I did not want and could do so with equanimity.

So I smiled, I asked, I watched, and I waited. I knew she had not expected me to be so bold or to drive such a hard bargain. The seconds ticked by. Then, with great cheer, she smiled and congratulated me on a long and fruitful career with the firm.

Damn it! No, No, No! This was not what I expected. Worse yet, it was not what I really wanted. She looked at me quizzically, wondering why I was not responding jubilantly to her generous offer. I had no idea what to do. Think, think, think . . . but nothing came. So I did what any sophisticated, independent young professional would do in such circumstances. I excused myself and went to the bathroom.

What was wrong with me? Why was I not ecstatic? Why could I not appreciate what was being offered? I looked at myself in the mirror and knew my mental game-playing days were over. I was not a business manager and could no longer pretend I was. I had to make a change.

I returned to her office a bit sheepishly, explained my change of heart, thanked her for her exceptional offer, and graciously declined it. It may have been one of the most liberating experiences of my life.

As I packed up my office, I enjoyed a moment of clarity. All the money and perks in the world really do not add up to much if you do not enjoy what you do. I knew I needed to find work that challenged me, inspired me, and satisfied my varied interests. I was ready to begin my search.

Shortly after my climb down the corporate ladder, I obtained an entry-level job on a television movie paying significantly less than my previous salary. You would have thought I had won the lottery from my Cheshire cat grin.

Since that first film job, I have worked with many successful and wealthy people who are not particularly happy. Those who find happiness seem to find it despite the perks, despite the money, despite the "stuff." They are the ones who march to the beat of their own drummer. They are the ones who live life on their own terms. They are the ones who listen to their authentic voice.

> **It is a delusion to believe dollars and perks**
> **can cure a suffocating job. It is a delusion**
> **to believe society's approbation can turn career**
> **lead into gold. Rely on yourself to determine**
> **the job characteristics that will satisfy.**

LOOK IN THE MIRROR, WHAT DO YOU SEE?

How do you see yourself? Are you a stunning diva who turns heads when you enter a room? Are you a meek and mild maiden who goes out of your way to remain anonymous? Are you a shrewd and confident businesswoman whom no one wants to offend? Chances are the world sees you exactly as you see yourself. Even Superman must keep this in mind.

Ideas for television shows come from many different sources. Some shows are based on a person's life story, some are derived from a successful feature film, some evolve from the creative genius of a writer, and some are adapted from a story or book. On one particular show, I, along with the director and other producers, joined together to turn a short story written by a well-known author into a television pilot. Despite being seven months pregnant, I eagerly packed my bags and headed for a popular tourist destination in the South known for its music, all-night celebrations, and fabulous cuisine where our show would be staged.

Because we were shooting in October, the show's creator invited the cast and crew to attend her annual "world famous" Halloween party—an event shared with about a thousand hand-picked guests. I debated for days about the perfect costume to wear. In my condition, only a pumpkin or Chinese lantern seemed appropriate. I should mention I gained fifty pounds during my pregnancy.

Anyway, on the night of the party, I put the finishing touches on my full-figured flapper costume and headed for the door when

I received an unexpected phone call. Apparently, one of our production assistants (PA) had been arrested on his way to the party. This PA was in his early twenties but barely passed for sixteen. He was unassuming, trustworthy, and gentle; not the kind of person to successfully spend a night in jail. I could not imagine what he had done to get himself into so much trouble.

Instead of making my way to the party, I drove directly to the police station to try to clear up whatever misunderstanding had landed our PA in the slammer. When I arrived, I realized the allegations were more serious than I expected.

Apparently, the PA had accepted an offer from our on-set security team (off-duty police officers) to borrow an authentic police uniform for his Halloween costume. While driving through congested city streets looking for the mansion of the show's creator, he came in contact with a group of on-duty officers. Thinking the PA was on the force, the police officers asked him questions that he obviously could not answer. Not wanting to lie, he came clean about his costume. Unfortunately, impersonating an officer in this particular town was a very serious offense. The PA was immediately handcuffed and manhandled into the back of a patrol car. This was just the beginning of his troubles.

To embellish his costume, he was wearing a Superman outfit under the police uniform. He wanted to impress the show's creator by incorporating different aspects of her show into his party "persona." Once he arrived at the police station and was booked, the arresting officer confiscated his police uniform leaving him arrayed in nothing but blue tights with a big red "S" on his chest.

The booking officer took one look at him and asked if he was gay. I should mention that Halloween is one of the busiest nights of the year at this particular police station. Consequently, the place was swarming with drunks who where having a good laugh at Superman's expense.

The PA was afraid to answer honestly about his sexual preferences and possibly become the victim of a hate crime, so he assured the officer that he was not gay. It was not until he was placed in a holding cell that he realized the import of the question. In order to maintain peace among its many prisoners, the station had two holding cells: one for homosexuals and one for heterosexuals. Our PA suddenly became entertainment for the macho men behind bars. Fortunately, after six hours of incarceration, we were able to post bail and spring him before he suffered serious harm to anything other than his dignity.

I relate this story to illustrate an important point: When we try to be something we are not, it can lead to serious trouble. And while I am happy to report I have never spent time in jail, I did have a similar "be true to yourself" experience on a full-length feature film I worked on a number of years ago.

I was hired by the director to produce a crime story about five roommates in their early twenties. In it was a scene in which two detectives come to the lead character's home searching for evidence of a crime. Most of the dialogue was written for the male detective, leaving only one line for the female detective to speak.

As we discussed our casting options, the director took one look at me and decided I would be perfect for the part of the female detective. I began frantically shaking my head from side to side while backing up in protest. It took all my restraint to refrain from screaming, "Not a chance in hell!"

"All you have to do is play yourself," he assured me.

"I don't know how to play myself!" I protested.

You should know that there is nothing in the world more frightening to me than being in front of a camera.

"It's just one line," he reminded me. "Anyone can do it."

Not anyone, I thought.

I wanted to tell him about my getting kicked out of a freshman acting class in college because I refused to act like a wilting flower. The teacher accused me of failing to exceed my comfort zone. "I have spent a lifetime perfecting my comfort zone! I can hardly abandon it for botany!" I wisecracked. Unamused, she pointed to the door. Seriously, I had no idea you could be kicked out of an acting class. I only hoped it did not mean a black mark on my permanent record.

Needless to say, from that moment on, I knew I was no actor. Give me a stadium full of people to whom I can lecture and I am in hog heaven. Ask me to pretend to be someone I am not, and my world and confidence start to crumble.

Despite my protests, the director insisted I perform.

When the big day arrived, I wended my way through hair, makeup, and wardrobe, dreading every moment. I practiced my one line over and over: "There is nothing here." "There is nothing here." But no matter how I tried, no matter how I varied the pacing and inflection, I still could not make myself believe myself.

I prayed to be struck by lightening.

The set was lit, the actors rehearsed, the marks set, and the director yelled, "Action." I stood there like a mannequin. My mouth was dry as the Sahara. My palms were slick with sweat. My armpits were stained—something you want to avoid when the scene requires you to reach up and grab something off the top shelf of a closet. At that moment, I would have preferred having my teeth drilled without Novocaine.

Take after take, the director tried desperately to extract even a minimally competent performance out of me. With each take, he became more and more discouraged by my spectacular lack of talent. I wanted desperately to give him what he was asking for, but it was beyond my reach. I was not and will never be an actor. I always knew it, and now everyone else did, too.

Fortunately, he had the good sense to cut my line from the film, but to this day I can rent the movie and watch in anguish as I impersonate an automaton. Having stumbled and fallen so ignominiously, I now know who I am. Among other things, I am a producer. That is what I am good at. That is what I enjoy.

Know who you are and what you want. Speak up, ask for what you are after, and decline to be what you are not. No one knows you as well as you do. Only you can honestly assess what is and is not right for you.

Stay grounded within your capabilities. You are the only who can determine what is best for you and what you can accomplish. A successful career path begins with a realistic appraisal of your own abilities. Resist well-meaning but misguided challenges.

STAYING THE COURSE

NO IS NOT AN OPTION

No is such an easy word to say. It is universally understood and often frees us from responsibility, commitment, even participation. And since it is such an easy way out, people overuse it when the alternative requires too much effort. "No, I can't get that for you." "No, that is not how we do things" "No, I can't help you with that." No, no, no! But must we accept no even from the parking attendant?

Many years ago, I agreed to produce a short film that was to be shot in New York City. The film was being financed, written, and directed by a casual acquaintance who was beginning his career as a filmmaker. This was to be his directorial debut, and he was planning on using the finished product as a calling card to open doors in Hollywood. Having no other opportunities at hand, I volunteered my time and talents to help make his aspiration come true.

New York City is a complicated place. For those with money, it is a mecca of fine dining, entertainment, and cultural activities. For the workingman, it is a daily grind. The limitations affecting the workingman held true for our film enterprise. With few resources, we were forced to beg, borrow, and steal (well, maybe not steal), making it exceptionally difficult to accomplish our mission.

Fortunately, most members of the crew were only looking for an opportunity to enhance their résumés and refine their skills, so they were willing to work for free. In return, as their producer, I promised to squeeze the budget to provide good food and a pleasant work environment.

Unfortunately, the director turned out to be arrogant without cause and fancied himself a cinematic genius. He spent the two weeks of shooting looking down his nose at just about everyone working so hard on his behalf. Despite my protests, he failed to see that these people were doing him a favor and that he needed to acknowledge it and demonstrate his appreciation. But he continued to alienate one and all.

The last night of the shoot, we were filming in a cemetery outside the city. We had worked later than planned and needed to vacate the premises expeditiously. Our authorized time had expired, and additional costs were piling up. Everyone was grabbing gear, rolling up cable, packing camera boxes, and storing lighting. As we humped equipment to the truck, the director remained in his chair ordering a production assistant to bring him hot tea.

The crew had finally had it. After ten days of taking orders from someone who could not even muster a simple "thank you," they said their good-byes as soon as the vehicles were loaded and bolted. The director and I were left alone in the cemetery in the middle of the night.

I soon realized my only transportation was the lone truck our disgruntled driver had left behind. The director had his car. Not only was he lazy beyond belief, he had no idea how to drive a stick shift, so his offering me his car while he drove the truck was out of the question. I disconsolately climbed behind the wheel of the truck and carefully maneuvered my way back to the city.

For those who have tried to drive in Manhattan (which takes real skill even on a moped), try doing it in a three-ton truck. I was an accident waiting to happen. Moreover, it was 2 A.M. and I had no idea where I was going. All I knew was that I needed to find some place safe to store the truck overnight so I could unload it in the morning. Since I was the one who had rented the camera, lights, and sound equipment, I was responsible for their safe return.

First, I tried parking on the street, but after driving around fruitlessly for half an hour, I accepted the fact that street parking was at such a premium, it was nonexistent. Next, I tried a number of parking garages but was turned away repeatedly. Either they were unwilling to accept vehicles so late at night, or they were already full. My appeals fell on deaf ears. I became intimately familiar with the word *no*.

Unwilling to accept defeat, I devised a foolproof plan. I decided to check into a four-star hotel, certain they would have a place to park my truck. I cared little about cost and was willing to pay out of my own pocket because I was exhausted and frustrated. I blew kisses at the valet as he drove the truck away; only to return a moment later when he discovered my truck exceeded the height limitations of the parking garage.

Realizing there was but one solution left, I parked the truck in the middle of the street and abandoned it. I went inside the hotel and took a seat by a lobby window and waited. Within half an hour, a city tow truck hauled my problem away. I knew that the truck would be securely locked in a police impound yard for the night and that I could retrieve it after a good night's sleep. By 3:30 A.M. I was safely tucked in bed accompanied by a satisfied grin; a grin that widened considerably when I later recovered the $350 it cost me to retrieve the truck from the director's father.

That was an early career, minor triumph of mine in resisting the word *no*, in refusing to accept it as an option. It has held me in good stead over the years in a business resistant to new ideas because it is otherwise drowning in creative submissions and desperate entreaties. Indeed, there are many more dramatic and inspiring examples of determination than mine, and a few are worth noting:

The story of *Desperate Housewives* and its creator, Marc Cherry, come to mind. To give you a little history, Marc began his career in 1988 right about the time a writers' strike was in progress; a terrible time for a struggling screenwriter to make it in Hollywood.

To make ends meet, he worked as a personal assistant to Dixie Carter until he was finally given a chance to write on the last season of *Golden Girls*. He went on to create *The Five Buchanans* and *Some of My Best Friends*. Neither show found a faithful audience and each was cancelled. Years passed with little work for Marc until he created *Desperate Housewives*, but even that proved to be a struggle. Four networks (HBO, FOX, CBS, and NBC) all passed on the show before ABC finally decided to shoot a pilot. An executive at ABC confirmed that Marc was living with his mother when the show finally received a green light.

Can you imagine how many times in his sixteen-year struggle Marc heard the word *no*? Yet, his perseverance paid off with a top-rated hit. In 2005, *Time* magazine named Marc one of the 100 Most Influential People of the Year due to the success of his show.

Seinfeld is another example. Despite having a reputation as being one of the worst-tested shows of all time, the show's creators believed in it enough to fight to keep it on the air until an audience could build. And what an audience it was.

These issues of negation, of course, are not exclusive to television. Feature films are an equally difficult medium. First, someone has to sell his or her idea for a project to a studio or independent investor, probably after pitching it all over town. Then, if someone is interested, the writer must write a script justifying the cost of making it. If financing can be secured, name actors and a director must be attached. Only then is the project likely to be made.

Hundreds of thousands of scripts have ended up in the trash heap because the right elements failed to come together at exactly the right time. *Little Miss Sunshine* took four years to make and came close to not happening at all. Even *Forrest Gump* almost failed to reach the big screen. With so many obstacles, it is a wonder films get made at all.

I believe the only reason some of these shows make it into production is because someone refused to give up. Someone was not willing to take no for an answer. I admire men and women who fight against such tough odds. We can and should learn from them.

Perseverance pays off. When you are unwilling to take no for an answer, you project a certain determination to which others can respond. When you are relentless in pursuit, you are likely to find success, and maybe even a good parking space.

> **Do not take no for an answer. This is easy to say and hard to do. But it has been proven time and again that insistence on yes is a fundamental character trait of successful people. When no thwarts your plans or goals, be exceptionally energetic in opposing it.**

LOOK IN YOUR BAG OF TRICKS

Sometimes what we are looking for is staring us right in the face. Sometimes we cannot see the forest for the trees. Sometimes we do not appreciate what we have until it is gone. But sometimes, just sometimes, a superhero can help.

Each show in my career has provided me with wonderful and unique experiences. Among other things, I have learned how to investigate a murder, capture a ghost, kidnap an undercover operative, and choreograph a ballroom minuet: talents obviously useful in everyday life.

On one particular show, I learned about the martial arts. It was a children's series featuring a group of teenagers who could transform themselves into superheroes to fight evil. While I was glad to have the work, the story lines lacked the creative spark I needed as a production challenge. As the first year turned into the second, I became discouraged and concerned I was destined for a life producing children's morning television.

Each week I was presented with a script proposing the same

old story line, which we would film the same old way: World-threatening incident occurs, kids called into action, they transform, they fight, they save the day, we all live happily ever after. The repetition was killing me with boredom, but I had made a commitment and planned to see it through.

Then one morning, I discovered a new way of looking at my job. As I walked from my car to my office, which was located on the second floor of our soundstage, I noticed one of our lead actors in full costume standing in front of the building smoking a cigarette. He was dressed in a white one-piece jumpsuit and held his helmet firmly by his side.

He suddenly threw his cigarette to the ground and quickly put on his helmet thus completing his "look." After all, he was one of the most popular children's characters of the day. I searched the parking lot to see what had caught his eye and motivated his transformation. Moving toward him was a young boy, maybe ten, being pushed in a wheelchair by his mother.

The actor, now in full character, strode forward and posed directly in front of the boy, fists on hips, legs spread apart. Time seemed to stand still. The child looked up in awe at the demigod before him.

His mother finally broke the silence. "We are so excited to be here. You are his favorite superhero of all time," she said, her voice unsteady. "His room is full of action figures and posters and . . . well . . . anything we can find of you."

The boy was too nervous to speak but his face expressed rapture and joy. I had never seen anything like it. I held my breath not wanting the moment to end. I was touched to the quick.

Finally, our actor bent down and took the boy's hand. With a little prodding, he was able to engage the boy in conversation. After some small talk, they made their way onto the soundstage where the boy would spend the day immersed in our fantasy world. His parents had requested this visit through the Make a Wish Foundation.

This experience allowed me to rediscover the value in what I was doing. I knew it was not Shakespeare, but to millions of children, it was pure magic and it mattered. I was determined to renew my commitment.

The job became more enjoyable. I debated with others the unique dangers of twelve-armed, six-eyed monsters. I tried to figure out what kind of spaceship would look authentic to kids. I suggested new and unusual karate chops. My enthusiasm was renewed.

For the most part, I am deeply grateful for the opportunities I have had to participate on the shows that have formed the fabric of my career. Many have been well written, well directed, and well performed. I have taken pride in having my name associated with them. Others have been less than stellar, obliging me to search for hidden or underlying value in order to maintain my enthusiasm and commitment.

For example, I have learned not to dismiss a script at first glance. Even if the story is lacking or the writing limited, I see if there is an opportunity to learn something new, to experience something unique, or to work with people I admire. I evaluate the totality of the show on its own merits. If I look hard enough, I believe I can almost always find something that will allow me to participate on the project with enthusiasm.

As another example, I remember being asked to work on a television movie about a serial rapist who would stalk women in his large apartment complex. Everything about the show offended me. The characters were flat and undeveloped, the violence was gratuitous, and the subject matter was offensive. But the producer was someone I admired and trusted, and I believed he would do everything he could to create a show that expressed reality without being exploitative. I agreed to accept the job.

It turned out that both the director and executive producer were creative, intelligent, and sensitive people who worked tirelessly to make the show worthy of an audience. While I was never able to embrace the subject matter, it was indeed treated with delicacy and respect. As part of the team, I was proud to say I helped make it happen.

Staying committed to your goals can be difficult at times. Perhaps you are not progressing quickly enough, perhaps the work you are doing is unfulfilling, perhaps you expected your career to develop differently. It will help if you look for value in all that you do along the way. Then, hold on tight to the goals you have set for yourself. Eventually you will succeed and the journey will have been worth it.

**You can stay committed to your goals
by digging deep to find some value in every work
experience. This technique will help you maintain the
drive you need to weather difficult times.**

STAYING GROUNDED

WHAT?! NO SOUFFLÉ!

When most people think of the entertainment industry, they think of glamour, award shows, elegant gowns, and fancy cars. Some think of money: lots and lots of money paid to stars like Tom Cruise or Jim Carey, who can demand multimillion-dollar deals for a few weeks of work. When I think of the entertainment industry, my thoughts often turn to food. Surprised? Most people do not realize this, but if you visit any film set, you will see that food is a major preoccupation of the business. Perhaps I should have ordered steak with that lobster . . .

Here's what I mean: We start each day with a completely catered breakfast. Sounds nice, huh?—someone else firing up the old frying pan. The best part is that we can have just about anything our little hearts desire. Order up! Pancakes, waffles, omelets, oatmeal, crepes, French toast, breakfast burritos, cheese blintzes, an assortment of cereals, fruits, donuts, and gallons and gallons of the world's worst coffee.

That is just the beginning. Six short hours later, as a result of those pesky union rules, we are all invited to sit down to a fully catered feast/lunch. This includes, but is not limited to, a variety of chicken, beef, fish, and vegetarian dishes; twelve or thirteen scrumptious salads; assorted breads and rolls; various soups; and a lavish offering of deserts—always à la mode—washed down with the world's worst lemonade.

Clearly, we need to work on the beverages.

Then, six hours later (assuming filming exceeds twelve hours a day, which in the eighteen years I have been in the business is normally the case—I think a blizzard stopped us early twice), it is time to eat again, and we all get in line for what is called a "walking meal." This is our version of fast-food dining: Chinese takeout, pizza, Tito's tacos, Mongolian barbecue, pasta, CPK, and on and on and on.

But wait! There is more. If for some inexplicable reason we experience a hunger pang or tummy grumble at any time of the day or night, we can always hop over to the craft service area to satisfy our cravings. What is a craft service area? It is an actual department staffed by two to four employees (completely disassociated from the hired caterer) who have the job of manning a snack bar around the clock.

Without doubt, this is a system designed to ensure bite-by-bite expansion. Based on my most recent calculation, I have gained and lost somewhere in the neighborhood of six hundred pounds over the course of my career. And this happens notwithstanding the deal I strike with the caterers at the beginning of every project: a deal affectionately known to them as the "Danielle four-step."

Step 1: The caterers and I meet at the beginning of the show while they are still eager to please me since I am the one who hired them.

Step 2: I gravely admonish them to (a) serve me only chicken, fish, and vegetables as I wish to preserve my health and (b) decline any requests or demands I may make for fat food no matter how heartrending my pleas.

Step 3: In time, I am overwhelmed by fatigue and frustration and go to the caterers pleading for pasta, steak, burgers, fries, and cookies galore. They desist.

Step 4: Beaten down by my constant begging, they give in, but only with lofty disdain. I gorge and enlarge.

I will not bore you with a complete list of snacks available at the craft service area since by now you are probably heading to the kitchen for your own detour and frolic, but the short list includes: cookies, candies, cheese platters, veggies (rarely touched), fruit, finger sandwiches, chili, quesadillas, dips, and chips.

Well, there it is. For those of us trying to maintain a healthy body, this is our cross to bear. What is even more disconcerting is that I, and everyone else in the industry, have come to expect it. Even though we do not need it and often wish we were not tempted by it, we get upset if the cornucopia of food is in any way diminished or denied.

"No fish option? Outrageous!" "Out of peanut M&M's? Unacceptable!" "What!? No low-carb, wheat-free, soy-based, fruit-infused double delectable? *I can't work like this!*"

It was in this frame of mind that I received a wake-up call one afternoon on set. I was standing in the catering line having just been served a steak-and-lobster combo when I began to complain about the quality of the béarnaise sauce. A newbie who was standing next to me was simultaneously praising the caterer and commenting on how unusual it was to have access to such a feast. I immediately realized how bothersome I had become. Not long ago I was a newbie too and would have been utterly impressed with, and grateful for, the bounty set before me. In the old days, I would have gladly accepted far less. But time had taken its toll and unjustified expectations had set in. I had come to expect not appreciate the perquisites of the business. I had started to resemble the type of person I often found pompously offensive.

I was at a crossroads. I could continue to maintain a high level of expectation such that little would impress me, or I could regain my sense of gratitude and appreciation. I decided to do the latter.

It seems to me we live in dangerous times. Many of us have come to expect the best of everything. We want it here. We want it now. And we want it with little or no effort on our part. What was once special becomes pedestrian and over time loses its luster. But not for me.

I looked down at the beautiful steak and lobster. Then I looked up at the troubled caterer who had literally slaved over a hot stove since 4:30 A.M. that morning and was hanging on my every critical word. I thanked him sincerely for a beautiful meal and a job well done.

Remember to be grateful for all that you have. Unfulfilled expectations can impair your sense of proportion. Instead of expecting everything just the way you want it, be grateful for what is offered and show your appreciation.

> **To be an effective manager, to be an appreciated co-worker, you need to beware of a creeping sense of entitlement and unjustified expectations. As your career advances, they can lead to arrogance and the loss of your sense of proportion.**

SUCKED INTO THE VOID

What do you do when your expectations at work have exceeded realistic bounds? How do you regain your sense of proportion? How do you climb down from that pedestal you built to honor yourself? Start with humble pie and no elbow room whatsoever.

Not long ago I started working on a new television series that was to be shot in Hollywood. I was excited to be part of the project because the scripts were edgy, hysterically funny, politically astute, and highly entertaining. Unfortunately, the production budget for each episode provided for less than half the money I was used to managing.

This parsimony reflected a paradigm shift in television programming that has occurred over the last few years. With the introduction of online media and hundreds of cable channels, shows no longer follow the standard network format. While programs such as *CSI* and *Grey's Anatomy* are still made for millions per episode with a top-dollar cast and a large writing staff, many shows are now produced for under a million dollars per episode. Often, the show's creator doubles or triples up as writer, actor, and, occasionally, director. In order to stay competitive with websites such as YouTube or MySpace, television has to offer a greater variety of cost-conscious entertainment.

On my new show, I was genuinely excited by the prospect of working with its gifted show runners and felt I could easily deal with the lack of financial resources; until my first day at work. As I was shown to my office, I began to feel I had made a big mistake. For the first time in many, many years, my office was "our" office, as in "no quiet space to call my own." I had to share the area with a few other people. This was not good.

I quickly realized the working comforts I had taken for granted were a distant memory: no personal assistant to place my phone calls; no couch on which to relax and clear my head; no driver to fuel my car; and no minifridge to hold my bottled water. I had to fend for myself. Imagine! I even had to learn how to operate a copier and set up a conference call all on my own. Sheeeesh!

By the end of the first day, I was decidedly dejected. It was not that I needed these things to be happy. It was just that their absence impaired my self-image. Without these staples, I felt less important.

The next day as I drove to work I had a lengthy cell-phone conversation with a good friend and mentor. As I lamented all that was lost, she suggested I reframe my thinking. She reminded me that because I had come to expect certain conditions, I was frustrated when reality did not conform to them. She also refreshed my memory on how excited I was on my very first film project despite the then less-than-desirable working conditions.

She reminded me that way back when I had been hired to work as a payroll clerk for a television movie production. Since the producers wanted the accountants near the set at all times, they established our office in half of a "two banger" (a trailer divided by a partition into two suites), with three desks tightly crowded into an eight-by-ten-foot space. Each time I entered or exited the trailer, I had to climb over my boss to reach or leave my work space. In addition, the drivers would sometimes park the trailer on a steep incline, causing our rolling chairs to gravitate to the lowest spot in the room. I became adept at writing with one hand while holding on to something fixed with the other. Since everyone on the show needed something from accounting sooner or later, folks often assembled outside the trailer, resembling a mid-depression unemployment line, while the trailer resembled a stuffed clown car.

Despite these substandard conditions, I could not have been happier. I was enjoying the work, excited by the opportunity, and eager to learn. Given the choice, I would have passed up a corner office to stay right where I was.

Now, many years and many offices later, I had apparently lost that unspoiled enthusiasm, that adventurous spirit that views each opportunity as a challenge. All I could see on the new show was a dimly lit office with no space of my own: an office where two show runners, two producers, and one studio head of production had to squeeze in to interview job candidates. We could have used a crowbar. I knew that if I did not change my outlook, I would be increasingly unhappy. I decided to follow my friend's advice and let go of my expectations. I stopped comparing everything to past experiences and tried seeing things with a fresh eye.

First, I took a good look around my office and realized I had everything I needed to do the job. Second, I got to know my co-workers really well and found they were wonderful people whose company I very much enjoyed. As I continued to focus on the positive, other benefits became evident. There were no prima donnas to pacify, and I was working with people who were not jaded by years in the business. In fact, these hard-working people were grateful for the opportunity. Everyone understood that compromises had to be made to perform the job properly and produce a quality show.

As time passed, our limited resources became a source of humor, which encouraged us to work more closely as a team. "We are too nice for things not to work out," became the show's motto. I was, in truth, delighted to be surrounded by kind, appreciative, industrious people who were willing to sacrifice for a higher good.

In addition, our limited resources inspired creative solutions. I was free to experiment, try new approaches, and find alternative solutions. It was refreshing to rethink my work style and develop new ways of accomplishing old goals.

I am not a Pollyanna. I do not advocate passive acceptance of reversals. I do, however, advocate a particular methodology to see you through when times are tough and options few. I advocate seeing the glass half full rather than half empty. I know that sounds trite, but the fact is we have the mental wherewithal to decide how we will respond to the world around us. Since every experience has both good and bad elements to it, why not choose to see it through rose-colored glasses?

You can ease the pain of career setbacks, reversals, and inertia by identifying and embracing the positive elements of your job situation. Seeing the glass half full is more than just an optimistic attitude, it is a mental bridge to better days.

COME ON, HOW DIFFICULT CAN SHE BE?

How would you like to have a full-time hairstylist, makeup artist, and costume designer at your beck and call? How would you like to have skilled artisans apply your lip gloss, disguise the bags under your eyes, give your hair a little bounce, select the perfect outfit, and make you look two sizes smaller? Sound too good to be true? Not for the biggies.

Many successful actresses in the film business come with their own "glam squads." Depending on the size of the show, this group will include, but is not limited to, a key hairstylist, a key makeup artist, a costume designer, a wardrobe supervisor, and supporting staff. If the show has a large budget, the retinue can also include a massage therapist, a full-time trainer, and a private chef. It takes a lot of people to perfect and project an image.

While it may sound frivolous, the glam squad plays an important role in the filmmaking process. Not only are the members of the squad responsible for making the actress look fantastic, they frequently become her confidantes and exert a significant influence on her mood throughout the day.

When an actress arrives on set early each morning (sometimes at 4 A.M.), she goes directly to the hair and makeup trailer. If the mood in the trailer is benign, with coffee brewing, soft music playing, and a nurturing staff in attendance, she will ease into the day feeling calm and relaxed. If, however, the trailer is filled with frenetic staff bickering amongst themselves and ignoring the star's needs, you can bet you will have an all-day unhappy performer on your hands.

After hair and makeup, the actress is provided with wardrobe. Usually the appropriate clothes are laid out in her personal trailer before her arrival on set. If she needs assistance getting dressed, a costumer will help. If you think costumes are just clothes, I beg to differ. What an actress wears can significantly affect how she feels and how she performs. This is especially true if the wardrobe is intrinsic to the character. An actress playing the role of a stripper needs to feel sexy, or her performance will fall flat. An actress playing a homeless woman will want her rags to feel authentic, or her character will not ring true.

But the glam squad's influence does not stop there. The amount of time a film company works each day is significantly affected by how well the squad performs its functions. If it is slow in getting an actress ready, the entire company must wait for minutes or hours with nothing to do. I cannot tell you how often I have stood idly by with a hundred other members of the crew waiting for an actress to come out of hair and makeup.

On any given day, an actress may have as many as four different looks depending on the scenes to be filmed. Each look requires the actress to return to hair and makeup and wardrobe for the appropriate transformation. This all takes valuable time away from filming. Consequently, production is often at the mercy of the glam squad, which must work expeditiously. The good squads can get an actress ready quickly without compromising her look or upsetting her in any way. The bad ones can bury you and bust the budget.

Of course, all this personal service, designer makeup, and specialty wardrobe costs money. Since the presence and participation of the glam squad is often negotiated and included in an actress's contract, the squad serves at her pleasure and not at the pleasure of production. Its primary purpose is to provide the actress with just about anything she wants, even high couture, exotic cosmetics, and fine jewelry. The end result is that the glam squad can break the bank if it is not "production friendly." If, for some reason, its members do not like you, there is a good chance the actress will dislike you as well. Then you are well and truly screwed!

Although I have worked with many exceptionally talented people in glam squads who were able to meet the needs of both the actress and production, the relationship can become adversarial very quickly, especially when the squad's demands are beyond the pale. Some of the more extreme demands I have received from glam squads include:

- A ten-ton trailer with pop-out sides for wardrobe (despite a small cast)
- The same for hair and makeup
- A full washer-dryer suite at each location
- Espresso machines
- A fully stocked refrigerator
- High-end stereo speakers
- Drivers or assistants to carry shopping bags from the mall
- Hand-sewn, hand-crafted wigs with human hair for day players
- $4,500 suits, $1,000 shoes, and $250 bras

Squad members often blink in confusion, or huff in disdain, when I ask, "Why didn't you buy this stuff at Target!? It would look just as good for a third the price." Perhaps they are not as well grounded as I am. Perhaps we move in different circles. Who can say? But the relationship is not always adversarial, and sometimes there can be very pleasant surprises. Let me give you an example:

On one recent comedy series, I was notified by the lead actress that she had hired a costume designer for the show before my arrival. This caused me great concern. First, I had not had the opportunity to interview the designer or check her references. Second, I had not had the chance to negotiate her as yet unset salary. Third, I had no idea if she could work within the confines of our limited budget and schedule. And fourth, since she had been hired without my involvement, I knew she had little motivation to please me. I also knew that in order to establish a healthy working relationship, I had to meet with her and set some boundaries right away. The truth was, because of the way she had been hired, I made assumptions about her and her work style that were unfair and later proved to be unfounded.

I expected her to be difficult and was almost certain she would ask for the moon. I waited for her to insist on the obliga-

tory pop-out trailer, a full-time alterations tailor, an elegantly ap
pointed fitting room, a driver to take her shopping, and a budget
that would cover French undergarments, Italian shoes, and numerous designer bags. I wondered how I was going to win her
support while denying her requests.

My expectations could not have been further off the mark.
She was friendly, unassuming, and eager to cooperate. When I discussed salary and offered an amount far less than she normally
commanded, she accepted willingly and replied, "I'm pretty flush
from the last show. I'm just excited to be a part of this one."

When I talked about her limited trailer space, she offered suggestions on how to improve it at reasonable cost. When I inquired
about cleaning and alterations, she actually offered to wash some
of the wardrobe herself to save money. And when I apologized for
the measly budget she would have at her disposal, she assured me
it would be plenty since she had already contacted several manu-
facturers to obtain free product placement.

I was so pleased I could have hugged her. Not only was she
talented, she was perhaps the most production friendly costume
designer I had ever met. She accepted our limitations, she respected the job we were trying to do, and she was willing to be
part of the team. Wow!

I realized as she left the office that I had become jaded about
glam squads. Yes, there were always going to be people in that
and other fields who would make unreasonable demands. But I
could not and should not assume they would all be prima donnas.
Some were as down-to-earth as I could wish and willing to collaborate fully.

**Mindlessly accepting stereotypes is a superficial way
to manage. Make an effort to give each new employee
or co-worker the benefit of the doubt, whatever his or
her vocation's public image. Assume full cooperation
and collaboration until proven wrong.**

AVOIDING LABELS

MY PART WILL BE PLAYED BY ...

We learn early that labeling or categorizing objects or people makes identification easier. A child learns to sort letters, numbers, and colors, all in an effort to organize his or her world. But as we grow older, we rely on labeling in ways that can be counterproductive. After all, the suit does not make the man.

It was in high school that I first felt diminished by a label. At the time, there were three stereotypes for kids: the popular kids, the jocks, and the stoners. By rank, popular was first, jock second, and stoner a distant third. Once you were labeled, there was no way out. In the trauma of adolescence, you felt stuck forever.

Sadly, high school was unkind to me. Though I tried out for numerous extracurricular activities, I could not seem to find satisfaction or success. I auditioned for plays, campaigned to be a senator, even auditioned for the song team—but to no avail. Finally, I found a place on the diving team, grateful to be part of a group but still displeased to be labeled a jock.

When graduation finally arrived, I was happy to leave high school's identification system and looked forward to social interactions where preconceptions would be abandoned and people would be evaluated on their own merits. In college, the tide turned for me, and I was able to triumph over adversity. Refusing to let labels keep me down, I found success in politics, social organizations, and academia and was singled out for honors at graduation. But the labels persisted, and throughout my career I have always had to contend with them.

In the film business, as a general rule, someone with television experience is all but excluded from feature films. People who produce reality shows are banned from scripted shows. Low-budget cable experience is insufficient for high-budget network employment. It is very difficult to cross over. Once you are "credited" with certain experience, the general assumption is that that is all you are qualified to do. I cannot tell you how many times I interviewed with feature directors who took one look at my résumé and decided I was not up to the task because of my television background.

On one occasion, I was told I was not qualified for a job in Los Angeles because I had been working exclusively out of town on location. I immediately called the studio executive and pleaded my case. I began by comparing the show for which I was being considered to the shows I had recently produced. I noted that in Los Angeles I would have access to the most qualified crews in the industry. On location, I often had to utilize local talent who lacked the requisite experience thus necessitating additional training and supervision.

I talked about the facility to be utilized. In Los Angeles, we would have a soundstage that was built specifically for filming. It would have high ceilings to accommodate sets. It would be designed with proper air conditioning to handle the heat generated by lights. It would have ample power to support any lighting design. It would have green beds (walkways built in the rafters) to provide easy access for grip and electric work. And it would be soundproof.

In contrast, on location I would have to convert an old department store, an embroidery factory, or even a brewery into a suitable soundstage. That necessitated altering the space by soundproofing it, modifying the power supplies, and installing air conditioning and temporary red light (keep-out) systems, all to make it film-friendly.

(In the interest of discretion, I decided not to tell the executive about the time I converted an embroidery factory in rainy Florida into a soundstage and, after the fact and to my horror, had to cover the entire 40,000-square-foot metal roof with roll after roll of horse-hair blankets to muffle the din during downpours. Well, we live and learn.)

I also discussed differences in the handling of labor contracts. When you film in Los Angeles, the contracts are prenegotiated so you know how much you will have to pay in salary and benefits. On location, you need to meet with and negotiate terms and conditions for all the crew.

Finally, I talked about the resources available in and around Los Angeles. Just about everything a script calls for can be purchased, rented, or manufactured in Los Angeles. That is not always so on location. Try finding a 1914 Stutz Bearcat automobile in a small town in Iowa.

Producing a show on location is far more difficult than producing one in town. Yet, the studio had categorized me as a location producer and not a local one. By showing the executive I was more than a label, I was able to prove I was the right person for the job. In the end, I was given the show and have been working in Los Angeles ever since.

But that was not the only label travail I faced in the film business. Another label that was incredibly difficult to overcome was that of certified public accountant. As I note throughout this book, my transition from accounting to production was a difficult one. That was because too many people held preconceived ideas about what an accountant should be and do. I had to overcome a truly ingrained set of assumptions. People saw me as a numbers cruncher. That meant I was analytical, organized, and fiscally responsible. But to others, it also meant I lacked creative vision. They surmised it was impossible for someone to be a good accountant and a good storyteller at the same time. They felt the two callings were mutually exclusive.

At one point, a successful development executive told me in no uncertain terms that I would never become a producer. She believed the best I could hope for was to work in the contracts department of a studio. In her mind, I was just a business suit. She could not see me as anything more than what I currently was. She was not interested in getting to know the real me and was satisfied to categorize me as she saw fit.

So for many years, I hid my credentials. Despite all the hard work that went into passing the CPA exam and the years of auditing that were required to obtain my license, I refused to be categorized solely as an accountant. It was too damaging to my film career.

Now, with many shows under my belt, I share my credentials with pride. I feel that all my qualifications have made me a better producer and I am no longer afraid to highlight them.

My advice is to resist being labeled at all costs. If someone categorizes you unfairly, speak up and show them they are wrong. By the same token, try not to label others. Take the time to get to know people as individuals with specific gifts to offer. No one fits any one category. We all are diverse and special in our own way. So refrain from using or accepting labels. That will help you move past stereotypes.

If you are unfairly or inappropriately labeled, your career will be slowed or diverted. If you unfairly or inappropriately label others, you will squander talent. Fight to get a chance. Bend to give a chance.

AN ARSENAL OF HIDDEN TALENTS

"Let your light shine!" "Share your gifts!" "Strut your stuff!" "If you've got it, flaunt it!" "Just get out there and show what you've got!" After all, the world can always use another helping hand.

Whenever I interview job applicants for a show, I always try to find out a little bit about their background. What are their hobbies? How do they spend their free time? Do they have a family? Pets? I do this because I have learned that some or all of their talents might prove useful on the project.

I remember shooting one day on location near a heavily trafficked local airport. We foolishly placed our set directly under the flight path. It was not until we started shooting a scene with dialogue that we realized the trouble we were in. Every few seconds, we would have to stop to let a plane go by. The actors were becoming increasingly frustrated and rightly so.

In jest, I told our location assistant to call the airport and redirect traffic. He assured me he would "get right on it," and I smiled at his appropriately sarcastic response. I turned my attention to minimizing scene interruptions. A few minutes later, the planes disappeared, and things quieted down.

"Well done," I jokingly told him.

"No problem," he responded.

He seemed sincere yet I did not consider for a moment that he had accomplished what I had asked.

"Are you playing me?" I inquired.

"No," he assured me. "They said they would use the alternate runway until we were finished." Holy cow!

Upon further inquiry, I learned that this underpaid assistant was an avid pilot who had flown for years and was friendly with the controllers in the flight tower. Who knew?

On another occasion, I worked with an assistant who had come to Los Angeles right from college looking for a way to break into the film business. He finally landed an entry-level job working as a writer's assistant on a television series. The job included making copies, fetching lunch, and answering phones.

After he had been with the show for a while and had established a relationship with some of the writers, he would make casual suggestions and offer disposable jokes to make dialogue funnier. Eventually, the writers started coming to him with ever-increasing frequency to add humor to their work. Now, he is a well-respected "punch up" artist in high demand and earns a great deal of money adding laughs to shows. Not bad for a guy whose throwaway talent was telling a joke. The fact is you never know where your talent or someone else's talent might lead.

Another example comes to mind: Several years ago, a writer/producer I currently work with was hired as an actress to star in a new pilot. Despite her best efforts, her performance was dreadful and she was going to be let go.

The director and head writer went to her trailer to tell her the bad news. Devastated by the turn of events, but thinking quickly, she asked if they might give her a job as a writer instead of an actress. They agreed, and happily, she has been writing successfully ever since.

I can also confirm that my own extracurricular activities have come into unexpected play upon occasion. Having studied dance my entire life, I often help choreograph smaller dance numbers on our shows. This worked well until one of our other producers decided I should also play the dance teacher in a particular scene. I was chary because of my antipathy to acting.

As I stood in the wardrobe trailer examining my skimpy costume, I had visions of ten million people seeing me shaking my booty in a leotard.

"Doesn't the camera add ten pounds?" I wondered aloud.

"I think so," our costume designer responded.

I handed her the tights, fled to my office, and hired someone else to take my place as the teacher. I also vowed to lose ten pounds in case I might be called upon in the future. As a dancer, of course, not an actor!

Then there is the issue of trying to acquire a new talent to supplement one's skill set. Coming up through the ranks and desiring to be a better producer, I asked the gaffer (lighting designer) on one of my show's if I could be an electrician for a day. He agreed provided I commit entirely to the job for twenty-four hours. I pledged to do so because I knew he would be counting on me as a member of the crew. Unfortunately, I picked a Friday to apprentice, just when we were filming a night scene out of doors.

Now, it happens that shows almost always save night work for the end of the week to be sure actors and crew get required turnaround time (rest) before being called back on set Monday morning. Union rules require this to avoid penalties, and the weekend ensures that it happens.

So my "day" started at 5 p.m., Friday, and ended at 6 a.m., Saturday. I worked like a demon because night shoots require a huge number of lights and very sophisticated lighting techniques. I wore a heavy tool belt for twelve hours, carried rolls and rolls of cable, helped the electricians set lights, helped the grips move stands, and watched the seconds tick by far too slowly. As luck would have it, it also started to snow. ("Gosh, Toto, I don't think we're in Hollywood anymore. This is Kansas.") When it was over, I crawled (still dressed) into bed, utterly exhausted.

No, I did not acquire a new set of skills. Yes, I did gain a profound respect for the work of film crews. And yes, I became a better producer for the experience. Maybe my new talent was just acquiring a higher level of awareness.

We all have hidden talents that can serve us well if we bring them out into the open. If you think you have something to offer, share it. If your co-workers have something to offer, find it.

> **You are more than the sum of your parts. Share hidden talents with others. Seek hidden talents from others. Effective management or performance is the full utilization of available skills and resources.**

STICKS AND STONES

It would be nice to think that name-calling went out of fashion at the end of elementary school. Unfortunately, it is alive and well today. Name-callers simply progress from loudmouthed bullies to manipulative adults who can wreak havoc on your self-esteem. When that happens, it helps to recall the schoolyard chant, "Sticks and stones can break my bones, but names will never hurt me" . . . but "useless in mind and body"?

I was working on a comedy series about a dysfunctional family when I became the punching bag for our leading lady. The show was problematic from the beginning. There were creative differences between the network and the show's writers. The show was costing the studio far more than originally anticipated, and the workload exceeded our limited resources. Each day we were incurring hours and hours of overtime.

A normal shooting day consists of twelve work hours with an additional half to a full hour for lunch. Anything over that comes at a significant premium. By the thirteenth hour, most crew members are into double time and are eligible for an assortment of additional fees referred to as meal penalties, night premiums, and forced calls.

Word finally came down from the network that "something had to be done!" We were given an ultimatum that we would have to complete each day's work exactly as scheduled. No more overtime would be approved. The bleeding had to stop. From that point on, everyone and everything came under intense scrutiny. The assistant director was pressured to keep the set moving more swiftly. The director of photography was told to light more quickly. And the director was told to block and shoot more expeditiously. The tension was so palpable you could cut it with a knife.

To add to our woes, a few of the actors were taking longer and longer to get ready to film. Often, we would find ourselves standing around, unable to shoot, while we waited for talent to arrive on set. Unfortunately, our studio executive happened to pay us a visit while this problem was occurring. She insisted that someone speak with the tardy, leading lady immediately. Our senior producer reluctantly offered to do so. I remember thinking how happy I was that this time it would not have to be me. Such conversations can be very unpleasant and can compromise a good working relationship if not handled properly.

The production continued as planned, and I gave no further thought to the issue. As the day came to a close and we were preparing to shoot our final scene, I exited the soundstage as the actress was entering it. I smiled and greeted her as always. She unloaded without warning. The gist of her tirade was that we were unfairly blaming her for the show's problems. I assured her that that was not the case. Unfortunately, she had heard through the grapevine that the studio had pointed her out as a problem that needed to be dealt with. As I later found out, the senior producer had avoided the issue completely. He had never bothered to talk to her.

The actress was ready for a fight. She began by telling me what a useless bunch of producers we were and how everything was our fault. Then she got personal. She began screaming that I was nothing but a simple-minded bean counter, that I was a useless waste of mind and body for whom she had no use, that I had not a single creative idea in my head, and that I had nothing useful to contribute to the show. She accused me of being one of those ugly little people who had nothing better to do than make her look bad.

For twenty minutes, I withstood the barrage trying desperately to defend myself, to maintain a sense of dignity, to present my case reasonably, but her words were so harsh, so painful that I left the set in pieces having been crushed by her outburst. Since that day, I have adopted a saying to protect myself in these situations (although I doubt I will ever again be subject to so nasty an assault), and it goes something like this: "It is not what someone says to you that matters, it is what you say to yourself when they stop talking that matters."

I did not have to accept the hurtful names she was calling me. I did not have to give her that type of power over me. If she had criticized me for something silly, such as being too bashful, for example, her comments would have rolled right off my back. I would not have given them a second thought. But in this instance, her comments really resonated with me. Being a waste of mind and body was especially hurtful. I was still learning to believe in myself, to trust my abilities and talents.

That day she got the better of me. Now, a few years and much reflection later, I would have handled the situation differently—

not by wildly defending myself, but by standing firm in my sense of self-assuredness. She needed to say what she said. She needed to protect herself out of her own fears and insecurities. At that moment, she was not interested in finding a solution or understanding the situation. She just needed to vent. But I did not need to own it or lose myself in it. In a strange way, her rant, in its very public and ugly forum, had nothing to do with me.

It is my firm belief that any conflict or misunderstanding between two people can and should be resolved in a respectful and professional manner. If you find yourself in a similar situation (outgunned and under attack), do not fight fire with fire. If you do, everyone will get burned. Take a deep breath, calmly see it for what it is, and give yourself permission to agree to disagree with someone else's assessment of you.

> **Try not to let words hurt you. It does not matter what someone says to you at work, however unkind. It only matters what you say to yourself when they stop talking. Vengeful retorts only diminish you in the eyes of others.**

AIMING JUST BEYOND YOUR REACH

MEN ARE JUST NATURALLY TOUGHER

My eight-year-old daughter recently asked me, "Why are boys so weird?" She was confident I could answer her question with perspicacity and precision. Of course, I could not. Men are a mystery to me and to most other women as well. They think, act, and behave so differently—so unpredictably. Even on the playground, they were more aggressive, more willing to take risks, louder, more forceful, and unfailingly interested in "yucky" stuff. So how do we compete against them? How do we suck it up?

I recently conducted an interview for a first assistant director on a cable comedy I was hired to produce. The candidate was a young man who had been recommended by our leading actress. I knew very little of his background but was certainly interested in talking with him because he came so highly recommended.

The job of first assistant director (1st AD) is extremely difficult under the best of circumstances and would certainly be so on this particular show because varying locations required numerous company moves. It was imperative that we find the right man or woman for the job.

So that you may better understand the complexity of the 1st AD position, let me share the job requirements with you. A 1st AD has overall responsibility for running the set. He or she is also the spokesperson for the director and the keeper and disseminator of all critical information. A 1st AD begins a project by taking a script and breaking it down into all its required elements: lists of characters, locations, sets, props, special effects, vehicles, stunts, specialty hair and makeup, background extras, and equipment. The 1st AD must also take into consideration actor availability, set preparedness, available manpower, time and chronology, efficiency of work flow, and day-versus-night requirements.

Once the 1st AD is familiar with all the required elements of the project, he or she will design a shooting schedule. This will determine the number of days it will take to film the show and the order in which the scenes will be shot. Scenes that take place in the same location will be clustered together. Actors' workdays will be consolidated to minimize hold days (nonworking days that are nevertheless paid days). Outdoor night scenes will need to be scheduled after dark (for obvious reasons). Neighborhood rules and restrictions applicable to filming will have to be observed. Time required to light scenes will need to be calculated. And all of this must support and accomplish the director's vision. It is a complex puzzle that requires intelligence and experience to assemble.

Once filming begins, the 1st AD will take charge of the set. One-hundred-plus crew members and cast will follow his verbal cues. He will be responsible for ensuring that all the elements required for the production are present and accounted for; that everyone is informed of the tasks to be accomplished; and that the company stays on schedule. A good 1st AD is a motivator, facilitator, communicator and expeditor and never buckles under pressure. In my experience, few earn top marks.

That is why my interview of the young man recommended by our star was so important. He was certainly personable, articulate and eager. But could he handle the job?

He handed me his résumé with an embarrassed smile. I looked it over and quickly concluded, as he already knew, that he had almost no relevant experience. He had graduated from the Directors Guild of America training program a few years earlier. He had only recently been elevated to key 2nd AD on an "all stage" (no locations) show and had only functioned as a 1st AD on a short film. He would be eaten alive, to coin a phrase, by our requirements.

I explained our needs in detail and the type of candidate for whom we were looking and was confident he would recuse himself. I was relieved when he agreed that he lacked the requisite experience and admitted that the task before him was daunting. But despite all that, he wanted to give it a try. *He wanted to give it a try?!*

Putting aside my reservations for the moment, I wondered whether a woman would be willing to take that kind of risk. The likelihood that he would fall flat on his face was almost certain, but it did not seem to deter him in any regard. I also found his callous disregard for the likely adverse effect of his inexperience on the show to be entirely consistent.

He reminded me of a production designer we had to hire for a show we filmed in the Northwest solely because he designed a stained-glass window for a self-centered creative executive who loved it. The designer had no working knowledge of the necessary arts of architecture, construction, set decoration, scenic painting, and vendor sourcing. As a consequence, when he decided to film a boy rocking in a rowboat, he built a complicated swing device to move the boat from side to side (requiring manhandling by numerous grips), which cost thousands of dollars, rather than spending a pittance to rent a simple mechanism to rock the camera for the same effect.

As I contemplated my applicant, I also compared him to another AD I had helped along the way. After years of toiling for me and others as a 2nd AD, she finally moved up to 1st AD, and I was pleased that I had positioned her to seize the opportunity when it arose. Unlike my applicant, she had been meticulous about gaining the necessary experience before taking on the job as a 1st AD. As a 2nd, she had watched, and learned from, the best. Then, after years in the 2nd AD position, she only moved up to 1st AD when she could work on smaller shoots to gain confidence and experience. Only then did she take on the responsibility of larger productions. I admired her approach.

My own early career developed much as hers: slowly and step by step. But, too slowly, with too many steps, as I eventually discovered. I realized this a number of years ago when I interviewed to be production manager of a very expensive dramatic pilot similar to *Miami Vice*. Before the interview, I did some research to learn about the people with whom I would be meeting. I was dismayed to learn that one of the producers (the one to whom I would be reporting should I take the job) had far less experience than I, yet had accomplished so much more in his career.

How did this happen? Had I inadvertently held myself back? Had I been too cautious and meticulous in gaining experience? Had my aversion to risk or fear of failure kept me from capitalizing on opportunities that came my way? Had I been less aggressive than a man would have been? Upon reflection, the answer was yes on almost all counts. So I decided to change my approach. I began looking for work that was slightly beyond my reach and beyond my comfort zone but not beyond by abilities. And it paid off as the years rolled by.

As for the 1st AD candidate, I thanked him and showed him the door. I decided, as always, to hire someone who could meet the requirements of the position. His arrogance and my former timidity reminded me that there was a happy medium between being too cautious and too reckless. That happy medium is somewhere between male aggressiveness and female reticence. While it is important to be prepared, it is equally important to take a chance on yourself.

Growth involves risk. We cannot be so afraid of failure that we are unwilling to try. We cannot overdo the need for preparation. Sometimes you will fail and sometimes you will succeed. Either way, it will be a great learning experience.

You must be neither too cautious nor too aggressive in taking on job responsibilities beyond your level of experience. Growth requires risk, which leads to reward. Aim slightly beyond your reach and comfort zone, but not beyond your abilities.

THAT'S WHAT BAND-AIDS ARE FOR

Do you remember the first time you rode a bike with your dad running alongside to keep you from falling down? Eventually, he had to let go, and you were on your own, barreling full speed ahead into the neighbor's new car. Do you remember at the pool when you sank like a stone hoping the lifeguard was paying attention and would give you another chance at life? If so, you know we all learn by trial and error. We make mistakes, correct our actions, and try again. Eventually, we are able to make it all the way down the street or to the side of the pool. Eventually, we get out of the rain.

Not long after I was admitted into the directors guild and became a network production manager, I was sent on location to work on a new series. I was young for the position and, having just received my promotion, knew I had a lot to learn. Fortunately, I was working for someone who had a great deal of experience and was willing to teach me. I knew I could count on him if the need arose.

Part of my job was to prepare the show's budget and approve the schedule that had been prepared by the 1st AD. Together, we would determine, among other things, which scenes would be shot each day, how long the work should take, where the scenes would be staged, what labor would be needed, what prerigging was required, and when each person would be called to work. Then, as the day progressed, the crew would look to me to decide when to break and what scheduling changes were needed if we were running late. I was confident I could handle the job.

A few days into the project, we were shooting an exterior scene when the skies opened up with a deluge. All filming stopped, actors ran for cover, crew quickly packed up sensitive equipment, and everyone huddled under pop-up tents to stay out of the rain. In the midst of the confusion, the director asked me, "What would you like us to do now?"

I looked around, wondering to whom he was talking. Whoa! It was me! The senior producer was on a location scout and, as I quickly learned, out of cell-phone range. I was all they had. Me, their fearless leader.

Everyone waited for an answer. Everyone waited for guidance. Everyone waited for a plan. Everyone was looking at me. I had to say something. I had to demonstrate I could take charge. I thought for a minute, looked over the schedule of the day's work, and made an executive decision.

"Let's move to the scene in the barn!" I commanded, certain that was the best plan of action. So the troops began to relocate: cameras, lights, chairs, monitors, props, wardrobe, and crew all moved through the mud to the new set. Unhappily, as soon as we arrived at the barn, I realized the roof could not keep out the rain, and it was leaking cats and dogs. We were as wet inside as out.

"Sorry . . . bad idea," I admitted, once everyone was settled in.

I briefly considered shooting in the rain. That was because producers often try to convince everyone else that a light rain will not show on film. It is far preferable and cheaper to do that than continuously moving to new sets. Of course, the droplets from the awning, the actors' wet hair, and the puddles in the background might be considered artistic failures, but only for the truly fussy. (Nowadays, of course, with hi-def, there is simply no way to ignore the patter of raindrops on the ground.) In any event, I decided to try another tack.

I looked over the call sheet for another plan. I spotted a scene that was to be filmed in the kitchen of the house we were using. "Let's move to Scene 18," I piped up. Before anyone could respond, I high-tailed it toward the house to show strong leadership. The director and assistant director followed right on my heels. The rest of the crew started packing, yet again, for another move.

The assistant director puffed up beside me. "We can't shoot that scene," he hissed at me. "The actors in the scene are not scheduled to arrive until late this afternoon."

What?! I stopped dead in my tracks, inches from the kitchen door. Since most of the crew had more experience than I, it did not take them long to come to the same conclusion. Scene 18 was out. I turned back to see a frustrated and soggy group of people staring daggers my way, all wondering how they got saddled with such a lightweight.

Finally, I did what I should have done from the beginning. I turned to my co-workers for help. Together, the director, assistant director, director of photography, and I looked over the schedule to determine how we might effectively utilize our time until the rain passed. We settled on a scene to be shot at the front door of the house under a porch roof that kept everyone out of harm's way. The crew breathed a collective sigh of relief knowing that their wild goose chase had come to an end.

Now, I can look back and laugh at my ineptness. But I learned from the experience and will not make the same mistake again. I am always prepared with a backup plan should lightning strike. I also know to include others in the decision-making process.

I have made many mistakes in my career, and I wear each scar with pride. It would be impossible to survive in this industry without falling down from time to time and learning from moment to moment. The key is to get up, brush yourself off, and keep on truckin'.

In times of trial, resist being the lone ranger.
Consult with your co-workers on the best solution.
Listen and learn to minimize your inevitable mistakes.

FOLLOW-THROUGH AND YOU

180 SANDWICHES IN 20 MINUTES

Have you ever felt like a short-order cook at home frantically whipping out meals to order? One child wants chicken fingers with ranch dressing, the other has recently become a vegan, and your husband still thinks meat and potatoes are a constitutional right. Be grateful you are not cooking for an army.

As I mentioned before, food is a mainstay in the making of any film or television show. Not only have workers become accustomed to culinary delights, film companies are required to follow union rules governing when and how often meals are to be served. If meals are not delivered on time, each employee is paid a meal penalty to compensate for the default. The penalties are paid as follows: $10 for the first half hour the meal is late, $15 for the next half hour, and $20 for any half-hour increment thereafter, until the meal is properly served. This can be very costly with so many cast and crew on set.

Now, breakfast and lunch are easy to manage since we have a full-time caterer near the set whose only responsibility is to prepare and serve meals on time. However, the dinner, or what we refer to as the "second meal," often becomes the responsibility of the craft service department. (It is referred to as a second meal because it is the second meal required; breakfast is a courtesy.) Usually, the craft service department will make arrangements with a nearby restaurant to provide the second meal. This gets tricky if filming is extended into the wee hours because most restaurants are closed.

To further complicate matters, we rarely know we will need a second meal until about two hours before it is required. Normally, we try to avoid serving a second meal by staying on schedule. But if we fall behind and film more than twelve hours, we need to make the necessary arrangements. Just you try calling a busy restaurant and ordering lasagna for one hundred ASAP; most just laugh and hang up the phone.

To be honest, meals are the bane of any producer's existence. Here is an example: We were filming a television show near MacArthur Park in Los Angeles. It was around 9 p.m., and I could tell we were going to be working much later than that. Thinking ahead, I asked our craft service specialist (a temporary replacement) to take care of obtaining a second meal I explained that we needed to do something special to help motivate our exhausted cast and crew. We were at the end of an especially hard week— fourteen-hour days, working under difficult conditions. Everyone was frustrated that we were so far behind schedule.

I knew a nice hot meal would boost everyone's spirits so I authorized craft service to spend double our normal budget. At 10:30 p.m., I went back to check on their progress but found no one around. Beginning to panic, I tried reaching the specialist on the walkie-talkie without success and eventually found her chopping vegetables and watching a DVD in the craft service truck.

"Where is the food?" I asked anxiously.

"Oh, sorry, I struck out. I couldn't find a restaurant close by that would deliver."

"Deliver!? We have twenty drivers standing around doing nothing! Surely one of them could have picked it up!"

"Well, no one could accommodate such a large group on such short notice," she mumbled, as she continued to watch her show.

Frustrated, I stepped forward and blocked her view. "So, why didn't you come and tell me sooner?"

"I was just about to," she said, licking her fingers as she put the finishing touches on her veggie tray.

"*We need to feed these people!*"

"I am," she said, proudly displaying her platter.

All I could think of was the angry mob that was about to descend on me and the thousands of dollars in meal penalties we were going to have to disburse.

I bristled at her, "I don't think you understand the gravity of the situation."

"What's the problem? We have an entire trailer full of snacks," she said, making a sweeping gesture with her hand. "I'll put out some chips and dip."

Then it hit me. "You've never worked on a union show before have you?" I asked.

"No. I was just helping out Frank. He was sick and asked me to fill in."

It was starting to make sense. She had no idea why the second meal was so important. By assuming she did, I failed to effectively communicate my needs. To the uninitiated, she was right, we did have plenty of marginal food available, and we had been eating it all day.

Nevertheless, I still had to find a solution to my problem. In half an hour, the cast and crew would take a break and would want something more substantial than chips and carrot sticks. I grabbed the nearest driver, a van, and a wad of cash and went looking for food.

About a block away, I found my solution: a Subway sandwich shop. Now, for a second meal to qualify as sufficient, it needs to be a hot entrée accompanied by a few side dishes, but given the circumstances, I was willing to settle for any kind of reasonable substitute. I ran through the front door taking the lone clerk by surprise.

"Quick, I need 180 sandwiches in twenty minutes," I said, pulling out my wad of cash to show I meant business.

"You gotta be kidding me!" he said, wondering if I was just off the funny farm.

"No, seriously, do I look like a woman who's kidding? I am desperate here, so please help me out. I need those sandwiches as quickly as you can make them."

Despite the panic in my voice, he refused to move. "Ain't no way I can get that many sandwiches done that fast, and I'm supposed to be closing soon." He looked at the clock, willing time to move more quickly.

In utter desperation, I did what any reasonably panicked producer would do in a similar situation. I jumped over the counter, put on a pair of gloves and grabbed as many pieces of bread as I could lay out to make sandwiches.

"Hey, you can't come back here," he said, trying to push me away. "Get back on the other side."

"Either help me or get out of my way!" I bellowed, mustard and mayonnaise flying.

"Seriously lady, if the owner comes in, I'll lose my job. You need to stop doing that!"

By now I was slapping sandwiches together on every surface. I was in a groove. The clerk realized there was no getting rid of me, so reluctantly, he started to help, and twenty minutes later the sandwiches were done.

I wish the crew had been as impressed by my perseverance as I was, but they did get a good laugh at the photo our driver took of me behind the counter. Fortunately, my heroic efforts paid off, to some degree. Only a few of the crew insisted on meal penalties that night. Most agreed to give me an A for effort and a pass on the penalties.

In the end, I learned three things from that experience. Well, four actually. First, make sure you give clear and concise directions. It also helps to explain just why you want something done a certain way. Second, do not take no for an answer. Third, I confirmed there is little future for me in the food service industry. And fourth, as a manager, you must assume responsibility for the actions of your subordinates.

When I say I confirmed there was little future for me in the food service industry, it is because my lack of skill had originally been established in an earlier culinary disaster.

Union rules require that each film production have a medic (registered nurse, emergency medical technician) on hand. In Canada, years ago, the medic could double up on tasks, and on a show I produced, the medic was also the key craft service supervisor. She was preparing a fruit salad for our little army when her assistant sliced open her finger, and she had to treat the injury on the spot and take the assistant to a clinic. I innocently entered the craft service truck as they departed, just in time to take a call from the production assistant on set pleading for food for a famished crew. An hour later, I was still assembling a disheveled and disjointed fruit salad, cursing the gods for their thoughtless prank. Later on, significant grumbling accompanied reluctant digestion.

Good managers give credit to their workers for a job well done. They also stand up and take the blame when a good worker fails. Ultimately, you are responsible for those you manage, and their follow-through is up to you.

You ultimately are responsible for the follow-through or lack of follow-through of your subordinates. Make sure you give clear directions and provide necessary support to ensure a positive outcome. Keep in mind that clear directions become even clearer when the reasons for them are fully explained.

THE SIGHT OF BLOOD MAKES ME QUEASY

Are you afraid of things that go bump in the night? Do you cower under the covers when you hear an unfamiliar sound? Do scary movies haunt your dreams for days on end, and if so, do you sleep with the lights on and the doors locked? You may have a date with the dead.

My father tells a story of his most eerie otherworldly experience. He was visiting the town of Skagway in Alaska, which was a conduit to the Klondike during the Yukon Gold Rush of 1898 and was founded to service and swindle the gold-crazy stampeders. The town and most of its vices were run by Soapy Smith, a thug and boss who cut his teeth on shell games, rigged elections, and saloon and gambling hall proprietorship. He was killed in a gunfight and buried in the remote town cemetery along with other, more upstanding citizens. Over the years, the cemetery became a tourist attraction.

My father decided to visit the cemetery early one morning and reached it down a lonely dirt road that paralleled an abandoned railroad track. At the cemetery, the breeze gently rippled the leaves of the giant trees in the grove enveloping the cracked and tilted headstones. The shade was dappled by sunlight revealing the exposed roots that had interwoven themselves under, around, and through the graves. It was lonely, lonely. My father sensed the presence of the dead. The hair stood up on the back of his neck. Man's primordial fear of the unknown sent shivers down his spine.

I too had an eerie experience in a cemetery while shooting a television miniseries in the Midwest. We were filming an artificial gravesite we had created in the corner of a real cemetery. The sky was truly dark and gray; the ground white with new fallen snow; the landscape barren and colorless. As the camera was about to roll, the director asked if we had some flowers to lay at the base of the headstone to brighten up the scene. Unfortunately, there were none readily available.

I looked out over the rows and rows of headstones and spotted a bright pink bouquet in the distance. I asked the director to hold the camera while I ran to retrieve it. As I bent down to pick up the flowers, apologizing to the deceased for my indiscretion and assuring him I would return the flowers promptly, I noticed that the name engraved in the headstone was the exact same name as that of our lead character in the miniseries. I shivered involuntarily and bolted back to the safety of our group.

Oh, I also made one of our junior production assistants return the flowers to the grave. As happened with my father, I was discomfited in the presence of the dead. But there was more to come, and the next time, the dead were above ground.

As part of my job, I am asked to find and employ specialists to assist us in making our shows as authentic as possible. If a show is about the CIA, we retain a retired agent. If a show features the growth and distribution of marijuana, we look for a weed connoisseur. If a show highlights a North American Indian tribe, we locate a Haida scholar. And if a show is about a coroner's office, we go directly to the source if the source cannot come to us.

Awhile back, I found myself entering the private sanctum sanctorum of a county coroner's facility. It was one of the busiest and most reputable in the United States. As the doors closed behind me, I berated myself asking, "Is there nothing you won't do for the good of a show?"

Normally, I look forward to learning experiences. It is one of the better parts of my job because I have access to places that discourage the presence of unauthorized personnel. I love the opportunity to observe and learn. On this particular day, however, I was frightened by what I was about to see. Even a friendly visit to the hospital makes me weak in the knees.

Our makeup artist, set decorator, and prop master accompanied me to the facility, and we were given a private, behind-the-scenes tour of every aspect of the coroner's operation. We steeled ourselves as bodies were weighed, tested, and tagged.

We spent time with a fingerprint specialist who created a way to rehydrate dead tissue and was proud to demonstrate his ability to extract fingerprints off particularly difficult specimens. We entered large refrigerated rooms filled wall-to-wall with corpses in repose; nothing like the organized drawers you see on prime-time television. We saw organ extractions and full autopsies. We saw nameless Jack and Jan Does. And saddest of all, we saw grieving families in pain.

Some of the elements of the coroner's operation struck me as completely incongruous, such as the gift shop offering towels, T-shirts, baseball caps, and key chains and the drop-dead gorgeous examiner who conducted field investigations of murders and deadly accidents with professional enthusiasm. Her description of accidents involving improperly secured children in car seats made me late for appointments for months as I tightened, re-strapped, and rebelted my daughter into her car seat before every journey.

The construction-site sounds of saws, grinders, and choppers necessary to swiftly harvest donated organs need no further description; nor does the unavoidable reduction of precious life to respectfully handled meat.

By the time we left the facility, we were intimately familiar with death. I had no idea then that its sounds, smells, and the images would haunt me for years to come. Given the chance to relive that day, however, I would do it without hesitation. Not because I have a morbid interest in the dead, but because I believe that my responsibility to create a good show must sometimes outweigh my personal discomforts. All of us felt we had to push past our limitations if we wanted to complete our work successfully.

It is true of other areas of film production, as well. Nowhere is this so manifestly obvious as in stunt work. To this day, I have never had a stuntperson come to me and say, "This is a little too much for me. I think I'll sit this one out." No, they do what the job requires. Having watched many in the profession prepare for a difficult stunt, I know for certain they feel fear; I know they doubt themselves; I know that sometimes they ache to declare, "It is better to say 'There he goes, than there he lies.'" But they push past all that and do the job they were hired to do. They follow through.

I remember one particular evening when I was standing by the camera at the bottom of a long, outdoor staircase leading down to a cluster of homes. In the scene we were about to film, the character was to fall down approximately forty steps to his death. The staircase was extremely narrow and made of cement, which further complicated the stunt.

We rolled camera, called action, and waited expectantly for the stuntman to begin his fall. Seconds ticked by as we watched him muster the courage to take the first step. I could only imagine how he must be feeling as I, standing safely below, felt terrified. Finally, he started his descent. Head over heels, over head, over heels, down the steep, hard surface.

The fall went on longer than I would ever have imagined; maybe time just stood still for me. He finally landed with a thud, lifeless at the bottom. When he began to stir at last, we all let out a collective sigh of relief. Thankfully, he was all right.

It takes a great deal of commitment, courage, and fortitude for film people to do what they do. They take their responsibilities seriously and conduct themselves with perfection in mind. You should approach your own commitments at work the same way. Give all you can, even if it is uncomfortable or requires you to reach.

When your performance review praises you for efforts above and beyond the call of duty, for unswerving dedication to completing the tasks at hand, and for placing the company's interests above your own, you will know you have pushed past your personal limitations and are doing the job you were hired to do.

CAN THIS ELEPHANT CURTSY ON CUE?

Have you ever tried to teach your pet a new trick? I have a tiny dachshund, a smooth little frankfurter that scoots around on frenetic legs chasing tennis balls, charging from couch to glass door to yip away malefactors, and leaping almost inches from the ground to snare treats. Despite my best efforts, he cannot sit on cue but that is all right because he cannot roll over either. I wonder if I might have better luck with something bigger? Perhaps an elephant.

While there are many things elephants can do—roll or pick up logs, balance on their hind legs, trumpet their presence, wear adornments, cuddle their babies, and shower their own backs—it does not seem likely that they can rise up on their haunches, cross one leg behind the other, bend their knees, hold up a skirt, and bend forward in a curtsy.

However, in film—when the actors are missing their marks, the director of photography is still lighting, a key prop has broken, the backdrop is too short, the schedule is shot, the budget is hemorrhaging, and the studio is screaming—can a director on the verge of hysteria and desperate for a hit cry out in frustration, "Can this elephant curtsy on cue?" I should say so. And everyone will do his or her best to make it happen, particularly the producers.

Filmmakers pride themselves on accomplishing difficult tasks. Even if the script calls for something extraordinary, they will try to provide it or go down fighting. Naturally, this becomes especially difficult when dealing with unpredictable and unreliable animals.

A few years ago, a good friend of mine journeyed to Asia to work as a first assistant director on a very large feature film. The script called for a lavish parade extending a quarter of a mile featuring ornate carriages, skipping children, prancing horses, thousands of cheering extras, and numerous regal elephants. To my overworked friend, the parade seemed comprised of thousands of different components.

In order for the production company to mount such an awesome spectacle, it hired an expedition master to determine the participants in the parade, the order in which they would march, the banners and bunting they would display, and where the parade would start and stop. The planning and preparation took months; the rehearsal took weeks.

Sadly, elephants are not always comfortable surrounded by thousands of people and unfamiliar livestock. To prepare them for the parade, the trainers decided to introduce them slowly to each participating unit.

One morning, the elephant trainers and the horse trainers brought their animals to an open field to give them a chance to familiarize themselves with the sights, smells, and sounds of each other. Extra trainers stood by to intervene in the event of aggressive behavior. The elephants were released from their transports, and the horses from theirs. Everyone stood stock-still: waiting, anticipating, dreading.

For a few moments, the meet and greet appeared uneventful. The horses looked at the elephants; the elephants at the horses. Zephyrs were sniffed; dirt pawed. Then, without warning, both species bolted in opposite directions, plunging deep into the surrounding jungle. Before the trainers could react, the animals were gone. Arresting the mad dash of a six-ton pachyderm departing at 15 mph was next to impossible.

Eventually, after much time and effort, the animals were rounded up and returned to their enclosures. Over time, a great deal of time, they were acclimatized, and the parade went off without a hitch. Round one for production!

That, of course, was a story of massed elephants. Individual elephants have minds of their own. A camera operator I know was filming a scene that required an actor to deliver his lines atop a discriminating behemoth. I say discriminating because the leviathan apparently did not care for the performance and shrugged the rider off his back and into the dust. What a critic!

All the film's horses and all the film's men could not get that thespian astride again. Fortunately, the trainers were well prepared, and a more forgiving elephant lumbered in to nail the scene. Round two for production!

When working with animals, I always expect the unexpected and am rarely disappointed. Except for a sloth that was exquisitely trained to do absolutely nothing, every other animal has surprised me in one way or another, and I have worked with them all: bears, caribou, panthers, mountain lions, rats, dogs, cats, birds, camels, zebras, alligators, squirrels, monkeys, chimpanzees, horses, bats, wolves, dolphins, seals, emus, ostriches, marmosets, macaws, iguanas, llamas, orangutans, gorillas, antelopes, potbellied pigs, rhinos, and, of course, elephants.

While filming a scene in which a mountain lion was to wander into the backyard of our lead actor's house and peer through the living room window to exchange looks with our star, I was once again caught short. Since we were working on a soundstage, we were able to "control" the environment: All unnecessary personnel were excused; all necessary personnel were cordoned off; the animal trainers were stationed just off-camera; and the lion was "restrained" by a safety line.

We rolled camera and called action. The lion moved through the frame, turned, looked at the actor, and then ambled away. The director called cut, and we congratulated ourselves on a scene well done.

Then, over the walkie-talkie, I heard, "I need everyone to stay exactly where you are. Nobody move." Unsure of what was happening, we joked that the lion was probably on the prowl.

Then we heard, "No need to panic but the lion is loose. Stay where you are until we can contain him."

Talk about a frozen tableau! We were posed for the long haul. No longer was the living room set a safe refuge. Somewhere out there in the dark was a hungry beast undoubtedly looking for its next meal. If memory serves, we forgot to breathe. Time moved with excruciating deliberation. Finally, the trainers found the cat and coaxed it back into its cage, and we were free to go. I got caught in the crush at the bathroom door. Round three for production!

On another occasion, I was directing a second unit that needed to film live rats. In the scene, our actor (pretending he's had too much to drink) hears something scurrying around inside the wall of his house. He takes out a gun and begins shooting at the wall. As the scene unfolds, the rats scurry willy-nilly through the house while the actor blasts away trying to wax them.

The first unit crew had already filmed the actor's side of the scene. It was up to us to film the rats scurrying around with fake ricochets popping up as they ran by. Despite our best efforts, we could not get the rats to cooperate. If we needed them to stand on a mark, they ran away. If we needed them to run away, they stayed glued to their spot. If we needed them to climb in a bowl, they ran around its base. Even bribery failed. In this age of plenty, cheese is apparently insufficient as a reward to rats and of no moment in convincing them to listen to reason.

In utter frustration, the trainer turned to me said, "I am so sorry this is not working the way you had hoped, but your producer was so desperate to save money that she refused to let us have the time we needed to train the rats properly."

Unfortunately, the producer was me, and he did not know it because we had never met before. I guess I had no right to complain. But despite the difficulties, we persevered and finally got some really funny footage. Round four for production!

Over time, I have learned some really useful lessons when dealing with animals. I try to give them as much training time as I can possibly afford. I make sure we schedule extra time during filming to cover the unexpected. I always insist that we have backup animals so that when one throws a tantrum and refuses to "come out of his trailer," we can nevertheless proceed. And I maintain a high level of optimism that things will work out, or almost work out, one way or another, to some degree, if the Gods so ordain. To date, that philosophy has served me well. Despite all the animals and all the missteps, I have never had a scene with animals that failed to work. Round five for me!

So, in a way, the answer is "Yes, the elephant can curtsy on cue." He can also hula, blow his nose, and shell peanuts standing on one foot. The truth is, almost anything can be done if a producer sets his mind to it.

"Must have it in two hours."

"No problem."

"They've doubled the price."

"I'll take care of it."

"They've discontinued that model."

"I'll find it."

"It's not available."

"We'll have it tomorrow."

Over the years, I have found that success is yours if you never give up. So perhaps it is time to add a goal-oriented attitude to your bag of skills. Say, "Yes, I can do that for you." Or, "Yes, I can make it happen." Or, "Yes, I will find a solution." Not only will you be more successful in your personal and professional life, you will set a good example for others to follow. Become that "can do" person that others want to emulate.

Be the person that makes things happen.
When yes becomes your standard response,
your co-workers know they can count on you to
get the job done. "Can do" people are prepared in
advance and expect the unexpected.

DEALING WITH DISAPPOINTMENTS

BOUNCE, BOUNCE, BOUNCE BACK

Do you know how to find that silver lining? Find the hope in hopeless? Make gold from lead? Some people just have a knack for it. No matter the circumstances, despite the disappointments, regardless of the setbacks, these optimists see rays of hope where the rest of us see gray skies. After all, do we really want our credo to be, "No matter how bad things get, they can always get worse"?

Throughout this book, I share my triumphs and achievements, but also my struggles, failures, and disappointments. From pain and sorrow, I try to mine nuggets of insight and wisdom to make each experience worthwhile. The experience I now share was one of my most professionally disappointing.

About five years ago, I was hired to coproduce a new pilot for a network drama. A talented writer who had built a solid reputation for himself in television had written the script. The show had all the makings of success: a skilled director, talented actors, and the financial resources to mount a beautifully filmed drama. The network was enthusiastic and seemed willing to support the project for the long run.

For months, I worked alongside a group of seasoned professionals, appreciative of the opportunity to contribute to a winner. I learned, I stretched, I struggled, and I gave it my best. Because I was part of the inner circle, I was allowed to participate in all aspects of the filmmaking process. I was a crucial part of the team.

When the pilot was finally complete, I was asked to begin planning for the highly anticipated series. I was so confident of my continued participation in the project, I readily agreed to locate potential stages and prepare a preliminary budget. Our team then dispersed while we waited for a formal pickup from the network.

I returned to my then home in the East to rest up and enjoy

the summer. For the first time in a long time, I was able to take full recreational advantage of the hiatus. Confident a job was waiting for me, I made no effort to network or look for future employment.

Then, one morning, I went to my local coffee shop, picked up the newspaper, and read that the show had received a twelve-episode order from the network the previous day. The story went on to praise the show and anticipate its future success. I was thrilled and waited for someone to contact me to let me know when to return to LA.

As the days passed without word, my confidence turned to concern. Why was no one contacting me? What had happened to disrupt my expectations? I decided to confront the issue and placed a call to my immediate supervisor on the pilot; someone who I believed was my friend. My phone call went unanswered and unreturned. Despite my hard work, no matter the nature of our relationship, he apparently was unwilling to return a simple phone call.

Shortly thereafter, I heard through friends that my position had been filled by another. I was bitterly disappointed. I finally mustered the courage to call an executive at the network with whom I had had a previous and positive relationship. I had to know what had happened. As I dialed the number, I felt like a jilted lover looking for closure.

Fortunately, the network executive took my call immediately. I asked if he could enlighten me about the hiring process. I explained that I certainly respected the decision not to recall me but that if there was some way I could improve my work—which must have been insufficient—I would be glad to do so and would be grateful for any feedback he could give me.

He had no explanation for me. He assured me that he was as disappointed and surprised as I was about the decision. He confirmed that the network was very happy with my work and would have gladly seen me return. All he knew was that the show runners decided to make a change. Apparently, the gentleman re-placing me had worked with the producers on other projects and had been unavailable for the pilot.

Unfortunately, I had to live with the disappointment without any real understanding of it. I felt at sea. I began to question my understanding of the business. If I could so easily misread the signs, believing my work was respected and appreciated, how could I trust my instincts in the future? To make matters worse, the show was a smash hit, and I could not share in its success.

I decided to talk to other producers who had experienced re-verses similar to mine. One had been replaced on three different shows in a five-year period. On one, he was blamed for being un-able to control the director and curb cost overruns. On another, the executive producer decided to give the show to a friend. On a third, he was unwilling to go over budget despite the show run-ner's insistence. Despite this run of bad luck, he was now produc-ing a top-ten show in its third season. The truth is none of these failures defined him. He was and is a respected producer who will continue to obtain work. I, too, am the same producer I was before my replacement. Nothing about the experience could change that.

Over the years, I have been on the other side of the fence. I have had to call people to let them know they would not be asked back. I know now that just because they were wrong for my show does not automatically mean they were deficient in any profes-sional respect.

Things change, people change, feelings change, requirements change; and sometimes we are affected adversely without culpa-bility. Do not let disappointments derail you. Change the things you can and accept the things you cannot.

**Treat disappointments as signals to change direction.
The sooner you pick yourself up and move forward,
the sooner you will be open to new opportunities.**

REDECORATE YOUR MIND

How easily can you alter your perspective? Change your point of view? Focus on something different? Think more positively? Become more creative? Why not let filmmaking train your mind.

Filmmaking, for the most part, is the utilization of a variety of illusions to tell a story. It is accomplished by and through the magic of sets, sound, makeup, wardrobe, camera work, and visual effects. Anyone stepping foot on a film set for the first time is usually surprised at how different things look from behind the camera.

Here is an example of how an illusion is created: We were producing a comedy series about a middle-aged married couple. In the story, the couple, trying eagerly to recapture lost youth, decides to attend a rock concert featuring one of their favorite bands. In the scene, the wife, having had a little too much to drink, climbs up on her husband's shoulders, lifts her blouse, and flashes the lead singer.

Organizing the scene was a challenge. First, we could not afford a big-name band to be on the show for just one scene. Second, we could not afford to fill a concert hall with background extras. Third, we could not show the fully exposed breasts of the lead actress on network television.

To make the scene work, we needed to think outside the box. With the help of the director, the other producers, the director of photography, a visual effects supervisor, our production designer and our lighting gaffer, we devised a plan that worked swimmingly.

We decided to build a small version of a concert stage complete with lighting trellises. Then, we hired a local band to pretend to play in time to a preselected song. Then, we brought in 85 extras (all we could afford) to fill the area in front of the stage.

On the night of filming, we carefully blocked (with the camera) what we would and would not see. We used the lighting trellises to cover the absence of a sea of rock fans. We shot behind the actress's bare back to simulate full-frontal nudity. We used specific lenses to limit the camera's eye. We tightened our footage of the band to frequently show hands playing, feet moving, and drumsticks beating. And we placed the camera high on a crane to shoot downward to disguise the absence of a real concert hall.

Then, to flesh out the scene, we hired a cinematographer to attend and film a real rock concert taking place in another state. He shot footage using the same type of camera, stock and lenses we normally use so the two pieces of footage would cut together. Our wardrobe department replicated the costumes of the real band.

By cutting together footage of a real band, a real audience, and our actors in a fabricated setting, we were able to sell the illusion that the show's characters had actually attended a rock concert. Filmmaking magic!

Other examples of film magic come to mind. A creative approach that impressed me was used on the *West Wing* television show. The president, Martin Sheen, was scheduled to give a speech on the back lawn of the White House in front of a large crowd. The cost of assembling the crowd would have been prohibitive. To solve the problem, the show's creators employed an imaginative technique to film the scene.

They photographed the president as he walked from the Oval Office through a long series of corridors to the back lawn. During his walk, they superimposed the ever-increasing sound of a large crowd off in the distance. When he finally reached his destination, they switched the camera back to his face and allowed the speech to begin. At no time did you ever see an audience, yet you were certain it was there.

Makeup also plays a key role in creating illusions. In certain films, an actor can be thirty in one scene and eighty in another. If the makeup is applied skillfully, the audience never questions the aging process in its willingness to suspend belief for art.

As to sets and backings, well, they can be quite effective too, providing a young producer knows her way around a film set. On

one series I helped produce, we wanted to depict our lead character living in a weathered house next to a harbor. We found an old
abandoned museum that offered limited access for filming and
was situated near the water. We decided to recreate the interior of
the house on a soundstage and to film all exteriors at the museum.
By using the soundstage, we could control light, sound, and
weather. The problem was what to show when the camera looked
out the window of the house. We needed to see the same view of
the harbor each time.

So we had a photograph taken of the harbor as it looked from
the museum. Then we blew it up and made it into a backdrop
(backing) that we hung and lit outside our set walls. To the audience, there was only one house, one harbor, and one view. You
could not distinguish between the two sites.

My selection of the original size of the backing was not my
finest hour. It needed to be large enough to cover both sides of a
corner window. Being somewhat inexperienced at the time, and
wanting to save money, I ignored the production designer's warning of "You'll need more," and said, "Don't worry about it.
Blame me if it's too narrow." Naturally, it was too narrow and
from certain camera angles you could "fall off" (see past) the
lovely harbor into a bleak soundstage. When the camera operator
exclaimed on the first day of filming, "Oh, oh, we've got a problem!," a solitary production designer's voice drifted in from off-
stage to inform one and all, "It's Danielle's fault."

There are many additional examples of film illusion. An imaginative technique used to enhance crowd scenes is the use of cut-
out people. There is actually a company that will come to your
location (usually a stadium or concert hall) and place paper dolls
in all the seats to give the illusion that the facility is full.

Shooting day-for-night is another way we modify reality. Let
us say we want to film a night scene at a popular bar. If the scene
takes twelve hours to shoot, we would have to be there from 6
P.M. to 6 A.M. to complete the work. Instead, we black out the
windows (building a black box with duvetyn and enough depth to

install a light) and create moonlight to give the sensation that it is night outside even though the sun is shining brightly.

Lastly, we use various visual effects (computer graphic images). They are perhaps the most effective way we have to alter reality. The field gets more and more exciting as technology advances. For example, we have used visual effects to place us in another city. We have created animals that can talk. We have filmed boating sequences in water pits on a soundstage, then used computer technology to place the boat in the open sea. When you think of *Jurassic Park*, you will remember it as a classic expression of the visual effects art.

All these experiences and techniques have broadened my perspective and have actually influenced me to look at work with fresh eyes. I know now there is always more than one point of view; there is always more than one way to solve a problem. Filmmaking has also trained me to find new and better ways of dealing with personal struggles and disappointments.

Whenever things do not go as planned, I try to change my perspective. I try to see events through another lens. Often, I can see the good in the bad; the opportunity in the disappointment; and the sincerity in the opposition. You also have the power to alter your perspective. You can choose to be devastated or reenergized and to turn a reversal into an opportunity. How you frame a situation is entirely up to you.

**When disappointed by a turn of events,
try changing your perspective. Look at it from
the point of view of others. Ask if it suggests a
new direction. Use it to inspire creative solutions.
There are two sides to every setback.**

CELEBRATING SUCCESS

YEA FOR ME!

We all love a good party, a chance to unite and celebrate. For most of us, any excuse will do: holidays, birthdays, sporting victories, and, of course, our child's milestone accomplishments. "She took her first step! Let out the streamers!" "Her first words! Cake for everyone!" "Her first eight-hour ballet recital! Drinks on the house, especially for me!" Toot, toot, toot that horn . . .

Not long ago, a group of friends invited me to dinner. They selected my favorite restaurant, a place I save for special occasions. As soon as we arrived, we treated ourselves to watermelon gimlets and something called a sex kitten, which I find embarrassing to say, much less order. Once our drinks arrived, my friends raised their glasses in a toast, catching me by surprise. They were toasting me!

The week before, I had found a publisher for this book and had been offered a plum assignment on a new television show. My friends, knowing how hard I had worked to achieve these goals, saw fit to celebrate. I was moved by their generosity and surprised by their gesture. In fact, I was a little uncomfortable being the center of attention, so I quickly turned the conversation to topics other than myself and enjoyed a wonderful evening with friends.

Perhaps I was uncomfortable because of the last time I was the center of attention. I had given a thank you speech as the honoree of a women's philanthropic organization for which I had done extensive fund-raising. I did not realize my blouse was unbuttoned and my racy bra exposed until a light breeze goose-bumped my skin on the way to my car. Perhaps that explains why the applause was so thunderously tepid.

Anyway, as I left the restaurant that night, I thought about how little time I had allowed myself for personal recognition. It had taken me eighteen years to achieve the success I was now enjoying. I had spent countless hours writing my book uncertain if it would ever find an audience. I had served a very long apprenticeship in film production. Yet despite the time and the hard work, I had only allowed myself a few moments to acknowledge my accomplishments. I realized how lucky I was to have friends who did for me what I could not do for myself.

Over the years, as with many women, I have moved quickly from one goal to the next, rarely taking the time to properly pat myself on the back. It made me aware that I was missing out on one of the most satisfying parts of life's journey. I realized that I needed to spend less time focusing on what I had failed to attain and more time on acknowledging and enjoying my accomplishments.

When we start out in life, we are bombarded with praise. Our parents, teachers, and coaches all build us up by heralding our accomplishments. Since we are evaluated constantly in our classes and activities, we learn to recognize and celebrate each milestone. But as we become adults, the opportunities for personal evaluation become fewer and fewer. Aside from an annual review at work, we often lack guideposts to measure our success. More than that, the measurements of success become uncertain and debatable.

As a freelance filmmaker, I am never formally evaluated. The only way I know if I am doing a good job is if I am offered another. Even that is not a sure way to know. Some of the most talented people in the business are out of work for long periods of time.

My point is that as adults we cannot always look to the outside world for validation and praise. Nor should we live without it. Instead, we should learn to "toot our own horn" from time to time, even if we are the only ones to hear it. We should set aside special moments to recognize our accomplishments, both large and small.

A good friend of mine spends a few minutes at the end of each day reflecting on the day's experiences. As part of her ritual, she identifies and acknowledges at least one accomplishment of which she is justifiably proud. I believe that in doing so, she enhances her own sense of worth and increases her self-confidence and self-esteem.

So celebrate your success. Take time to acknowledge your accomplishments and reward yourself when a goal is reached. The reward can be anything: a day at the spa, an hour of quiet time, a box of chocolates, a wink in the mirror, or just a pat on the back. You may not think your arm can reach that far, but I promise it can.

Celebrate your successes, whether large or small. Take time to acknowledge and reward yourself for a job well done. The cumulative effect will nurture a confident self-image.

SUMMARY OF RULES

FOLLOWING YOUR PASSION

RULE 1 In choosing a career, visualize it from finish to start by asking yourself the following questions: Will I have no regrets? Will I have pursued my dream? Will I have had fun? If the answer is yes, you will know what choice to make now, and money will likely follow.

RULE 2 Do not let fear stand in the way of following your passion. Strive to preserve your childhood confidence that all things are possible. Perseverance, courage, and hope will get you where you want to go.

KNOWING WHO YOUR ARE AND WHAT YOU WANT

RULE 1 It is a delusion to believe dollars and perks can cure a suffocating job. It is a delusion to believe society's approbation can turn career lead into gold. Rely on yourself to determine the job characteristics that will satisfy.

RULE 2 Stay grounded within your capabilities. You are the only who can determine what is best for you and what you can accomplish. A successful career path begins with a realistic appraisal of your own abilities. Resist well-meaning but misguided challenges.

STAYING THE COURSE

RULE 1 Do not take no for an answer. This is easy to say and hard to do. But it has been proven time and again that insistence on yes is a fundamental character trait of successful people. When no thwarts your plans or goals, be exceptionally energetic in opposing it.

RULE 2 You can stay committed to your goals by digging deep to find some value in every work experience. This technique will help you maintain the drive you need to weather difficult times.

STAYING GROUNDED

RULE 1 To be an effective manager, to be an appreciated co-worker, you need to beware of a creeping sense of entitlement and unjustified expectations. As your career advances, they can lead to arrogance and the loss of your sense of proportion.

RULE 2 You can ease the pain of career setbacks, reversals, and inertia by identifying and embracing the positive elements of your job situation. Seeing the glass half full is more than just an optimistic attitude, it is a mental bridge to better days.

RULE 3 Mindlessly accepting stereotypes is a superficial way to manage. Make an effort to give each new employee or co-worker the benefit of the doubt, whatever his or her vocation's public image. Assume full cooperation and collaboration until proven wrong.

AVOIDING LABELS

RULE 1 If you are unfairly or inappropriately labeled, your career will be slowed or diverted. If you unfairly or inappropriately label others, you will squander talent. Fight to get a chance. Bend to give a chance.

RULE 2 You are more than the sum of your parts. Share hidden talents with others. Seek hidden talents from others. Effective management or performance is the full utilization of available skills and resources.

RULE 3 Try not to let words hurt you. It does not matter what someone says to you at work, however unkind. It only matters what you say to yourself when they stop talking. Vengeful retorts only diminish you in the eyes of others.

AIMING JUST BEYOND YOUR REACH

RULE 1 You must be neither too cautious nor too aggressive in taking on job responsibilities beyond your level of experience. Growth requires risk, which leads to reward. Aim slightly beyond your reach and comfort zone, but not beyond your abilities.

RULE 2 In times of trial, resist being the lone ranger. Consult with your co-workers on the best solution. Listen and learn to minimize your inevitable mistakes.

FOLLOW-THROUGH AND YOU

RULE 1 You ultimately are responsible for the follow-through or lack of follow-through of your subordinates. Make sure you give clear directions and provide necessary support to ensure a positive outcome. Keep in mind that clear directions become even clearer when the reasons for them are fully explained.

RULE 2 When your performance review praises you for efforts above and beyond the call of duty, for unswerving dedication to completing the tasks at hand, and for placing the company's interests above your own, you will know you have pushed past your personal limitations and are doing the job you were hired to do.

RULE 3 Be the person that makes things happen. When yes becomes your standard response, your co-workers know they can count on you to get the job done. "Can do" people are prepared in advance and expect the unexpected.

DEALING WITH DISAPPOINTMENTS

RULE 1 Treat disappointments as signals to change direction. The sooner you pick yourself up and move forward, the sooner you will be open to new opportunities.

RULE 2 When disappointed by a turn of events, try changing your perspective. Look at it from the point of view of others. Ask if it suggests a new direction. Use it to inspire creative solutions. There are two sides to every setback.

CELEBRATING SUCCESS

RULE 1 Celebrate your successes, whether large or small. Take time to acknowledge and reward yourself for a job well done. The cumulative effect will nurture a confident self-image.

4

Management Techniques

FINDING VALUE IN OTHERS

WHO LET THE COWS OUT OF THE BARN?

What makes a job interesting? Is it the people, the project, or the creative process? For me, it is variety. What I enjoy most about my work is that every day is different: different story, different people, different problems. The only constant is that whatever can go wrong will go wrong, just about the time you run out of (1) money, (2) time, or (3) your mind. And it really gets interesting when bovines are involved.

Back in the nineties, I was producing a very low-budget feature in the rural South. The script setting called for a middle-class house surrounded by green pastures and a picture-perfect barn. We found such a house in an unusual neighborhood. From the street side of the development, all the houses looked like any other ranch-style community in a suburban setting. From the back side of the development, one was literally transported to farm country. The house had a pristine lawn in back leading to a huge pond. On one side of the pond was a red barn, which served as the gateway to a cow pasture. It was absolutely perfect!

Fortunately, the house was owned by a lovely older couple who were thrilled to be making Hollywood history. Unlike most property owners, they were willing to let us do anything we wanted to their home except we were never ever to leave the barn door open. Apparently their cows were prone to meandering. I assured them that we would take proper care and then sent them to a nice hotel as part of their compensation.

Shortly before we began filming, I was asked by the local film commission to approve a political hire: someone with clout wanted his son to break into the business and I was a means to that end. I brought him in for an interview and was singularly unimpressed. He spoke in an inaudible whisper and continually looked at the floor. His shoulders were slumped forward as if he were trying to hide inside himself. He had no experience, and I was certain he would not do well in such a high-pressure business as ours. But his father was determined, and after all, I had the perfect job for him. He could guard the barn door!

Finally, filming began. The first morning was pretty uneventful but as the day wore on it became painfully clear we would need to film past our curfew: a curfew agreed to by the neighbors, the film permit office, and the local police. While I was simultaneously working on an extension of time and trying to keep our grip department out of jail (something about an altercation with a group of KKK members), I kept getting interrupted via walkie-talkie by my political hire. I politely told him I would get back to him as soon as I could. Then, I went back to the problems at hand. I bribed the neighbors into cooperating by sending them off to a catered meal, promised the borrowed police officer a walk-on role, and begged the film permit office for a revised permit. With so much going on, I had completely forgotten about our new employee. About an hour later I noticed part of my crew gathered in the street.

"Is now a good time?" my political hire asked, having magically appeared at my side.

"A good time for what?" I asked. "What's everyone doing?"

"That's what I've been trying to tell you," he said. "The director wanted to film a scene inside the barn."

"So?" I answered.

"He made me open the door."

Before he finished, I jumped off the patio and rushed to the end of the driveway.

"Oh God, no!" I started to run down the street. "No! No! No!"

It seems our cows had taken over the neighborhood and were wreaking havoc in all the yards. They were contentedly sampling the floral delights. I realized from the middle of the herd that I had no idea what to do. I could not push them back toward the barn. I could not ride them in. I could not tie a rope around all of them and drag them back. And worst of all, who was going to help me? I was the boss. People were looking to me for direction. Dollar signs appeared before my eyes as I began to imagine the cost of the damage. To make matters worse, the neighbors would soon be returning home after their nice catered meal. *I had to get rid of the cows!*

The political hire stayed by my side, patiently waiting for my next move. I was stumped. In utter desperation, I picked up my walkie-talkie and politely asked if anyone knew anything about cows. Laughter echoed from inside the house and out. I guess that meant no. Then my political hire asked in his sweet southern drawl, "Well, ma'am what would you like to know?"

Losing my patience, I barked, "Well for starters, *how the hell do I get the cows back in the barn?!*"

"Oh, do you want my help with that?" he offered.

"Yes, I want your help with that!" I snapped. "What should we do?"

He thought for a moment. "Well, I would just call them in."

"Of course! What was I thinking?" I turned toward the herd and said sarcastically, "Hello there nice cows, would you please follow me into the barn. No pushing or shoving. There's room for everyone." The cows ignored me. Strange.

My sarcasm was completely lost on him. "I don't know about that," he said. "They're not too smart, and I don't think they understand what you're saying."

"Well then, perhaps you could speak to them," I suggested.

And so he did. To this day, I have never seen anything like it. He began to make this weird sound, something between a "moo" and a "hee-haw." Immediately, the cows stopped chewing, raised their heads, and then fell in line behind my unassuming pied piper, and followed him right back into the barn. That was it; he had the skill. He had the know-how. He had a hidden talent, and I had precipitously dismissed him as someone with nothing to offer.

The film business is an unusual business. Unlike others that require a specific set of credentials and/or degrees, anyone can pursue a career in entertainment regardless of, or despite, his or her formal qualifications. I have worked with a grip who had a PhD in philosophy, a production assistant who spoke six languages, an ex-lawyer who was happy to perform manual labor, and an Olympic athlete who was willing to start as a writer's assistant.

The lesson I learned is this: Do not prejudge subordinates. You may think you know all you need to know about them but you do not. Often, they will surprise you. They may have something to teach you. They may be there to set an example for you, to inspire you, or to challenge you. In my case this unassuming boy was there to save me. In his sweet southern way he had a solution to my problem. In that moment, I was reminded that I was no better or worse than he was. We were just different. We each had something useful to bring to the party.

In an earlier chapter, I discussed avoiding labels and uncovering hidden talents as an essential part of personal development. Here, it is an affirmative management technique and bears repeating.

Therefore, whenever I employ new people, I try to reserve judgment. I try to get to know them. I try to seek out their hidden interests and gifts, and in doing so I can usually surround myself with an exceptional pool of talent.

Everyone has a skill to share.
Make an effort to know your employees and in the
fullness of time discover their hidden talents.

A LITTLE SHANTY TOWN

Who out there does not love a rags-to-riches story? We all cheer
when we hear about some poor small-town girl who risks everything to follow her dream, leaving family and friends behind and
making her way to Hollywood with only a few dollars in her
pocket. On the brink of starvation, she uses her last few cents to
buy a cup of coffee when—*poof!*—she is discovered and ushered
into a life of fame and fortune. I keep waiting for this to happen
to me, but curiously, it does not. Still, I wonder what certain people have that makes them stand out and how one learns to recognize unique talent, especially in the boonies.

The closest I came to discovering this was in a little shanty town
in Mexico. We had been sent to Mexico City to produce a television
movie about the cocaine trade. The story began in a remote village
where a poor family grew coco plants as a means to survive. Once
the crop was harvested, the youngest son traveled down river in a
handmade canoe to bring his product to market. The journey was
long and treacherous for a seven-year-old traveling alone.

For days, the director, producers, and casting department
brought in young actors to read for the part. As time wore on, the
director became more and more concerned that he could not find
the person he was looking for. The success of the show hinged on
the boy's performance. As we got closer to shooting, everyone
started to discuss casting the part back in the States or postpon-
ing the shoot altogether. Having run out of casting options, the director decided to focus on location scouting, leaving the casting
department to look for more possibilities for the part.

Several of us ventured out together to find locations. The days
were long and the journeys treacherous as we bounced along un-

paved roads in remote parts of the country. Finally, we found ourselves on an unmarked street lined with small clapboard shacks. They were aged and worn, with dirt floors, tin roofs, and no running water or electricity. There may have been twenty homes in all. Outside, the children played with makeshift toys and wore tattered clothes. Some were barefoot. At the end of the road, and in complete contrast to the rest of the area, a palatial estate surrounded by an impenetrable wall stood in solitary splendor.

We drove to the end of the road, parked our vehicle, and made our way to the entrance. The estate was fortified by a large wrought-iron gate with no doorknob or doorbell to signal our arrival. We foolishly stood out front yelling *hola!*, waiting for someone to respond. Finally, a groundskeeper came to our aid. He seemed cautious at first, surprised to see a group of Americans on the doorstep. We explained why we were there and asked to speak with the owner. A few minutes later, a young woman appeared. She had long blond hair, a slender build, and spoke perfect English. She was not at all what we expected.

We quickly learned that she had spent most of her life studying in the States and had returned home after her mother's murder. The property had been in her family for generations and was once a successful coffee plantation. It had been the only source of employment for most of the townspeople. Now that the place lay dormant, she felt personally responsible for the townspeople's care, struggling to carry on her mother's legacy. She was living far from the people she loved, removed from life's simple conveniences, and had only her staff to protect and keep her company. We were intrigued by her circumstances, and she was grateful for the diversion. We spent the rest of the afternoon together.

With pride she showed us around. There were acres of lush gardens, a small Catholic chapel, buildings where the coffee had once been processed, and her spacious and beautifully appointed home. The more we saw, the more excited we became. This would be the perfect home for the drug lord in our story. She agreed to let us come back to film.

As we drove away, our director asked if we could stop the van for a moment. Tired and cranky, we entreated him to drive on, but he insisted. As he jumped out with his camera in hand, I assumed he was looking to shoot stills of our new location. Instead, he focused his lens on a little boy playing in the dirt. The boy became more animated as the shutter snapped.

After a while, the director asked our translator to join him. He needed help assuring the boy's father that we meant no harm. The three talked at great length. The rest of us stewed in the van eager to return to our hotel. Finally, the director hugged the little boy, shook his father's hand, and announced that he had found the star of our show. *The star!?* What on earth was he thinking?!

Here was a poor, uneducated child with no formal training. He had never been past the end of his street much less asked to perform in front of hundreds of people, numerous cameras, and lots of equipment. Could he learn in a few days what some professionals took years to master? Could he memorize all his lines and deliver them with conviction? Would he fold under pressure? As I sat worrying, our director rejoiced, thrilled with his find.

When the filming began, we all wondered how this little boy would fare. We watched in awe as he came to set each morning prepared and full of enthusiasm. With great courage, he listened and learned, doing whatever was asked of him. He said his lines, hit his marks, and gave a terrific performance. When it was time to say good-bye, I was sad to see him go. He had been an inspiration to us all.

Looking back, I wondered what the director saw that day. Was it the way the boy looked? Was it his inquisitive nature? How did the director see potential where the rest of us saw nothing? Perhaps he was willing to look harder. Perhaps he was more open to possibility. Either way, the affair left a lasting impression on me. I have learned that sometimes talent can be found where you least expect it. If we open ourselves up to all possibilities, who knows what we might find.

With experience, you will develop an ability to spot talent, which is everywhere. But you must be and remain open to finding it, even where you least expect it.

WHO TO HIRE

WHEN ONLY THE VERY BEST WILL DO

Is there risk in hiring someone who is better at the job than you, someone more qualified, better trained, or with more experience? I suppose if you are afraid of being outperformed or outshone, you might shy away from such people. But what if you cannot do it alone?

In the beginning of my career, I felt enormous pressure to be completely knowledgeable in all areas of production, afraid that if I could not answer a question or solve a specific problem, I would be something of a failure. It was an exhausting time for me. No matter how hard I tried, there was always so much more to learn. I finally realized that I could never keep up in a field where technology was constantly changing and where there were so many specialized areas of expertise. I decided there had to be a better way.

I realized that instead of knowing everything, it was acceptable to know a little bit about a lot of things. If I did not have all the answers, I could hire extraordinary people who did. I realized that I could continue to be a vital part of the team by finding the right person for the right job.

To illustrate, I have scripted a couple of scenes from a fictional television show along with a series of questions that would need to be answered before filming begins:

EXT: SMALL SUBURBAN HOME—NIGHT

DALE, a young man in his late teens sneaks from his home as the rest of the world sleeps. Quietly, he pushes his car down the street to avoid waking his parents. When he reaches the end of the block, he gets in the car, starts the engine, and drives away.

EXT: REMOTE DUSTY ROAD—LATER THAT NIGHT

As wind and rain batter the car, Dale struggles to keep from sliding off a dirt road and into a ditch. Windshield wipers fight to keep the deluge of water from obscuring his vision. He peers into the night searching for something. Finally, he stops the car and refers to a map taped to the inside of his windshield. On the seat beside him is a sketch of a mythical-looking dragon. Satisfied with his location, he puts the car in gear and continues on. Before he can accelerate, something slams into the side of his car almost flipping it on its side. He hits the gas, burying the tires deep into the mud. Another blow sends his car lurching forward. The tires spin wildly, trying to gain traction. Finally, they take hold distancing him from his attacker. He searches his rearview mirror but sees no sign of life. Relieved, he turns back to the highway as a four-hundred-pound dragon slams into the road inches from the front of his car. Dale swerves to avoid it, losing control of the car and slamming into a tree. Mercifully unharmed, he jumps from his car and flees as the dragon swoops down to grab him. He loses his footing and falls headfirst down a steep embankment, landing bruised and bloody at the bottom.

Here are some of the questions that would need to be addressed for this scene to become a reality:

LOCATIONS

- Should Dale's home be built on a back lot or should we find a real home in which to film?
- Where can we find an old dirt road that will meet our production needs and support the script?
- Do we need to close off an existing road to make this shoot possible and would the city even allow it?

TRANSPORTATION

- What type of car should Dale drive?
- Should we rig the car so it will be easier for the actor to push down the street?
- How many matching cars do we need since at least one will be damaged?
- Does the car need to be reinforced so the crash will not hurt the driver?
- How do we create the sensation that the car is under attack?
- How do we get the car stuck in the mud?

PROPS

- What will the map and sketch look like?
- Who will create them?
- What will the dragon look like?
- How will the dragon be manufactured?
- Will the dragon be animatronic or CGI?

SPECIAL EFFECTS

- How should we create the wind and the rain?
- How do we get the dragon to fly?
- How do we set the tree so it will not collapse when hit?

VISUAL EFFECTS

- How can we enhance the look of the dragon with computer graphics?

STUNTS

- What parts of the scenes should a stuntman perform?
- What parts of the scenes should the actor perform?
- How do we keep both of them safe?
- Should the car hit a real tree or a manufactured tree?
- How should we choreograph the fall down the embankment?

WARDROBE

- What should the actor be wearing to hide the stunt pads?
- What clothing will help hide the stuntman's real identity?

CAMERA/GRIP/ELECTRIC

- What type of cameras should we use?
- How many cameras do we need?
- What type of film should we use?
- Should we shoot on real film or video (hi-def tape) stock?
- Should part of the scene be shot in slow-motion?
- How do we light the scene to create the right mood?

MAKEUP/HAIR

- How should we create the bruises and blood?
- Will we want to use prosthetics?
- Does the stuntman need a wig?

OTHER

- How much will all of this cost?
- How long will it take to bring it together?

Even a few scenes like these require the skill and expertise of a variety of professionals. As in most businesses, it takes a team of people to accomplish lofty goals. As you can see, it would be unrealistic for one person to be expected to handle all this on his or her own. I certainly could not. But if good people are hired who know their business, it all becomes quite manageable.

Let down your guard and admit you do not know and cannot know everything. Accept help from others and make your professional life a lot easier. I, for one, am grateful and appreciate those people who know more than I do in their chosen field, and I take comfort in knowing I do not have to carry the burden alone. I can now pride myself on those things that I do well, in particular finding and hiring the very best talent.

To ensure performance at the highest level, do not let your pride stand in the way of hiring the best.

THE BALL THAT NEVER BOUNCES

What makes a good employee? Is it someone who gets along well with others? Is it someone who rarely makes a mistake? Is it someone who is ambitious and does whatever it takes to get ahead? Or is it the person you can count on to follow through each and every time?

We can all sadly recount instances when someone promised to do something then failed to follow through, leaving us in the lurch. Since we often take people at their word, a broken promise comes close to being a lie. What is worse, we often rely on other people's work to support our own. When they fail, we fail.

People who do not follow through in the film business are soon looking for a new career. Lack of follow-through is simply not tolerated because each department counts on the others to support the work it is doing. It is such a collaborative process that no one is willing to work alongside people who are unreliable.

The work is fast and furious, making the quest for perfection extremely difficult.

People are often asked to accomplish impossible tasks. "Can you get one hundred pink flamingos by tomorrow?" "Can you dress three hundred refugees by morning?" "Can you change the color of this car in an hour?" "Can you rig a bathtub that overflows for the next scene?" If someone says it can be done, they had better be able to deliver, or the result can be disastrous. Try filming an air rescue without the helicopter, a wedding without the gowns, or a basketball game without the court. Film is a visual medium that requires all elements be present when needed.

When we prep a new show, we spend a great deal of time discussing what the director wants. Each department goes to great lengths to manufacture, rent, or purchase exactly what the director has requested. If something the director wants is unavailable or cannot be made within our resources, everyone must know far enough in advance so changes can be made. Any and all questions are asked and answered so that, hopefully, there will be no surprises. The day before the shoot, a call sheet is handed out detailing every item needed for the following day's work. Everyone comes prepared. You never, ever want to surprise a director in the middle of a shoot by saying, "Sorry, I couldn't get that for you." In our business, it just is not done.

In addition to all this, the director has the option of asking for things as they come to mind. A scene may not be working as planned, and the director might think a different prop would help. The company might arrive on a new set to find the green walls clash with the actors' wardrobe, and all the costumes have to be changed. A scene in a bar might play better in a restaurant, which means food has to be in evidence. The point is that requirements are constantly changing in the film business, and those who are successful are able to take the ball and run with it. They must deliver under the best and worst of circumstances. Those that do are resourceful, creative thinkers who will stop at nothing to get the job done right. Perhaps that is why film people can accomplish so much in such a short period of time.

For some people, follow-through is a way of life. It is a measure of professionalism. These are the people you want on your team; people you can depend on who will never drop the ball but instead will keep several in the air.

> **Hire and value most those employees ready,**
> **willing, and able to follow up and follow through.**
> **Judge performance and, if possible,**
> **offer incentives based on these criteria.**

NOW I'M DESPERATE, YOU'LL HAVE TO DO

What happens when the best and the brightest are simply not available? What happens when we have to work with the second tier or, God forbid, the bottom of the barrel? For women, it is like booking an appointment with Laurent D. only to be styled by his brand-new assistant. Whether in our personal lives or in business, how do we succeed when we are so often forced to settle?

There are many reasons we are forced to hire less qualified people. Perhaps there is insufficient time to do a thorough search, perhaps our first choice declines our offer, perhaps the selection committee does not share our vision, or perhaps the local talent pool is limited.

When filming on location, we often hire locally to minimize cost. This saves having to transport and house the entire crew. So when we choose to shoot in a remote part of the country, we know we will often be working with people who have limited experience. When this happens, it is up to management to make sure that the job is done properly.

A number of years ago we were filming a miniseries based on a best-selling novel. In an effort to be authentic, we decided to shoot the show in the same Midwestern town identified in the story. We agreed to bring experienced personnel from Los Angeles to head each department, then to hire everyone else locally. One of the local hires was the camera loader. A loader is someone who hauls the equipment around, keeps the gear clean, organizes the camera truck, and loads and unloads the film. Although it is an entry-level job, it is important that it be done right.

Most camera departments work out of a large five-ton truck. The truck is lined with shelves on either side and has a darkroom in the front where processed film is handled. The crew using the truck includes the director of photography, the camera operator, a first assistant camera (focus puller), a second assistant camera, and a loader. If there is more than one camera, the crew doubles in size.

The loader we hired was passionate about photography but had limited experience on a film set. She was thrilled to be part of the show, and since she was strong, willing and able, we felt she could handle the job. After some basic training, she set to work.

Her first few days were pretty uneventful, then things started to unravel. We were filming in an expensive home just outside town and had just finished a very emotional scene, which left everyone tired and irritable. As the crew set up for a new scene, the camera operator tried to contact the loader to remind her to bring him a new piece of equipment. When she failed to respond via walkie-talkie and did not return with the gear, we started to worry. We immediately sent a production assistant to look for her, but she was nowhere to be found. Frustrated, the second assistant camera ran to the truck to get what was needed.

When he returned, he came running over to me. Apparently he had found the loader and needed my help. I was immediately concerned that she had been hurt and quickly followed him outside.

"I think she's in there," he said pointing to the empty camera truck.

"I don't see anyone," I responded, stating the obvious.

"Not in there," he exclaimed, a little annoyed. "In there." He gestured toward the darkroom.

I listened for signs of life but heard nothing. "You sure?" I asked.

"I thought I heard someone talking, but when I knocked, no one answered."

The two of us jumped into the truck and knocked on the darkroom door. "Hello, is anyone in there?" I shouted. We stood with our ears to the door patiently waiting. "If you're in there please say something?" I felt rather foolish talking to a possibly empty room.

As we were about to leave, a little voice called out, "Yes, I'm here." The second assistant camera and I turned back toward the door.

"Are you locked in?" I asked.

"No . . ."

We waited for more, but nothing.

"What's she doing?" the second assistant camera whispered.

"I have no idea," I whispered back. "Could you please open the door?" I asked.

"No, I don't think I should," she replied.

"Why not?" I was starting to lose my patience. "You can't stay in there forever."

The second assistant camera decided this was as good a time as any to bring up more bad news, "We need to get in there soon," he told her. "They're running out of film on set."

That helped. She started to cry.

"Sorry," he said.

I decided to try another approach. "I would really like to help you, but I need to know what's going on."

"You think she has someone in there?" the second assistant camera whispered. Oh! I had not considered that!

"I'm alone," she assured us. "I think I might have messed up the film. I'm afraid to open the door."

My heart sank. You never want to say "messed up" and "film" in the same sentence.

"What do you mean 'messed up'?" I asked.

"I started to unload the film but something went wrong, and it spilled out everywhere. I can't get it back in the mag."

"How long have you been in there?" I asked.

"A really long time," the second assistant camera helpfully volunteered.

"I can't see my watch but I would guess at least an hour," she replied.

The second assistant camera had heard enough. Before I could stop him, he ran to the set to get backup.

"OK, let's not panic," I said. "Maybe we can talk you through this."

"But what should I do?" she replied mournfully.

What was I thinking? I cannot even load my fully automatic snap-and-shoot. I was going to be of little help. Before I could answer, the truck was aswarm with people. The entire camera crew, the director, the assistant director, and the executive assistant were all squeezed inside, and everyone was talking at once. The assistant director wanted to know what film was ruined so he could schedule a reshoot; the director was wondering what to tell the actors; the camera crew was arguing about how best to rewind the film; and I was trying to keep the loader from becoming more upset.

Finally, we came to our senses. Nothing we were doing was getting us any closer to a solution. We decided to let the first assistant camera stay with me and help since he had the most experience with the equipment. The rest of the crew went back to the set to try and complete the day's work.

So, with great care and patience, the first assistant camera talked her through the process of respooling the film. Time passed slowly, but eventually she found her way out of the darkroom and into the light. The film was fine, and aside from her bruised ego, all was well. She even got a standing ovation when she returned to the set.

I could not fault her for what happened. She was new and lacked the experience and training she needed. A more skilled professional would never have found herself alone in a darkroom with film unraveling at her feet. It was a risk we were forced to take when we decided to employ someone less qualified.

When these situations occur, you need to acknowledge a person's lack of experience, provide additional support, and, above all, keep cool. We all know it is easy to manage people who are at the top of their game. It takes real skill to bring out the best in those who have not yet arrived.

> **When you are forced by circumstance to
> hire people who are less qualified, keep your
> expectations reasonable and be sure to provide
> additional support and supervision.**

CHECKING REFERENCES

DIG FOR GOLD

"But it was just a little white lie! Everyone else does it!" Or do they? When is a white lie not a lie? When is it merely an exaggeration of the truth? And when is lying acceptable, if ever? What if no one is harmed? What if it helps a person to get ahead? What if the liar is me!?

I believe honesty is black and white. Either you are telling the truth or you are not. There is no in between, no gray area. When someone is caught in a lie, it defines him or her. The character of the liar is compromised, and I for one no longer care to do business with this person. Sound harsh? Perhaps. But who wants to be surrounded by people who cannot be trusted?

Recently, I found myself sitting across from a potential employee, reviewing her résumé. She came highly recommended and I was eager to find a position for her on our show. As I reviewed her credentials, I noticed that she had worked on a film I was associated with years ago. I like when this happens because nothing beats the firsthand experience of working with someone you worked with before. Unfortunately, I do not have the best memory and often forget people I have worked with a few months ago, much less five or six years ago. I wracked my brain trying to place her. Then, something unusual in her résumé caught my eye. Her former job title gave me pause for concern. I read it, then re-read it, hoping there was some mistake. I was certain that only one of us had enjoyed that particular job title on that particular show and was pretty sure it was me. Uh-oh, someone was lying.

When I told her I had worked on the project as well, she became visibly uncomfortable. She tried to steer the conversation in another direction, but I brought her back on point. I asked what her responsibilities were, who she had worked for, what her greatest challenges were—intimate details only someone on the project would know. She failed to answer my questions and became rather defensive. Finally, she admitted in exasperation that she had embellished her résumé "just a little."

In addition to losing all trust in her, I could not help but think she was rather dense. If you are going to lie about your experience, try not to appropriate your interviewer's former job.

I began to wonder how many applicants over the years had lied to me to get a job. How many had sat across from me and fibbed to my face? And more importantly, what was the nature of their lies?

I started to talk to various people about the way in which they constructed their résumés and found that there were essentially two schools of thought on that: some believed in complete honesty and others had no trouble stretching the truth. Those that stretched the truth manufactured all sorts of fictions. They listed shows on which they had never worked, they enhanced their titles to appear more experienced, they took credit for responsibilities they did not have, and they increased their levels of pay.

I realized that I needed to take greater care in obtaining accurate information on potential hires. In addition to asking questions about the quality of their work, I needed to make a far greater effort to verify dates of employment, titles, responsibilities, and compensation—not only on their most recent projects but also on those dating back a number of years.

I have found that, without exception, the more detailed you are in your verification efforts, the more successful your hiring will be. Whenever possible, use the Internet to verify information listed on a résumé, rely on the advice of mutual acquaintances whose opinion you trust, track down (by networking) and talk at length to employers the applicant intentionally omitted from the résumé, and keep detailed notes during the interview so you can cross-check all information received.

It is sad that we have to protect ourselves from a dishonest few, but it is better to do the job properly the first time and employ only the most honest and reputable people rather than do it a second time under far less advantageous circumstances.

> **Take the time and make the effort to properly verify any and all information pertaining to job applicants before hiring them. In particular, track down former employers not listed on the résumé.**

SHERLOCK'S GOT NOTHING ON YOU

How does someone obtain a reliable reference on a potential employee? In my experience, it is very, very difficult. Our litigious society makes it dangerous to honestly criticize anyone, even if they deserve to be singled out. I show the greatest restraint when commenting on previous employees. Instead of saying things such as, "She likes the sound of her own voice," or "Keep the coeds locked up when he's around," I use words like "challenging" and "oddly-qualified"—words that have no meaning. This being the case, how do we protect ourselves from hiring people who will make our lives a living hell? How do we protect ourselves from the overindulgent and the sticky fingered?

As with most employers, I have been burned more than once by bad hires. On one particular occasion, I hired a costume designer to create the look and style for a new series. The candidate had years of experience, interviewed well, and had a strong résumé. She had also worked for one of our producers in the past, and he gave her a glowing recommendation.

About two weeks into the show, she began charging us for weekend work in addition to her normal salary. Before long, her entire crew was coming in on Saturdays to get "caught up" at considerable cost to the company. Her excuses for the overtime varied. "The actors aren't happy with their wardrobe, so I need to make some changes," or "The executive producer specifically asked for this late Friday night," or "The script came out late, and we needed to prepare." While the answers seemed legitimate, something did not ring true. I decided to do some investigating.

I began to notice that she was frequently unavailable during the day and that her crew seemed unusually overworked. We were filming a relatively easy show, so this did not make sense. It did not take long to realize our costume designer was double dipping; brazenly working on two shows without either one's permission. No wonder she was working weekends, she had to make up for all the time she was absent.

Her behavior was totally unethical. She had lied to both shows about the work she was doing, and then charged us for overtime she had not earned. Not only was she stealing from the company, but she was forcing her staff to lie on her behalf. She was fired summarily.

Another unfortunate situation developed with a prop assistant whose job was to assist the actors on set. He would provide them with any prop or item they needed to touch while on camera. Throughout the season, a number of props in his care disappeared without explanation. Since he was such a personable guy and an incredibly hard worker, it never occurred to us to suspect him of wrongdoing. However, one night he was caught red-handed stealing an expensive piece of equipment. Again, he was fired on the spot.

Looking back, I had to ask myself what could have been done to prevent the hiring of these two malefactors. The answer was easy. I could have done a better job in obtaining accurate references. I decided to redo my reference checks to see what information I could glean the second time around. What I learned, unfortunately, came as no surprise with hindsight. The costume designer had a reputation for double dipping and had been caught on more than one occasion. The prop assistant was known for "losing" things and could not be trusted. How did I miss such important information?

First, in the case of the costume designer, I relied too heavily on only one reference. I stopped checking after our producer gave her the thumb's up. Regrettably, the producer was unaware of her extracurricular activities. Second, I put too much value on the references given to me by the prop assistant. He had obviously only listed associates he knew would sing his praises. All in all, I had been lazy and failed to properly verify their work histories.

In retrospect, I could have taken advantage of numerous opportunities to gain the information I needed. I could have checked with the costume designer's union to learn about the shows to which she had been assigned. I could have talked to people with whom she had worked in the past. And I could have talked with actors to see if she had provided them with exceptional service.

In the prop assistant's case, I could have checked with his prior shows to determine their level of loss and damage. I could have talked with his union to see if any grievances against him were on record. And I could have talked with our vendors to see if they were replacing props in his care too frequently.

The point is, you need to dig for useful references. As they get harder to obtain because of the legal climate, you need to find new and creative ways to extract them. If someone is not forthcoming, try a new angle or read between the lines. Look to someone's peers for information, check with their subordinates, and reach out to vendors for whom they have worked. Never, ever limit yourself to just the immediate supervisor.

And remember the Internet. Websites like MySpace and Face-book, which are popular social networking sites, can also provide useful information about a potential candidate. A quick Google search of the applicant's name might bring up additional information of interest. Finally, professional networking sites such as LinkedIn and Jobster, Inc. can be useful reference tools for employers in all fields.

By trying a creative approach, you can find a wealth of information to help you make the best decision possible and avoid being taken to the cleaners.

> **Be especially creative and energetic when seeking references. The most useful information may come from the least likely source.**

MAKING THE DEAL

VARIETY IS THE SPICE OF LIFE

Why do you need to work? Do you simply require the income to pay your bills and put food on the table? Are you the kind of person who requires a title to define who you are? Do you have to get out of the house because you can no longer spend twenty-four hours a day socializing with a toddler? Or do you need the rush of the "deal" to feel alive? Here is one look through the lens of self-discovery.

Those of us who need to work approach it in different ways. What may be satisfying for one may fall short for another. This diversity causes us to seek different forms of compensation. It is shortsighted to assume that those we wish to hire want only money. The truth is that cash is not our only bargaining chip. In fact, there are numerous ways to reward someone for the work he or she does.

To illustrate, I am reminded of four different directors of photography (DP) I hired for four different shows. They all had similar skills and performed similar functions: to help design the look of the show; to determine how it would be shot; and to select the camera, film, and equipment to be used. It was also their responsibility to hire personnel for and manage the camera, grip, and electric departments. All four of these DPs were talented and successful in their own right, but each approached the job opportunity very differently.

The first DP spent most of his career shooting smaller, independent features. He had done well financially but was not getting the notoriety he desired. He wanted to be sought after by higher profile shows. When it came time to negotiate, he was less interested in the financial incentives and more interested in the exposure our show, a network prime-time drama, could bring him.

The second DP had years of experience in both features and high-profile television. He was currently on his third marriage and had two small children to raise while putting his older kids through college. He had just purchased a very expensive home and was strapped with alimony and child-support payments. He was looking for as much money as possible.

The third DP was an artist who was young and quirky. While he insisted on being fairly compensated, he was not at all interested in being rich and famous. His only criterion for taking the job was to be part of a project in which he believed. He asked: Was the story compelling? Would he be able to fulfill his artistic goals? Would he be working with like-minded people? Could he pursue his passion?

The fourth DP was looking to take on a more challenging role. For many years he had been recognized as one of the best

DP's in the television business. He had done all he could in his field and was ready to move up to a new position. He wanted to be challenged in a new way by being given a shot at directing.

All these people were looking for something different: more exposure, financial gain, artistic challenge, or new opportunity.

By being sensitive to each individual's needs and by aligning them to the needs of the project, you too will be able to negotiate deals that are fair and equitable for all parties and meet everyone's goals.

Everyone is looking to be compensated appropriately.
Make the effort to learn what candidates really
want and need before negotiations begin.

YOU GET WHAT YOU PAY FOR

Do you subscribe to the old adage, "You get what you pay for"? Think how often we try to save money by purchasing the least expensive appliance, only to have it break hours after the warranty expires. Or how often we hire the cheapest contractor, only to find his work is faulty and needs to be redone. Based on these experiences, does value always cost money? How about when you are at the end of your rope?

We would all like to have the resources to pay top dollar to ensure quality performance, but sometimes our financial situation does not allow for it. In my work, I am hired to deliver a project for a certain amount of money, that is within budget. It is my job to be fiscally responsible and save money wherever I can. If I fail, there are others waiting in the wings to replace me. I have no choice but to make sound business decisions. So how do we reconcile the need to be frugal with maintaining quality?

We all know that if a job is not done right, it can cost dearly. We also know it is easy to break the bank if we do not look for ways to save. In my experience, each situation has to be assessed separately. When I take on a new project, I begin by laying out a budget. I look to see what areas of the budget are most important to the success of the show. I consider what the cost in time and money will be if significant mistakes are made. And I look for ways to cut corners without jeopardizing the project as a whole. Then, based on these factors, I determine where the money should be spent.

On one television movie, the writer had written a fantastic stunt sequence for us to shoot. In the story, a group of hitmen go after our hero. After being chased, he finds himself trapped on the roof of a downtown high rise. He is surrounded, unable to defend himself, when his courageous sidekick suddenly appears dangling thirty feet from a helicopter on a rope ladder. In desperation, our hero leaps off the building and grabs hold of his friend. The two men hang on for dear life as the helicopter flies them to safety. Not an easy thing to shoot on a TV budget.

In order to make this work, we needed an aerial coordinator, a helicopter pilot, a stunt coordinator, a number of riggers, and a couple of stuntmen. Since this stunt was incredibly dangerous, we needed to take special care in the people we hired. Each person involved had to have complete and total trust in the other members of the team. Skill and experience were everything. After a great deal of research, numerous interviews, and in-depth reference checks, we assembled what I felt was a top-notch group. We all felt confident that we could deliver what the writer had written.

About two weeks before the shoot, I received a phone call from our studio executive who was growing increasingly concerned about the cost of the show and had decided to find ways for us to scale back and save money. I could tell by the sound of his voice that he felt he had discovered something worthwhile. Apparently, he had found a local helicopter pilot we could hire to handle the sequence. Not only was the guy willing to work for a lower rate, but as a local, he could save us a great deal of money in other areas. We would not have to pay travel time for the pilot or the aircraft, we would not have to cover the extra cost of fuel, we would not have to pay for storing the copter overnight, and we would not be required to pay any housing or per diem allowance, such as hotels and food. All in all, the studio executive was right. On paper this seemed like an obvious choice. He quickly faxed me the new pilot's résumé.

I reviewed the résumé and brought the pilot in for an interview. He interviewed well, had experience in the film business, and seemed capable. But for some reason, I could not help feeling uneasy. I kept asking myself why I was resistant to change. Why was I not excited about saving all this money? Was I hesitant because I had not found this candidate myself? Was I hesitant because I was reluctant to reprep the sequence? Or was there something more important at stake? Whatever was going on, I needed to make sure my motives were clear before I went back to the studio with my decision. I thought about it for a few days, consulted with other producers, and then decided I needed to fight for the pilot I wanted from the beginning.

In this case, I really believed that a stunt of this magnitude warranted extra expense if for no other reason than the comfort level provided by the initial pilot. He was a seasoned professional with a stellar reputation who had done this type of stunt before. I felt completely confident in his ability to deliver and admired his emphasis on safety. Unfortunately, the studio was not convinced that only one person could do the job and continued to refuse to pay more for the service. We went around and around, unable to agree on who to hire. At one point, I exclaimed in frustration, "God forbid that something should go wrong with this stunt. Will it have been worth saving a few thousand dollars?!" To my surprise, this finally tipped the balance, and the studio agreed to support my decision, and we proceeded as originally planned.

I should mention that the stunt went off beautifully. As the sun set over the city, a helicopter graced the skyline with two young men hanging by a rope ladder, five hundred feet above the ground. We watched in awe as they disappeared over the horizon.

As I stood on that rooftop, I was overwhelmed with a sense of relief that everyone was safe, and sincerely grateful we had been willing to pay for the best.

Quality costs more. Assess each situation and determine where value is most important.

Value comes at a price, so be prepared to
pay extra when circumstances dictate,
to fight for the quality you require, and to justify
the decision financially or otherwise.

YOU SCREW, THEY SCREW, WE ALL GET SCREWED

Have you ever met someone who would do anything to save a buck? They will nickel-and-dime you until you are so fed up you want nothing further to do with them. They ignore the principles of a successful negotiation and are only interested in meeting their personal goals. And in the end, even this does not work, and they end up losing more than they save, particularly if the opposition is organized.

I watched this situation unfold while setting up a new television series. The parent company had a longstanding reputation for being excessively frugal; so much so that they often alienated people in the industry. Additionally, the company was new to television, having worked exclusively on low-budget features. My experience taught me that any show could be made either on a shoestring or with enough money to pay down the national debt. The key to success was how you handled expenses, so I decided to give the company the benefit of the doubt and do business their way.

The first task was to hire the crew. Fortunately, the unions had recently negotiated and ratified the terms and conditions of their contracts. Salaries were clearly defined on a rate sheet that all shows filmed in Los Angeles were required to follow. With this information in hand, I hired the people I felt were best suited for the job. As the weeks progressed, I took pride in knowing we had a fantastic crew.

About three weeks into the project, I was called into a budget meeting to discuss the projected expenses of the show. We went through the budget line by line discussing ways to save money and bring down costs. I defended the areas where I felt we needed the money and gave in where I thought we could save prudently. When we finished a grueling day of negotiating, the company was still not satisfied with the bottom line. Much to my surprise, one of the executives instructed me to strike a better deal with the unions. I tried to explain that their contracts were nonnegotiable, but he insisted that I make it happen. As an added inducement, he implied that if I could not accomplish the task, he knew others who could.

I went back to my office feeling incredibly frustrated. I had never heard of the unions giving special consideration to a show like ours. The industry as a whole had already agreed to this season's contract. Who were we to ask for special consideration? Even our labor lawyer did not see how I could get a better deal.

Either way, I was screwed. I had already hired the entire crew at contract rates. I had negotiated in good faith giving my word; something I take very seriously. Now, I was looking for ways to undercut the people I valued most. I had even encouraged some to turn down other jobs in order to work for me, all based on terms to which I had agreed. I was now being asked to go back on my word to save a few bucks. The whole thing was disheartening.

I decided to contact a union representative with whom I had a long-standing relationship to see what we could do. He informed me in no uncertain terms that the rate sheet applied, and there was no room to negotiate. I had nowhere else to turn, so I called the executive back and told him what I had learned. I suggested he bring in someone else if he felt that person could do a better job. I explained that our crew had already been hired, and any change might jeopardize their loyalty. I was especially concerned we would lose the entire construction department, which had recently been offered another show. He told me he would get back to me.

A day later, one of his junior executives called me with his response. First, I was to fire the entire construction crew immediately. "Screw them if they don't want to work at a lower rate," he insisted. Then he gave me the name of the new construction coordinator I had to hire. Lastly, he told me to continue negotiating with the unions.

Had no one heard what I said? I had already hit a wall! When I asked for suggestions on how to negotiate a better deal, I was told to threaten taking the show to another country. Since we were now days away from filming, we both knew the threat was nonsense.

I could not believe this was happening. First, I was being asked to fire a group of people I deeply admired. Second, I was being asked to lie to people with whom I had spent years building a good relationship. I had no idea what to do.

When my construction team heard the news of my dilemma, they were only too happy to leave. They had a better offer for more money on a different project anyway. I cannot tell you how sad it made me to see them go. But not as sad as the company was going to be.

Apparently word also got out around town, and when I called the unions again, they told me that not only was I not eligible for lower rates the company was insisting on, I now had to pay higher rates than I had previously committed to. *What?!* I had never heard of such a thing.

While our company was suggesting we fire people without cause and looking for ways to cut pay, the unions had taken it upon themselves to respond in kind and had found a loophole to penalize the show. In the end, I had to notify all my employees that they would be making more money than expected. You can imagine how disappointed they were.

I can never confirm this, but my feeling is, had we played fairly from the start, had we been respectful of the contract, and had we honored the deals we made, we would have been treated fairly in return. Instead, we screwed, they screwed, and we all got screwed.

> **Treat people fairly regarding compensation.**
> **Above all, keep your commitments**
> **and you will be repaid in kind.**

MOTIVATION AND PRAISE

OK, EVERYONE—GROUP HUG

We all want to be recognized and feel valued at work. Most of us want to grow in an environment that supports and encourages us. As employees, we want to be praised and rewarded for our contribution. In short, we want to feel successful and fulfilled. And when we are fortunate enough to find such an opportunity, we thrive giving those we work for our very best. So why, then, do many managers fail to create this type of environment? Especially on a raging river.

Early in my career, I was given a rare opportunity to oversee the second unit of a major feature film that was to be shot in several locations in and around Canada. My job was to produce all the stunt work; a job that seemed beyond my then level of expertise.

The stunts we would execute included extensive white-water rafting, a runaway horse and carriage, a caribou stampede, and a rock quarry explosion. It was difficult work that required skilled labor. Since I had been brought in from the States, the Canadian crew had been selected for me, and I did not have the opportunity to hire the experienced people I felt were necessary. Unfortunately, film production was at an all-time high in that part of the country and experienced crews were hard to find. Since I was relatively new at this, I went along, although it gave me cause for concern.

I found the local crew approached things differently from the way I was trained. Without giving them the benefit of the doubt,

I assumed they were doing things wrong—quickly finding fault with their actions. Instead of trying to understand their approach and learn something new, I condemned them for not doing it my way. Yet, I was unable to articulate why my way was better and became increasingly frustrated while openly criticizing what I did not understand. The more frustrated I became, the less enthusiastic they were. The more they feared my scrutiny, the less we accomplished. I was creating a vicious cycle of which I was initially unaware.

I was especially hard on our first assistant director whose job it was to communicate the director's wishes, run the set, and ensure that all elements were available when needed. As I have mentioned, being a first assistant director is one of the toughest jobs on a film crew since the day's success rests squarely on your shoulders. If a company does not make its day (complete its work on time), the first assistant director is held responsible.

After a few months on the project, it came time to shoot the white-water scene. In this scene, a boy and his dog struggle to stay afloat on their handmade raft, which careens down a series of rapids. The raft had to be carefully lowered into the canyon by helicopter, then cabled off until we were ready to launch. Extreme white-water rafters had been hired to oversee safety during the sequence. They would lead and follow the raft as it raced down river in case things got out of hand. Finally, we had six cameras secured at various points along the river wall that were hanging precariously over the water to film the scene. For this stunt to work, everything had to be timed perfectly, with everyone working together like a well-oiled machine. Our first assistant director was struggling to keep it all on track despite my critical voice. Finally, having had enough, she turned to me, handed me a walkie-talkie, and told me to supervise the camera work myself.

I was paralyzed. It was so easy to find fault with everyone else, but not so easy to do it myself. Instead of apologizing for being such an ass and giving her my support, I took the walkie-talkie and got in position, praying I would not screw up. The director called action, the cables were released, the raft lurched forward, the stuntman held on, the cameras rolled, the safety team flew by, and the scene was executed with perfect precision—except for my part. Since I missed the cue, the camera team I was supervising turned on the cameras too late. By the time the cameras rolled, the stunt was over, and we were filming an empty river. Like a rookie, I had ruined a fabulous shot: a failure the crew witnessed with a certain degree of pleasure.

I realized that my own fear and insecurity made it impossible for me to treat members of the crew with the respect they deserved. As their boss, I should have guided, motivated, and praised them. Instead of listening to and valuing their input, I found fault. Instead of acknowledging that we were all green, I tried to hide my inexperience by distancing myself from them. All in all, I behaved badly and poorly managed the people who had been put under my supervision.

I am happy to say that I am no longer the supervisor I was back then. Now, I see myself as part of a team. I accept that I do not know everything and that it is OK to learn from others. I realize that everyone needs to be praised for a job well done. And I no longer focus on the negative and accept the fact that everyone is allowed to make mistakes. These changes have made me a better manager and made my work much more rewarding. Now, when I walk on a film set, I am greeted with warm smiles, strong handshakes, and sometimes heartfelt hugs.

**To be a good manager, see yourself as part of the team
and readily offer praise for jobs well done.
Resist negativity and nonconstructive criticism.**

I'D CRAWL THROUGH BROKEN GLASS FOR YOU

Have you ever noticed there are people whose presence seems to light up a room? When you are with them, they effortlessly make you feel important. They also seem to bring out the best in others. What is it that makes these people special and can we become like them? I think we can. Except perhaps for the truly boorish.

It took me a long time to realize how significantly I could affect the people I worked with: how my behavior toward others could change their behavior at work. I started to notice that we are all interconnected and that for each action there is likely to be a predictable reaction.

I had been working with the same group of people on a television show for about three months. My job was to analyze the script, budget and schedule the show, oversee and approve all expenditures, hire the crew, find the locations, act as a liaison between the director and various departments, negotiate all deals, solve any problems that crept up, and keep the company on track. With so much to do, I rarely had time for small talk, preferring to get straight down to business.

One particular day, I went to the set to discuss a new lighting setup with the best boy. It was his job to order all specialty equipment for the electrical department, and I wanted to make sure we were in agreement on what the company needed. I found him at the back of the electric truck and immediately launched into a discussion of the issues at hand. He sat quietly watching me as I rambled on. When I finished, he smiled and teasingly said, "Good morning, Danielle. How are you today?" I ignored him and went back to my concerns. Again, he politely said, "Good morning, Danielle. How are you today?" I started to get irritated as time was being wasted. Could he not see we had serious things to discuss? Matters of urgent importance? As if reading my mind he said, "Don't you get it? A few seconds of your time can make a huge difference to people."

"Fine," I muttered. "Good morning."

He laughed, "I suppose it's a start." We returned to our discussion.

The next day, I again came to the set. As always, I was completely focused on the work ahead, but his subtle message had stuck with me. I took a step back and decided to extend myself. When people passed, I smiled and wished them a good morning. At first my crew seemed surprised, but then I could see how happy they were that someone had taken the time to acknowledge them. I realized that I had been so focused on my own responsibilities, I had forgotten what a difference a simple act of kindness could make.

I started to look for new ways to engage people and took a serious interest in their responses. I began to ask people for their opinion and input. The more I asked, the more valued people felt and the more they became an integral part of the project. I also noticed that when someone was involved in the decision-making process, they were more committed to it and less likely to complain. People seemed happier with the way things were going.

Then I decided to extend the idea even further. I started to take a personal interest in people, not as their friend but as someone who could challenge them and help them meet their own particular goals. For example, I allowed them to suggest ways their department could better support the script. I also encouraged them to create special props or a better way to choreograph a fight scene that would make the show better.

I believe this approach has had a profound effect on the way people react to me. Recently, while on a film set, I overheard a private conversation between two of my employees. One of our new hires turned to our key grip and asked, "What's the boss like?" His response was, "I'd crawl through broken glass for her." That may be the best compliment I ever had.

Make an effort to bring out the best in others.
Be gracious, be interested, be sincere.

WHO SAID WORK HAD TO BE WORK

Do you work for the kind of person who expects you to stay late even though your work is finished? Do you feel you have to be a constant presence in the office in order to be noticed and to get ahead? I used to feel this way until I spent a summer in the Midwest and all that changed. Until I was used and abused.

I had been offered a show with a very successful producer working as his production accountant. Having worked in this capacity for years, I was eager to take on more responsibility and to advance my career. After an in-depth discussion, he agreed that if I took the job, he would support and teach me in any way he could. In return, I was prepared to give him 110 percent. I was excited to work with someone new from whom I could learn and who might provide me with additional opportunities.

We found ourselves working in a town of 25,000 people, many of whom were fascinated by the film business. While the people could not have been nicer, often showering us with gifts and baked goods, the town itself took some getting used to. At night, we would return to our ratty hotel rooms located downwind from the meat-packing plant. For entertainment, we would frequent the pool hall or the local strip club, both popular spots with the locals. Even our dining experience left much to be desired. Since pig farms were plentiful, pork was readily available, and all vegetables were deep fried. As time wore on and the town became more suffocating, so did the job.

Instead of providing the challenging experience I had hoped for, the producer only seemed interested in the hours I was working. He expected me to arrive by call (the time the shooting crew reports to the set), often as early as 6 A.M. Then he would insist that I stay until the company was fully wrapped, sometimes as late as 10 P.M., six days a week. At first I was happy to put in the hours and help in any way I could. But as time wore on, it got harder and harder to maintain my enthusiasm. Although he kept promising to give me more responsibility, he never got around to it, making the days painfully long. I felt overqualified and underutilized. Since I was often able to complete my accounting work early, I became a clock watcher.

About halfway through the shoot, another job opportunity presented itself. A producer I had previously worked for called to offer me the production supervisor job on a new pilot. Although the two shows overlapped, he was willing to wait for me to finish the show on which I was working. Thrilled with the news, I shared my good fortune with my co-workers, who were all equally pleased; all, that is, except for my boss. Instead of congratulating me on this wonderful opportunity, he merely reiterated that I not leave him until his show was finished, which, of course, was the plan. He then mentioned how "surprising" it was that someone would hire me as a production supervisor since "surely there were more qualified people available." I was furious.

What was the point of working sixteen hours a day trying to please someone like this? What a complete and total waste of time the effort had been. I realized by keeping me at his beck and call, he was more interested in controlling me than supporting me. More importantly, I realized that evaluating a subordinate solely on the hours he or she was working was missing the bigger picture. It was more important to focus on the employee's accomplishments than the number of bare hours he or she worked.

Now that I manage others, I have adopted this philosophy. Work until the work is done, then go home and have a life. No one needs to sacrifice everything for the job. We all need balance in our lives and that means valuing family, health, spiritual growth, recreation, and work. I firmly believe that the more balanced we are, the happier we are, and the better we will perform on the job.

Value overall performance; not just time worked.
An employee with a balanced life is a better employee,
and that balance should be encouraged and supported.

HOW AND WHEN TO SAY GOOD-BYE

NICE GUYS FINISH LAST

I prefer to think of people as being inherently good, honest, and hard working. Some might find this a bit naïve and would suggest that evildoers lurk around every corner, but that is not the world in which I want to live. Instead, I focus on what is good and decent in people and try to understand and tolerate what is bad, at least until the loot is discovered.

As with any business, dishonesty and theft occur in the entertainment world. I have seen company assets disappear without explanation on more than one occasion. On one show, I returned from lunch to find my desk missing (no kidding). On another, I watched as a crew member walked off with a pair of Tiffany lamps. Once, a fleet of company vehicles simply drove away and are no doubt in Cuba by now. Electronics are especially popular: television sets are commonly lifted, as are computers, cell phones, and high-tech gear. Sometimes employees will submit illegitimate receipts for reimbursement or will accept kickbacks from dishonest vendors. The sad truth is theft happens. Even the nicest people can turn out to be the worst offenders.

A few years ago, we were filming a drama about a government agency in charge of world intelligence. Due to the nature of the show, our prop room was stocked with the latest in technology: mobile phones, computers, surveillance gear, and audio/visual equipment. Additionally, one of our sets was a "world surveillance" station that was dressed with wall-to-wall flat-screen monitors. All in all, the company spent a fortune on equipment.

Throughout production, various props began to disappear: a digital camera here, a notebook computer there—never enough to reveal the source of the problem but certainly enough to call attention to it. Although we had our suspicions, we were unable to prove the items were actually stolen or by whom.

Aside from the missing items, the prop department seemed well run. The three-member team worked especially hard, was professional, creative, and, above all, adored by the actors. Hell, I loved them too. As a result, we could not bring ourselves to believe any of them would act in a disreputable manner.

Finally, the season neared its end, and we found ourselves filming the last scene of the last show on the last day. Some of the departments decided to get a jump-start on wrap. Wrap is the time when everyone closes down operations. Items that were rented are returned. Assets that were purchased are boxed, inventoried, and stored. All outstanding bills are paid, and the show closes its doors.

The video playback department, which was responsible for the surveillance set, began to pack up all the equipment. Computers were to be returned to prop storage and the monitors to a rental company. As the team finished taking the last of the equipment to their truck, one of the most expensive flat-screen monitors came up missing. The head of the department appeared in my office in a panic. "Where could it have gone?" he asked. "We turned our backs for less than a minute."

At first I assumed the crew had packed the monitor away without realizing it, but a search of the truck turned up nothing. We all knew that if we did not find the monitor soon, it would be gone forever, costing the company thousands of dollars. We searched every storage room, office, set, trailer and truck. Security set up an exterior checkpoint so that no one could get on or off the lot without being searched. We looked for hours but could not find the missing equipment.

When we had accomplished all that we could and were ready to give up, one of our video techs stumbled onto something unusual. By accident, he tripped over a cable at the back of the stage and noticed that a piece of plywood had been strategically placed over a hole in the base of the set. The set had been built on risers so that all the power cables could run under the floor. At this spot, the cables had been pushed aside, and the plywood was blocking the opening. Our video tech got down on all fours, removed the plywood, and peered under the set. "Well, looky here!" he said. Our flat-screen monitor was just where someone had left it.

We quickly replaced the plywood and told the video tech to go home and say nothing about what he had discovered. Clearly, someone had hidden the monitor, intent on stealing it later. Well, he was in for a big surprise. We waited until the company was finished wrapping, then positioned a security team to lie in wait.

Around midnight, after everyone had gone home and the stages were dark, someone appeared through one of the side doors and approached the back of the stage. With a flashlight to guide him, he made his way to the hole, removed the board, crawled under the set, and took possession of the stolen monitor. Ever so quietly, he headed for the exit. Before he reached the door, Security threw on the lights catching him red-handed. None of us could believe our eyes. It was a man from the prop department we all really liked and respected; someone we believed in and trusted; someone we would have happily hired again.

I may have been duped that day, but I learned a valuable lesson. People have to earn your trust. Until they do, you must accept the possibility that they will take advantage of you. Even people you think are fantastic can harm you in the end. In hindsight, I should have made changes to the prop department when equipment started to disappear, not waited until things got out of hand. By being nice guys and trusting too freely, we sometimes fail to see what is really going on and quickly put an end to it.

Save the benefit of the doubt for people who have repeatedly earned your trust. Be cautious with others. If anyone abuses your trust, show them the door promptly.

YOU CAN'T MANAGE THEM TO GREATNESS

It is sad and disheartening to fire someone you really like, perhaps as difficult as breaking up with that very nice guy who just brought you flowers. In the business world, we often retain employees longer than we should, hoping things will get better. We go out of our way to help them, make excuses for them, and try to fix their mistakes. But no matter how hard we try, we cannot overcome their shortcomings, and in the end the relationship must end. And well before shock and awe set in.

This particular story is about the painful break up of a set decorating department. Set decorators are the people who take an empty space and bring it to life as the visual backdrop for a story. They are responsible for decorating anything from a war-torn barracks, to a 1920s dance hall, to a futuristic space station, to a rainforest. Whatever the mind can imagine, these people can create. They provide flooring, window treatments, artwork, furniture, practical lights, fixtures, greens, and accessories: everything it takes to make the set look authentic.

What makes their job particularly difficult is the limited time under which, and the limited resources with which, they must work. When a new television season begins, a crew of eight people is given four to six weeks to design, shop for, rent, install, and decorate all the permanent sets. The permanent sets are those that will be filmed repeatedly during the run of a show. For example, the permanent sets on NUMB3RS would include the police station, a university classroom, and the lead characters' home. Imagine trying to decorate your entire home in four weeks in addition to a police station and a schoolroom! The task can be overwhelming and requires special skill.

Within the set decorating department, the person in charge of the money and manpower is called the leadman. Each day he (or she) must keep track of the hundreds of assets being acquired by the staff. The leadman must keep tabs on where the money is going, how much has been spent so far, and if there is enough left to finish the job. The leadman is also responsible for scheduling the crew and making sure there is enough manpower to do the job correctly. We rely heavily on this person to keep the department on track and to notify us of any potential overages.

On this particular show, our leadman was relatively new to the job but had worked within set decorating departments for years. He had the complete support of the set decorator who had brought him to the show. They both assured me that together they could handle all responsibilities without difficulty. Based on the leadman's overall references and this joint assurance, I decided to hire him. In my experience, some of the best employees are those who step up to new opportunities and responsibilities.

Shortly after we started filming, I asked to see a breakdown of the money spent to date. The leadman assured me that he had completed the report but was having trouble with the computer program. Wanting him to succeed, I helped him assemble the necessary paperwork, doing most of the job myself. I was certain that with a little help and encouragement, he would perform well. A week later, he again failed to produce the updated report. This time he asked for a waiver. We were running out of time, and he felt he needed to focus his attention on completing the sets instead of the paperwork. He was already putting in fourteen hour days. How much more could I ask of him? I offered to bring in help, but he assured me the department was fine. "There is no need to worry," he said. Reluctantly, I agreed. I understood the importance of being film-ready, and I could see how incredibly hard he was working. Aside from the paperwork, the sets were coming together beautifully, and everyone was happy with the job he was doing.

Sometime after that, the production accountant came to see me. According to her records, we had expended our entire labor budget for decorating and still had two weeks to go. I immediately called the leadman to find out what was happening. He confessed that he was way over budget in labor costs but was planning to offset it by savings on purchases. He apologized profusely for not notifying me sooner and assured me everything was under control. By now I knew in my heart we were in trouble. But we were so close to completion and he was trying so hard, I decided to wait a little longer hoping things would turn out satisfactorily.

Big mistake! When all was said and done, the sets were $50,000 over budget. On a television budget, this is not good! Even though I had not personally spent the money, I was ultimately responsible for the cost of the show. I had hired him, I had co-managed him, and I had kept him in place long enough to do real damage. Now, I had to fire him.

Sadly, all of this could have been avoided if he had been let go earlier. From the start, it was clear he did not yet have the experience or the skills necessary to succeed as a leadman. Unfortunately, I was so certain that I could manage him to greatness that I failed to appreciate all the warning signs. By taking him under my wing and making excuses for him, I did us both a huge disservice.

When you keep a floundering employee on too long, his reputation is diminished and his confidence severely set back. Additionally, you will have to earn back the trust and respect of the people who hired you. By hanging on too long, you make the situation worse, much worse.

> **Do not prolong the inevitable. If someone is**
> **failing to perform, let him or her go. By keeping**
> **this person on longer than you should,**
> **you do harm to all concerned, particularly yourself.**

ADIEU TO YOU

Is there a way to fire someone positively? Is there a way to cushion the blow and perhaps uncover a new and better direction? If so, it really helps to have a decent memory.

A few years back, I was asked to work on a television series that was to be shot on a tropical island. I could not believe my good fortune and daydreamed of working in flip-flops and tank tops. Naturally, I jumped at the chance to get away from the real world and immerse myself in paradise. What could be better than a working vacation with white sand, crystal blue water, mango daiquiris, and a few new friends?

Shortly after arriving on location, we realized the island had a limited supply of seasoned actors, and it became clear we would need to fly most of them in from New York or California. Among other things, it was my job to approve and oversee travel, and I took it upon myself to ensure the actors were treated properly. Whenever a new actor arrived on set, I made it a point to greet him or her personally and make myself generally available to provide assistance.

On one particular day, a very tall and handsome actor in his late twenties arrived from New York. Unfortunately, I was in the middle of a crisis: something about needing a trained dolphin for the next day's shoot while being far from Sea World's training facility. Anyway, I could not give him the attention he deserved. Instead, I quickly greeted him and turned my focus to the problem at hand. Seeing I needed help, the second assistant director stepped in to guide the actor toward his wardrobe fitting.

Much to my surprise, the actor ignored the second assistant director and began following me, asking if he could have a moment of my time. Based on prior experience, I was certain he was about to launch into some ridiculous diatribe about being a strict vegan and needing his special food flown in from the mainland. I was completely surprised when he asked if I remembered him.

I hate questions like these. One, I have the world's worst memory, and two, I meet roughly one hundred and fifty new people on each show. At one or two shows a year for eighteen years, well, you get the picture. However, I did not want to offend him or seem rude. I wracked my brain hoping something would register, but I still had no idea who he was.

"I am so sorry," I said. "I have a terrible memory. Have we worked together before?"

He decided to throw me a bone. "Yes, as a matter of fact we have." He smiled, wryly.

Well, that narrowed it down to roughly five thousand people. I waited for more but he was not forthcoming "Could you give me a hint?" I pleaded.

"It was not under the best of circumstances," he shared with a twinkle in his eye.

I had no idea where this was going, but I knew I did not like it. He clearly was enjoying my discomfort.

"Seriously? Don't you remember? (pause) You fired me!" he noted.

Oh, crap, crap! Please let this not be happening.

"Now do you remember?" he asked, certain that I would.

I still had no idea who he was, and this really surprised him.

"One of the most memorable moments in my life, and you don't even remember it!"

I felt like an idiot just standing there, nonplussed. "I am sorry," I said, not knowing what else to offer.

"Wow, you must fire a lot of people!"

I decided to change course. "Did you deserve it?" I asked, interested in the circumstances.

He laughed, surprised at my question. He thought for a moment. "Yes, I guess I did."

Phew!

He continued, "I was a production assistant on a movie you produced in Atlanta. You were pretty unhappy with me most of the time—with my showing up late and not being where I was supposed to be. I'm surprised you don't remember. Anyway, after a few weeks, you called me into your office. I knew what was coming, but it didn't go down the way I thought it would. Instead of throwing it in my face, you told me to stop wasting my time in a job that didn't mean anything to me. You told me I had talent and potential that could be put to better use. You told me to go out and find what I really wanted to do in life, and that I could be really good at something. So I did. And here I am, traveling first class."

And then it came to me—the cocky young kid who had crossed my path years ago. I remembered our encounter, and I was glad to see he had taken my advice and made something of himself.

But he was not yet finished, "So I just wanted to thank you. If you hadn't kicked me out on my ass, I might still be grousing, making a lousy four hundred bucks a week."

We both knew he was easily making ten times that now. We laughed and parted company, but that exchange left a lasting impression on me. In my career, I have had to fire many people. No matter the circumstances, it is never an easy thing to do. But it is important to remember that letting someone go does not mean they are irretrievably incompetent or incapable of finding success. It just means that they have not found the right place to shine.

Let us be honest. Most of us have been let go at least once. I was fired as a waitress and relieved of my duties on my first production managing job. These were painful times, but I believe they helped force me to work harder and to redirect my energy toward something that was better suited to my talents.

When I am working with an employee who is failing, I look to see if he is receiving the support he needs to succeed. I ask myself: Am I clearly communicating my expectations? Am I giving him enough time to complete the tasks required? Does he have the tools necessary for the job? If, and only if, I can say yes to all these questions, do I consider terminating his employment.

Once the decision is made, I prepare an inventory of his strengths so that they can be highlighted and discussed. No one likes to fire an employee, but it can be a whole lot easier to do if you focus on the employee's capabilities and keep his dignity intact.

When you are forced to fire someone, use it as an opportunity to help redirect the person's energy to something better suited to his or her talents and interests. Focus on someone's strengths rather than emphasizing weaknesses.

FISCAL RESPONSIBILITY

SPEND A THOUSAND TO SAVE A PENNY

How often have we heard the phrase "penny wise and pound foolish"? The people who practice this type of fiscal responsibility are frequently ineffective. Having worked with a few of them, I have learned the hard way that there are fundamentally two ways to approach fiscal responsibility: The first is to squeeze every last dime out of something until there is nothing left with which to work. The second is to find constructive ways to save money by hiring good people and running an efficient enterprise. I prefer the second approach. Especially if a budget is tight, tight, tight.

Being fiscally responsible is not just about saving money. It is about working smart. It is knowing what you have and what you can afford, then making the best use of your resources. It is making smart choices that benefit the company as a whole. And it is about being fair and decent to everyone from the janitor to the CEO.

We can compare the two basic approaches and determine which works best. To begin, let us assume we are about to produce a television show that will likely run over budget. How can we save enough money to make the project feasible?

The first group, the penny pinchers, might go through the budget line by line looking for ways to save. Here are some of the ridiculous suggestions I have heard:

SUGGESTIONS	WEEKLY SAVINGS
Pay the five assistants $400 instead of $450 a week	$250
Cut out the expensive snacks	$500
Do not let people buy Uni-ball pens	$35
Do not reimburse gas receipts	$1,000
Limit cell-phone reimbursement	$200
Disallow Starbucks	$500
Rent only one Port-a-Potty on location	$70

After all this brainstorming, they have saved a total of $2,555. Wow! Hardly seems worth it. These same people also consider you irresponsible if you suggest reducing an actor's pay from $85,000 to $75,000 a week to help rein in spending. Go figure!

Here is how the fiscally responsible group applying sound management principles might approach the problem. First, they would hire the most seasoned director, producers, and writers they could find. This is crucial because you need people who are not only creative but flexible and realistic. (Surprisingly, we often have to work with new, young, hip directors who have no real experience. As a result, they are unable to make a decision and often change their minds at the last minute. Each time they ask for something different, it costs the company money. On the other hand, by hiring people who are experienced, you are better able to stay on budget and work efficiently.)

Second, they would be pragmatic about what they can and cannot accomplish in the time available. They would lay out a schedule, determine its feasibility, discuss alternatives, and do whatever it takes to ensure that the funds available will support what they hope to accomplish.

Third, they would respect and recognize everyone's contribution. They would know that the better employees are treated, the harder they will work and the more cost-effective they will be.

Finally, they would keep everyone focused. By clearly setting goals and minimizing distractions, they would steer the team in the right direction.

This type of thinking will yield far better financial results than monitoring office supplies or eliminating fancy coffee. How? Because employee turnover, excessive overtime, and wasted resources will be avoided. The net savings will be far greater than a few pennies pinched.

Be smart about how and where you try to save money. Good management (realism, flexibility, clear goals, and high morale) will beat penny pinching every time.

WHO'S PAYING FOR THAT?

As my mother (and possibly yours) used to say, "You cannot have whatever you want, whenever you want, all the time." With such sound advice, I learned early that you have to make choices: "Do I want to make the car payment this month or buy the new Kate Spade bag?" "Do I want to pay off my credit cards or invest in those Gucci sunglasses?" The truth is most of us need to make compromises in our everyday lives. We have to earn, save, and bargain-hunt to make the most of what we have. But what about the people who are used to having it all? People who are unfamiliar with the meaning of the word no. How do you deal with them? Do you take away their toys?

In Hollywood, there are a number of very wealthy people (not just actors) with fat bank accounts, more cars than days in the week, and private jets to whisk them from place to place. Their reality is very different from ours. Having worked with many of the rich and famous, I have found that the concept of financial responsibility can be foreign to them; it is something they have heard about but never had to practice. So how do you tell someone who is used to getting what he wants when he wants it that he cannot have it? Especially since we rarely (well, never) have enough money in the budget to give everyone everything they desire?

On most shows, preproduction begins when we make a list of those things each department will need. Camera, grip, and electric will need to rent equipment and purchase expendables. Locations will have to lease properties for filming, obtain permits, and pay for police and security. Set decorating will need to rent or buy furniture, decorations, floor and wall covering, hardware, and artwork. Wardrobe will have to buy shoes, undergarments, coats, shirts, pants, dresses, and jewelry. Construction will have to buy wood, drywall, paint, and nails along with renting tools to create the sets. Props will have to manufacture or purchase anything the actors use in a scene. Stunts, special effects, and animal wranglers will all have special expenses that need to be taken into account. And there will be salaries to pay, offices to set up, supplies to purchase, computers to rent—it all costs money.

Once we know what the show requires, the director, producers, and writers need to decide where to spend and where to save. The first place to look is the script. What do we absolutely need for the script to work and what can we live without? Eventually, compromises will have to be made, and some things will have to go. For some people, this is not a problem. For others, this is especially difficult. So what do you do when you are working with people who are predisposed to having it all and are not willing to make sacrifices?

I have found that there are three ways to deal with this problem. The first and most obvious approach is to just say no. Stand firm and hold your ground refusing to give an inch. This tactic used to work when budgets were carved in stone and directors were less sophisticated; now it just makes people mad. When I have tried it, I have ended up alienating the very people I needed to work with the most. Or they simply threatened to pay for it themselves. This might sound like a great solution, but I am here to tell you it is not. You either end up looking cheap, or they never cough up the dough, leaving you hanging when the bill comes around. I recommend staying away from this strategy.

The next approach is to just say yes to everything. This might be a great way to make friends and put a smile on everyone's face, but it will not go over well with your boss or the company. An unwillingness to rein in spending in the film business often results in huge overages, which can be career-ending. You might want to avoid this strategy and the unemployment line, both.

The third and most successful approach is to offer choices to avoid forcing people to accept or oppose. Encourage a dialogue. For example, if I were to say, "Can we lose the scene where the car drives through the car wash with its top down?" The likeliest answer would be, "Of course not! We need that scene or the whole show falls apart!" Instead, I might try, "Would you rather include the car wash with the top-down scene or that amazing love scene on the wing of the bi-plane? I can't imagine a better ending to the show." Then they have to make a choice, and hopefully they will choose parsimoniously.

When you are trying to encourage people to acknowledge the financial realities of a project and to make concessions to work within your means, it helps to keep them informed, allow them to contribute to the decision-making process, and give them viable options from which to choose. A decision made collaboratively has the best chance of being supported.

> **Being financially responsible does not necessarily mean imposing restrictions from above. Involve others in the decision-making process. Where you can, give them options. That way everyone will support the difficult choices that have to be made.**

WE CAN'T AFFORD THE CHIMP

As I have observed, life is full of financial choices. Do we buy groceries or splurge on dinner at a fine restaurant? Can we afford a full-body massage or will a half-hour facial do? Should the bonus check go into retirement or be invested in a pair of Manolo Blahniks? Life is just one financial decision after another. Hopefully, over time, we learn to make the right choices. Even if the bride must throw the maid-of-honor into the wedding cake.

Learning to make the right choices holds true in the film business and, indeed, any business. On any given day, I might make a hundred decisions that affect our production's financial position. How to divvy up the pie? To be honest, I find this challenge quite enjoyable. After all, it would be terribly boring if all I had to do was hand out money. It takes real creativity to stretch a dollar as far as it will go. Over time, I have learned that to maximize resources, alternatives must be considered.

I will give you an example: I was recently presented with a script that told the story of a film production company that bought the rights to a new chimp cartoon they were certain would bring them success. As part of the story, the production company mistakenly tries filming two live chimps attached to motion control sensors as a promotional stunt for the cartoon. All hell breaks loose, and the live chimps attack a group of filmmakers, leaving them bruised and bloody.

Immediately upon reading the script, I contacted the writer with my concerns. In my experience, chimps are extremely expensive to work with and require numerous trainers because they can also be extremely dangerous. It would take months to train the chimps properly, would require stunt performers to stand in for the actors, and would take days to film in order to assure everyone's safety. None of this was possible on our limited schedule and budget. But the writer did not want to lose the live chimp sequence.

After numerous discussions, we decided to keep the story as scripted, but when we got to the scene where the live chimps attack, we replaced them with one small (well-trained) monkey who could jump on actor after actor without injuring anyone or breaking the bank. The writer added a line of dialogue to explain one monkey rather than two chimps, and the story held together beautifully. Rather than throw out the whole story, we simply made choices that allowed us to protect the integrity of the script.

To better explain this process, let me walk you through another example in more detail: Let us say we want to film a wedding scene as part of our show. The script calls for the wedding to take place in the Crystal Cathedral in California with five hundred guests in attendance. The wedding is an evening affair and everyone is required to wear black tie. While the guests wait for the ceremony to begin, the bride discovers her groom ravishing the maid-of-honor in the bride's sitting room. All hell breaks loose and a cat fight ensues. The fight moves from the sitting room to the reception hall that has been set up for the party. The hall is decorated with a large catered buffet, a twelve-tiered wedding cake, and a champagne pyramid fountain. The bride throws her maid-of-honor headfirst into the cake, which topples over, sending the champagne fountain and its glasses crashing to the floor.

We know we cannot afford the scene as scripted, but any changes we make must preserve the writers' vision. How do we maintain the integrity of the story and keep it visually interesting while respecting applicable financial limitations? The following is a list of suggestions that might make the scene doable:

CURRENTLY SCRIPTED	SUGGESTED CHANGE	SAVINGS
Crystal Cathedral	Fancy hotel	$10,000
500 guests	200 guests	$32,500
Evening affair	Day affair	$5,000
Black tie	Elegant but casual attire	$5,000
Bridal sitting room	Women's bathroom	$10,000
Buffet in evidence	Buffet not yet set up	$3,000
Stunt fight	Tame push and shove	$2,500
Breaking champagne flutes	Avoid breaking glass	$5,000

By changing the venue for the wedding from the Crystal Cathedral to a fancy hotel, we save thousands in location fees and achieve greater flexibility as to when the shoot can be scheduled. Having fewer extras saves payroll. Changing the scene from night to day makes it easier to light, saving money in both equipment and manpower. Changing the event to a casual affair saves the cost of formal attire and reduces the amount of hair and makeup required. Changing the scene from a sitting room to a women's bathroom saves thousands on set dressing since a bathroom does not require furnishings. Eliminating the buffet dramatically cuts down on the cost of food. Choreographing the fight differently saves thousands on stunt doubles. And finally, omitting the breaking glass saves the cost of manufacturing candied glass champagne flutes. (We use candied glass instead of real glass so that no one gets hurt.) By implementing these changes, we maintain fiscal responsibility by making the scene more affordable.

When you are working with limited resources, you have to find creative ways to stretch your dollars. Try looking at novel alternatives to accomplish the same results. Offer suggestions to help people consider other options.

Perhaps one day I will work on a show that has so much money I will not have to worry about divvying up the pie. Until then, "Since we can't afford the chimp, would you consider a marmot instead?"

> **When you have limited financial resources,**
> **be creative in seeking low-cost alternatives**
> **that accomplish the desired result.**

CRISES AND REVELATIONS

GET THAT AMBULANCE OUT OF MY SHOT!

We would all like to think of ourselves as indispensable, certain that no one could do our job as well as we can. When we think about calling it quits, we dream about the crippling effect our resignation would have on those who have offended us. We fantasize that our employers would be unable to carry on without our genius. Well, the sad truth is we are all replaceable. Even when tragedy strikes.

On my very first show, I was hired as a location accountant to sit in a trailer and process payroll. All day long I labored in front of a calculator crunching numbers so that the cast and crew could get paid. Day after day I found myself tackling a never-ending mountain of paperwork. The job lacked creativity and glamour, but what did I care. I was in the game. So there I sat, not twenty feet from where the real action was taking place. Three times a day, I would peek my head out of the trailer to watch the shooting crew in action. That was exciting.

Since I was still determining the direction of my career, I used this opportunity to explore where my interests and skills might fit in. Could I shop for clothes all day as a member of the wardrobe department? Did I have an eye for color and design making me an asset to the art department? Could I use my hands to build and maintain props? Each day, I would try to visualize myself in a new role. Then it hit me: stunts! I could be a stuntwoman. It would be far more interesting than pushing paper, and it would force me to stay in shape. I had visions of hanging out with really buff stuntmen while making a major contribution to the production. With what little I knew, stuntpeople were treated like royalty. And of course my experience as a gymnast, parachutist, and springboard diver, along with my love of fast cars, was all I really needed.

Having made my decision, I waited patiently for our lead actress's stunt double to show her stuff so I could watch and learn. In the story, our heroine had to flee a gang of bad guys to save the day. I know, not terribly original. Anyway, the chase was to take place high atop a series of downtown buildings. To escape, the stuntwoman was to jump from the roof of one building to another over a two-hundred-foot-deep chasm. While the crew set out to prepare, our stunt team engaged in an extensive discussion with the director. I watched them collaborate, very much wanting to be part of their exclusive team.

Finally, when everything was set, the cameras rolled, action was called, the chase ensued, and my heroine leapt high into the air. Time stood still as I watched her soar overhead. Then awe turned to panic as it became clear she was off her mark. She barely cleared the landing, and then went crashing down, breaking both her ankles in the process. As she lay there in agony, the director yelled cut, crew members went running, and an emergency response team carried her downstairs and loaded her into an ambulance.

Before I could catch my breath, someone shouted, "Moving on." Without missing a beat, the director of photography was setting up another shot, the crew was relighting, a new stuntwoman stepped forward, and the first assistant director screamed, "Get that ambulance out of my shot!"

What an illuminating crisis! I decided then and there that perhaps stunt work was not for me. Perhaps there were other more challenging and satisfying careers I might try that would not land me in a hospital bed. The experience also helped me realize that no matter the circumstances, and no matter how good you are, there is always someone who can and will take your place.

No matter the circumstances, accept the fact that you are replaceable. Never make a career decision assuming they will scramble to keep you. Be confident and competent, not arrogant.

WHO HIRED THE WOLF THAT WON'T HOWL?

There are certain natural behaviors we expect from animals. A chicken will lay its eggs, a male dog will lift its leg, and a wolf will howl at the moon. Or will it?

I have learned over the years that animals rarely behave the way you would like them to. I have worked with a donkey and camel who thought they were lovers, refusing to be separated for any length of time. I have employed a grizzly bear that would only perform if you fed him massive amounts of marshmallows dipped in cod-liver oil. And I have dealt with a herd of caribou that were so stupid they would follow each other over a cliff if you let them. But my worst experience was with a pack of wolves high up on a glacier in the Rockies.

Wolves are difficult by nature. They constantly jockey for position within the pack. Left to their own devices, they would fight to the death for alpha status. When working among them, great care must be taken. Electrical fencing has to be strategically placed, cages have to be positioned within reach, and there has to be just the right number of trainers to orchestrate the wolves' every move—all to ensure their safety and the safety of those around them. Sometimes even hair and makeup must be applied so their fur is a matching shade of gray. Needless to say, the whole thing can be a circus.

On this particular movie, I was assigned to produce the stunt and animal footage, which included photographing a pack of wolves sitting high on a mountaintop howling at the moon. I assured the company I could easily handle this. We searched for days to find just the right spot, consulting a lunar map to ensure we would have a full moon as our backdrop. We made plans to transport our entire team along with cameras, lights, grip equipment, props, and so on to the top of a glacier. When all the plans had been finalized and we were ready to go, we spent the entire day moving everything into position.

Helicopters would drop down into the valley, pick up a small group of people and their equipment, then head back to the top of the mountain. Back and forth we went until everyone was in place. Lights were set, cable was run, sound equipment was powered, and the cameras were placed. Finally, when the moon was just so, the trainers brought out the wolves and put them on their marks. The atmosphere was perfect.

As film ran through the cameras and tape recorded sound, we waited for the wolves to do something. Seconds turned to minutes. We watched them. They watched us. Nothing happened. Time passed, and everyone looked confused. Where was the howling? Realizing we were at a standstill, I stopped the cameras and turned to the trainers. "Why aren't they howling?" I asked.

"Sometimes they don't feel like it."

"What?!" I started to panic. I had just assumed that when the time was right, they would want to cooperate. "But they have to!" I said. "We've come all this way. They have to do something!"

The trainer thought for a minute. "We could all try howling. Sometimes that gets them in the mood."

So I turned to my trusty crew. "Could you all please howl at the moon?" Everyone started to laugh, but it was not a joking matter.

"Do we get some kind of SAG contract?" a smart-ass grip asked.

"No one is leaving this glacier until those dogs sing," I snapped.

So in unison, fifty of us gave it our all and howled as loud as we could.

The wolves, while mildly amused, chose not to participate. They eventually grew tired of us. A few lay down in the snow, one cleaned its paw, another pulled at its chain. Eventually, we gave up and grew quiet. "Why isn't this working?" I asked.

"Maybe we don't sound like real wolves. It's probably throwing them off," a trainer said.

You think!?

She continued, "Maybe if we had a tape of real wolves . . ."

So without delay I sent our production assistant back down the mountain to fetch a tape of howling wolves. The rest of us sat in the dark for what seemed like an eternity trying to keep warm. Finally, the helicopter returned, the tape was handed over, and we were back in business. We all resumed our positions, the wolves were removed from their cages and put back in place, the cameras began to roll, and the sounds of wolves pierced the night. Only they were not our wolves. Our wolves just became agitated, wanting to know where the sound was coming from. I was completely flummoxed.

By now we had been on the mountain much longer than originally planned. The crew was cold and tired, and we still had hours of work to get everyone home. So in utter desperation, I did what any good producer would do. I improvised by feeding the wolves peanut butter. While the wolves licked and chewed, the trainers used hand signals to get them to lift their heads. My hope was that with their mouths moving and their noses pointed skyward, we could simulate what looked like howling and put the sound effect in later. The whole thing looked utterly ridiculous and ended up on the cutting-room floor.

Had I done my research properly, I would have known that there was a chance the wolves would not cooperate. Instead, I made an unjustified commitment and missed a deadline. Being new to the business and young and naïve, I was eager to please and made promises I could not keep. Did I deliver? In this case the answer was a clear and resounding no.

We all want to please the people for whom we work. Taking initiative, following through, and accomplishing goals are what makes us good employees. But we need to be careful. By overreaching and not preparing properly, we run the risk of failure. Even our best intentions can end in disaster if we are not careful.

Think carefully. Make sure you can deliver before you make a promise you cannot keep. Over time, you will be respected for your realism and candor.

FIREWORKS FROM HELL

Don't you just love the Fourth of July? I know I do. It is a time when friends get together to share a picnic on a warm summer night while the high school band plays "Stars and Stripes Forever." Then the sky explodes in a cascade of color: reds, blues, and greens that light up the night before ending in a breathtaking finale. Well, that has nothing to do with my story.

Try finding a competent, reliable fireworks technician the week of July fourth. I am here to tell you it is virtually impossible. But—that was my assignment. We were working on a television series about a family with eight children who were attending a hometown fair to celebrate the fourth. In keeping with the story, the production designer had created a spectacular set with games and rides. The wardrobe department and casting filled the set with perfect extras. The director painstakingly laid out his shot list in advance so that everyone was properly prepared. The camera, grip, and electric departments were ready to execute his vision. All I had to do was find a fireworks person who could provide the appropriate bursts of light in the deep background when the camera was rolling.

Because it was the week of the fourth, every fireworks company I contacted was unavailable. After all, the fourth was their one big night of the year. I was beginning to think I would have to set off the fireworks myself when one of the more reputable firms said they knew someone who could handle our project. He came with glowing references. We met; he seemed knowledgeable and was willing to work within our budget. I hired him immediately so as not to lose his services at such a busy time of the year.

The big night for the shoot finally arrived, but where was my guy? I called his shop, his cell phone, and his home with little success. As the rest of the crew labored away, I ran around chicken-without-a-head style, unsure what to do. I left message after message hoping my man would respond. Anxiously, I watched as the big set lights were brought out, and the crane was assembled. Everyone was in high gear except for me. I stared at my phone willing it to ring.

Finally, it did. One of his associates had retrieved my frantic messages and was offering to help. He could not imagine what had happened to my technician but told me he would send out a replacement team. About fifteen minutes later, the guy I originally hired pulled into the lot. Relief washed over me. I ran to greet him and watched as he fell out of his car too drunk to stand. Apparently, the local pub interrupted his journey.

A few minutes later, two of his associates showed up and got down to business. They assured me that they were completely sober, apologized profusely for their supervisor's behavior, and further assured me that they could get the job done. They showed me their credentials and promised they would deliver exactly what I had hired their boss to do. Then they went about setting up for the shoot. My drunken friend hugged me for the third time, then curled up on a sound blanket and fell asleep.

About an hour later, everything was set to go. The sun was down, the actors had been rehearsed, the lights were up, and the cameras were in place. The assistant director asked everyone to take their places so that filming could begin. I moved to my spot near the monitors.

Now for those of you who have never seen a film being shot, it takes hours to record a single scene. The scene is shot over and over again. This is done to obtain shading in performances from the actors and a variety of perspectives from the cameras. It gives us choices in editing when we piece a scene together. Keeping this in mind, we often reset the same scene over and over again. Props, such as food that is being eaten or a cigarette that is being smoked, must be restored to their original state for each take. Each time the director yells action, the actors return to their starting point and play out the scene in the exact same way as before. It is an exercise in repetition. In order for the fireworks to work properly, the fireworks team has to set off the same explosives in the same color each time. Our contract provided for this, and I had no reason to believe it would be a problem.

We all took our places. The director yelled action, and the actors began their dialogue. Suddenly, huge explosions lit up the sky. The fireworks were so high and wide the camera missed them entirely. The shot was unusable, and the director was furious. He kept yelling, "Cut! Cut! Cut!" but the fireworks kept going—one explosion after another, with no end in sight. Everyone started yelling for me to do something. Already at a full gallop, I flew across the set to where my fireworks team was set up.

Oblivious to the chaos they were causing, I found them sitting back admiring their show. "*What are you doing?!*" I yelled. They seemed surprised to see me. "*Turn it off! Turn it off!*" I screamed.

It took a minute for my bleatings to register, then they scrambled to shut the display down. I waited in agony for the explosions to cease and the dust to settle. When all was quiet, I assessed the damage. This debacle had cost us our entire inventory of fireworks. With all eyes on me, I had to walk back to the director and notify him that there was nothing left to shoot. There would be no more fireworks to color his scene. It was a disaster.

We had blown thousands of dollars in fireworks for nothing. We got none of it on film and had to temporarily shut down production, wasting both time and money. How could this have happened? How could things have gone so wrong? Without their boss to guide them, the technicians misunderstood the nature of the work we had requested. They executed a fireworks show the way they always had, not the way a film company required. In short, the night was a miserable failure.

Sometimes the universe just conspires against us. Had we shot at another time, we would have had more qualified people from which to choose. Had I hired someone who was sober, the night would have gone off as planned. Sadly, everything that could go wrong did go wrong, and I was stuck with the blame. Even though most of these things were out of my control, I was ultimately responsible.

So I did what any good professional would and should do. I apologized for the dismal failure, accepted responsibility even for those things I could not control, and then just let it go.

**Sometimes things just do not work out
despite your best efforts. Be forthright about it,
accept responsibility, and move on.**

SAFETY

KABOOM!

Anyone who has recently visited a comedy club knows the joy of improvisation. The element of surprise entertains and delights us. By being free of structure and expectation, creativity can come alive. But there are certain times improvisation is not appropriate, certain times when we do not want to be surprised. No one wants to be operated on by a heart surgeon who works "off the cuff," or be represented in an audit by an accountant who likes to "wing it." Similarly, no one in the film business wants to be involuntarily surprised by special effects or to exclaim, "What the hell was that?!"

Special effects personnel are responsible for a variety of jobs. They create the bullet hits caused by a shooting gun. They create wind, rain, and snow on the ground or in the air. They design and install plumbing to make faucets and fountains work. They lay in smoke or fog for a background effect, and they rig explosives so that various objects will blow up at the right time. A good effects crew is golden. A bad one can cost you dearly in time, money, and safety.

I cannot tell you how often everyone on set has waited for an effect to work properly: a bullet hole to ooze blood, an arrow to fly straight, a rain to soak an actor. If an effect is not executed properly, everything comes to a grinding halt, leaving the crew standing around eating donuts.

While these are minor irritations, they fail to compare to the real damage a poorly run special effects department can cause. Since special effects personnel often work with high explosives, they can pose a serious risk to themselves and others.

I have seen an explosion in an abandoned warehouse cause numerous windows within a city block to shatter because the effect was not rigged properly. I have seen an explosion cause a car to rocket so high into the air everyone had to run for cover. One poorly timed explosion at a rock quarry blew up before the camera crew could get into position. And of course, there is always the explosion that has been detonated but does not go off, sending some poor guy or gal into harm's way to disarm it.

To be a special effects expert requires considerable training, a fearless mindset, absolute attention to detail, an eye toward safety, and, above all, an unwillingness to fail. When the risks are so high, there is no room for error.

We have a duty to ensure our employee's safety by hiring only the most qualified personnel, to make sure that all safety precautions are met, and to provide the time and money necessary to prepare and execute the work properly.

> **Give considerable thought to the safety of your employees. Do not compromise on time, money, or the use of qualified safety personnel to protect them.**

THEY CAN ALWAYS SEW IT BACK ON

I always wondered why companies post signs with slogans such as: "It's been 36 days since a company employee was injured on the job." Is this a way for the safety department to show its effectiveness? Do the companies think it makes people more cautious? Does it show that management really cares? And if these signs are posted, how do people feel when an accident happens and the sign then reads: "It's been one whole day since we hurt anyone!"

Different jobs have different degrees of danger. A window washer hanging thirty stories above the ground obviously has more accidents than the copy boy in an office, though we do know paper cuts can be pretty nasty. Unfortunately, the film business is replete with danger: helicopters crash, electricians get shocked, grips get hit by heavy equipment, trainers are bitten by angry livestock, stuntmen get thrown from cars, special effects teams get burned, and construction crews get their fingers cut off. Sometimes I feel our entire industry is an accident waiting to happen.

There are a number of factors that contribute to this. The first is that the film business runs on a tight schedule. We are constantly watching the clock since we are usually trying to accomplish more work than is reasonably possible within the time allowed. This forces people to work faster than they should. The second is that incredibly long days often exceeding twelve hours make people tired and careless, which can compromise their safety and the safety of others. The third is that as audiences become more sophisticated, the stunts and effects become more complicated, forcing us to take greater risks. And finally, because many positions in film do not require any formal education, some employees do not have sufficient training to execute the tasks expected of them. It is up to management to monitor these factors and ensure that the show is maintaining the safest work environment possible. But how is this accomplished?

The first task is to identify the dangerous work being executed and to compensate the risk taker properly. In our business, we do this by paying additional fees for work the industry deems dangerous. If a stuntperson executes a difficult stunt, he or she is paid additional money called a "stunt adjustment." The adjustment can range from $100 to $500 per action.

If a camera person is required to operate the camera near a dangerous activity (such as helicopter work or water work), he or she is paid a hazard fee. By requiring companies to pay additional fees, we call attention to danger and take special care to minimize accidents.

Another way to focus on safety is to let employees know how valued it is. This can be done in a variety of ways. One way is to limit the amount of overtime people are allowed to work. A tired crew is an unsafe crew. (We have all heard stories of people falling asleep at the wheel after a sixteen-hour day.) Fortunately, most studios are very concerned about this and set limits on the number of hours to be worked.

Another way is to insist the work area be kept neat and clean. In our industry, we conduct a walk through, a special activity in which management and crew walk the sets to identify potential hazards. Is a cable likely to trip someone? Is a rope tied off where someone could get caught up in it? Are ladders placed in the fire lanes blocking emergency exits? By requiring that a work area be properly maintained, management signifies the importance of safety.

And finally, the strongest message is sent when management refuses to allow workers to participate in activities that are too dangerous. Perhaps an actor wants to drive his own getaway car, or a director wants a camera operator to hang out the back of a racing truck, or a director of photography wants an electrician to place a light too close to a power line. When these situations arise, a producer must stand firm in his or her conviction that safety is not to be compromised.

Over the years, we all learn to use our intuition and experience to detect situations that could be potentially dangerous. Remain ever diligent in protecting the safety of your workers and try to set an example for everyone to follow. After all, it is better to be safe than sorry.

> **Communicate safety concerns, eliminate
> safety hazards, and oppose unsafe practices.
> Your attitude and concern should set the standard.**

SPLAT!

Are you prepared for an emergency? Are you the type of person who keeps a level head when things go wrong? Do you immediately take charge, or do you faint at the sight of blood? Mothers, for example, learn quickly what category they fall into. When their little angel decides to jump off the roof to see if he can fly, or sets his sister's hair on fire, they are forced to act immediately and soon discover how they perform under pressure. Indeed, how would you perform far above the ground?

Aside from the rare household mishap, most of us are not confronted with extremely dangerous situations very often, unless, of course, you spend time on a film set. In the film world, it is not unusual to stage car crashes, set people on fire, or send them flying high above the ground. So how do we ensure the safety of our employees? One way is in the level of our preparedness.

The following illustrates how a stunt might be planned and executed, how we try to maintain safety, and how we cope when tragedy strikes.

On a recent project, the script called for a martial arts fight to be carried out high above the ground in a cluster of trees. You might recall *Crouching Tiger, Hidden Dragon* as an example of this type of fight choreography.

We started by hiring a group of highly skilled artists from China to stage the sequence. Then we hired a local stunt coordinator to oversee the stunt department and two stuntwomen to double for the leads in the fight. Since the principal actors were not trained for this type of work, the stuntwomen were carefully selected to duplicate their appearance in every respect. We found two women who had extensive martial arts training, had worked with flying rigs, and had the perfect look. Once these women were selected, we choreographed the sequence.

First, we had to find a grove of trees that not only looked beautiful but could support the weight of the stunt. The trees had to be the proper distance apart to hide the stunt rig and cables and to make the stunt easier to accomplish. Once the location was selected, the riggers (a group of people who specialize in engineering cable rigs) began setting up the sequence.

Second, proper safety harnesses had to be selected, fitted, and approved for both stuntwomen to wear. Then the wardrobe department was consulted to ensure the costumes would hide the harnesses but in no way interfere with movement or safety. In addition, the two stuntwomen worked with hair and makeup to fit wigs that looked natural but would not hinder their ability to see.

Third, once the rig was up, the choreographed stunts were rehearsed again and again until everyone involved felt comfortable and secure.

Finally, a group of us met to devise our emergency plan. The stunt coordinator, the rigging crew, the stunt doubles, the director, the director of photography, the first assistant director, the on-set medic, and I talked through how the stunt would be shot and what we would do if something went wrong.

When it finally came time to shoot, everyone got into position and settled down. We turned the set over to the assistant director, who talked us through the plan. In case of an emergency, everyone on the set knew who would take charge, who would be allowed to approach an injured person, who would be allowed to communicate with emergency personnel, where the closest hospital was, where the emergency vehicles were standing by, and who would accompany the injured person in the ambulance. If only we were this well prepared in our daily lives. Nothing was left to chance. Everyone was familiar with the plan and prepared to follow it to the letter.

The cameras started to roll, the director yelled action, and the stuntwomen began their fight. Back and forth they flew from treetop to treetop. It was an amazing sight to see. Then without warning, a harness snapped, someone screamed, and one of the stuntwomen fell twenty feet to the ground. She lay motionless for what seemed like an eternity. Then, as quickly as it happened, the plan kicked into gear. Critical information was relayed, appropriate personnel came to her aid, and she was rushed to the nearest emergency room. Fortunately, she got the care she needed and made a full recovery. But without that plan in place, things could have turned out very differently and very badly. We all acted properly that day because we knew what steps to take. We had considered all the variables and had rehearsed our actions over and over again in our minds.

You may not be able to prevent all accidents from happening, but you can be prepared when they do. Always have a plan in case of emergency. You will be glad you did.

Prepare an emergency plan in case of accidents and confirm that your co-workers know it in advance.

THE MAKINGS OF A GREAT BOSS

MY SPECIAL THANKS TO ...

You may have discerned by now that this book is about lessons learned, not individual personalities. Thus, while I have generally declined to name names, I would like to take this one opportunity to honor two producers who have acted as both mentors and friends. I do this to illustrate the characteristics of a great boss so we can all learn from their example.

The first producer is John P. Flynn whom I have known and worked with for over sixteen years. Together, we collaborated on at least ten projects including pilots, miniseries, television movies, and episodic dramas. All in all, we spent almost forty months together working throughout the United States.

John is one of the few people I know who is genuinely happy to share his wisdom and experience with anyone willing to learn. Anytime someone asked him a question, he took the time to answer it fully no matter how busy he was. He was open to having people participate in all areas of the filmmaking process, even if their job did not allow for it. He believed that for people to be satisfied with their work, they needed to learn and grow and feel challenged.

Confident in his own abilities, he took chances on all of us, allowing us to try new things. Throughout our working relationship, John allowed me to push past my own limitations. He provided a safe environment to learn and to grow. He never failed to offer praise when I got something right and gave me the confidence to continue and succeed. He allowed me to fail without repercussion—stepping in to correct only when necessary. He opened doors for me, creating new opportunities to advance in my career. I can honestly say I learned more from John than anyone else with whom I worked.

The second producer is Mark Burley. Mark and I produced over thirty-five hours of television together. We worked with children, animals, special and visual effects, various stunts, difficult studios, and eccentric talent.

In my view, Mark approaches work with just the right balance, always keeping things in perspective. Although he engages in a high-stress profession, he never plays politics, loses his temper, or takes his frustrations out on others. In fact, just the opposite is true. He is one of the most thoughtful, honest and straightforward human beings with whom I have had the pleasure to work. When you join one of his shows, you know it will be an enjoyable experience. Not only will he treat you well, he will employ like-minded people who believe work should be inspiring and fun.

Our time together placed us in a number of difficult situations. By watching and listening, I learned how to effectively deal with difficult people, to surround myself with the best employees, and to be true to my convictions. He taught me to lead by example, and I am fortunate to have been part of his team.

At one time or another, we all get the opportunity to work with people we admire and respect: to learn from them, to listen to what they have to say, to follow their example, and to know they will teach us something new. And the more we learn, the better at our jobs we become.

Watch, listen to, and learn from the best. You will know them when you meet them because you will be inspired. They will share their knowledge and treat you with consideration. Emulate them.

YOU'RE ALWAYS A BOSS TO SOMEONE

No matter who you are or what you do, at some time or another you will be the boss of someone else. Whether you are the president of your parent-teacher association or the president of a Fortune 500 company, you will have the opportunity to guide and motivate others. How well you perform this role is entirely up to you. Even if you are homeless.

For those of you lacking confidence in your management ability, here is my general advice: Manage people the way you would like to be managed. It is as simple as the golden rule: "Do unto others as you would have them do unto you."

This idea really hit home one afternoon while we were shooting a television show in downtown Los Angeles. We were about to film a "walk and talk" (two actors walking and talking) along a freeway overpass. Beneath the overpass was a colony of homeless men and women living in cardboard boxes. The area we were filming was littered with trash and unspeakable debris, and no one on the crew wanted to deal with it. Also, the actors refused to work near such squalor, and production came to a screeching halt. We scrambled to find a professional cleaning company but had little success on such short notice. Even if we found one promptly, by the time it arrived and resolved the problem, we would be hours behind schedule.

While we discussed our options, our location manager asked if he could give one of the homeless men some money to start the cleanup. By the location manager's side was an elderly man dressed in ratty clothes and smelling of booze who clearly had not bathed in days. I could see he obviously needed the money. I was skeptical he would succeed but figured, "What could it hurt?" At worst, we would be out a few dollars.

The homeless man shook my hand and profusely thanked me for the opportunity. He offered to bring along a few friends to help. Within minutes he returned with his two-man crew. We gave each of them a twenty, some cleaning supplies, and put them to work.

To my surprise, the three men went about their business carefully and efficiently and with great dignity. They swept and mopped and picked up trash until the street was spotless. The elderly man shared in the work. He took charge and managed the others. He gave them suggestions, praised them when they did well, and followed up to ensure we were satisfied with their performance. Because of his management style, they exceeded our expectations and departed feeling supported and appreciated.

Having dismissed the elderly man at first, I was sincerely impressed by his attitude and his actions. I was impressed by the way he took personal responsibility for the people working under him and his insistence on a job done well. Here was a man who could not keep a home, could not put food on the table, and could not live within society's norms, but he was able to manage others with care and compassion.

There are lots of theories on how to manage, but there are no hard-and-fast rules to follow. You will know you have done well when you can bring out the best in the people around you. When those in your charge are working hard and efficiently not because they have to but because they want to, you will have succeeded as a boss.

**To the extent you can, as part of your management
technique and style, manage employees
the way you would like to be managed.
It is the golden rule of supervision.**

SUMMARY OF RULES

FINDING VALUE IN OTHERS

RULE 1 Everyone has a skill to share. Make an effort to know your employees and in the fullness of time discover their hidden talents.

RULE 2 With experience, you will develop an ability to spot talent, which is everywhere. But you must be and remain open to finding it, even where you least expect it.

WHO TO HIRE

RULE 1 To ensure performance at the highest level, do not let your pride stand in the way of hiring the best.

RULE 2 Hire and value most those employees ready, willing, and able to follow up and follow through. Judge performance and, if possible, offer incentives based on these criteria.

RULE 3 When you are forced by circumstance to hire people who are less qualified, keep your expectations reasonable and be sure to provide additional support and supervision.

CHECKING REFERENCES

RULE 1 Take the time and make the effort to properly verify any and all information pertaining to job applicants before hiring them. In particular, track down former employers not listed on the résumé.

RULE 2 Be especially creative and energetic when seeking references. The most useful information may come from the least likely source.

MAKING THE DEAL

RULE 1 Everyone is looking to be compensated appropriately. Make the effort to learn what candidates really want and need before negotiations begin.

RULE 2 Value comes at a price, so be prepared to pay extra when circumstances dictate, to fight for the quality you require, and to justify the decision financially or otherwise.

RULE 3 Treat people fairly regarding compensation. Above all, keep your commitments and you will be repaid in kind.

MOTIVATION AND PRAISE

RULE 1 To be a good manager, see yourself as part of the team and readily offer praise for jobs well done. Resist negativity and nonconstructive criticism.

RULE 2 Make an effort to bring out the best in others .Be gracious, be interested, be sincere.

RULE 3 Value overall performance; not just time worked. An employee with a balanced life is a better employee, and that balance should be encouraged and supported.

HOW AND WHEN TO SAY GOOD-BYE

RULE 1 Save the benefit of the doubt for people who have repeatedly earned your trust. Be cautious with others. If anyone abuses your trust, show them the door promptly.

RULE 2 Do not prolong the inevitable. If someone is failing to perform, let him or her go. By keeping this person on longer than you should, you do harm to all concerned, particularly yourself.

RULE 3   When you are forced to fire someone, use it as an opportunity to help redirect the person's energy to something better suited to his or her talents and interests. Focus on someone's strengths rather than emphasizing weaknesses.

FISCAL RESPONSIBILITY

RULE 1   Be smart about how and where you try to save money. Good management (realism, flexibility, clear goals, and high morale) will beat penny pinching every time.

RULE 2   Being financially responsible does not necessarily mean imposing restrictions from above. Involve others in the decision-making process. Where you can, give them options. That way everyone will support the difficult choices that have to be made.

RULE 3   When you have limited financial resources, be creative in seeking low-cost alternatives that accomplish the desired result.

CRISES AND REVELATIONS

RULE 1   No matter the circumstances, accept the fact that you are replaceable. Never make a career decision assuming they will scramble to keep you. Be confident and competent, not arrogant.

RULE 2   Think carefully. Make sure you can deliver before you make a promise you cannot keep. Over time, you will be respected for your realism and candor.

RULE 3   Sometimes things just do not work out despite your best efforts. Be forthright about it, accept responsibility, and move on.

SAFETY

RULE 1   Give considerable thought to the safety of your employees. Do not compromise on time, money, or the use of qualified safety personnel to protect them.

RULE 2   Communicate safety concerns, eliminate safety hazards, and oppose unsafe practices. Your attitude and concern should set the standard.

RULE 3   Prepare an emergency plan in case of accidents and confirm that your co-workers know it in advance.

THE MAKINGS OF A GREAT BOSS

RULE 1   Watch, listen to, and learn from the best. You will know them when you meet them because you will be inspired. They will share their knowledge and treat you with consideration. Emulate them.

RULE 2   To the extent you can, as part of your management technique and style, manage employees the way you would like to be managed. It is the golden rule of supervision.

5
Responsibility without Authority

KNOWING YOUR POWER

WELCOME TO PARADISE

I often feel the world would be a better place if only you and I were in charge. Surely you agree. How frustrating that despite profferment of our best ideas, we are held back by people for whom we work. How frustrating that we lack the power and authority to put those ideas into practice and see positive results. Perhaps our efforts are compromised by our supervisors' limited vision or lack of understanding. Perhaps if we were artistes.

Years ago, I was hired to manage a new television series to be shot on an island. The show was to primarily take place inside a five-star resort hotel, which we decided to build from scratch. It would become the show's permanent set. As I have noted before, a permanent set is a structure that is photographed repeatedly during the making of a television series. Think of the emergency room in *ER* or the courtroom in *Law and Order*. These are the sets in which the characters spend most of their time.

In order to construct our hotel, we imported a production designer from Los Angeles to create the look we needed and to oversee the construction and decoration of the project. Since the town in which we were shooting had plenty of skilled labor, we agreed to use a local construction coordinator and local carpenters. We even lucked out when we found an abandoned brewery whose rooms we could use for our soundstages. The rooms featured high ceilings, cement floors, and ample refrigeration.

Constructing a hotel set is similar to constructing the inside and outside of a real building, even though building permits are not required. You still have to provide for framing, drywalling, painting, wallpapering, flooring, lighting, and molding; and you have to install hardware, appliances, counters, landscaping, and plumbing. The only difference is the time line. A real hotel might take a year to complete: we had six weeks.

Before construction can begin, the producers, director, cinematographer, and production designer review the designer's plans for the set. Color choices, architectural detail, sight lines, lighting sources, entrances, exits, and overall flow are discussed. Once everyone agrees on the look of the set and the cinematographer feels confident it can be photographed properly, the design is approved. Then the construction coordinator calculates the cost of construction.

Once that is done, we usually have to make modifications to our design since we rarely can afford everything we want. Compromises are made and plans revised until we have a set we find aesthetically pleasing and is one the budget can support. Once construction begins, we try to stay as close to the original plans as possible so as not to incur unapproved overages. To track costs, a weekly cost report is prepared that compares budgeted figures to actual expenditures. If this report is prepared accurately and on time, we know if we are over or under budget and can make necessary changes. This is extremely important since money is being consumed very, very quickly.

On this particular show, it did not take long for us to realize the production designer was going to break the bank during construction. He failed to provide detailed plans to the construction department when promised, causing delays in the work schedule. He repeatedly asked for additions that were not originally approved, causing cost overruns. He failed to communicate his ideas clearly, causing work to be performed incorrectly. He constantly changed his mind, causing work to be duplicated unnecessarily. And he failed to apply logic to his architectural designs, causing a waste of both time and money.

This created unique problems. For example, he insisted the set for a bungalow be built three feet off the ground, which in turn caused the unnecessary elevation of all associated equipment and the utter befuddlement of the studio executives. As I tried to explain his logic and the related costs, restating his nonsense about sight lines, I knew I might as well be arguing for the benefits of deep-fried Twinkees. We all knew it was ridiculous.

Everything this production designer did cost the company money; a fact he seemed to care little about. When I tried to talk to him about financial overages, he reminded me he was an "artist" and could not be bothered with such trivial concerns. I sensed from the first day that we were headed for trouble. But how much trouble? With all the problems, it was impossible to provide accurate cost reports. We had no idea how far over budget we were going.

Had it been up to me, we would have sent the production designer home on the first flight out of town. But because he was friendly with the executives, no one was willing to let him go. My repeated protests fell on deaf ears, and I quickly realized he was not going anywhere anytime soon.

As the situation grew worse, I knew something had to be done. We decided to bring in a more seasoned construction coordinator from Los Angeles to try and keep the project on track. I figured that if I could not replace the production designer, I could at least bring in someone to police him. Although the local construction coordinator was competent, he lacked the strength and confidence to stand up to the production designer when necessary and to refuse his demands to spend money frivolously.

As soon as our new construction coordinator arrived, he informed me that we were badly behind schedule. In order for the set to be ready on time, we would need a lot more manpower. He also concluded the materials had cost far more than projected. When all was said and done, we were hundreds of thousands of dollars in the red. As soon as I was notified, I did what any frustrated producer would do: I went to the producers' trailer, banged my head against the wall, and sent expletives heavenward.

I stayed there a long time and thought about where I had failed. Perhaps I should have complained louder, longer. Perhaps I should have raised a red flag sooner. Maybe if I had provided more specific examples of the problems I was having others would have listened. The truth is, there were any number of ways I could have handled the situation better than I did. Given the chance to do it over, I would certainly have tried a different approach.

But I also recognized I was not alone. We had all played a part in this fiasco. The production designer, construction coordinator, and other producers had contributed to the problem. It was not my fault or burden to carry alone, and I needed to stop berating myself over it. I needed to own up to and apologize for those setbacks over which I had control and to let go of those I did not.

You cannot be held entirely responsible for mistakes if you are not given the sole authority to make decisions. In the business world, you will have responsibility without authority time and again. If failure occurs, take responsibility for your share, but let others own up to their own mistakes.

Recognize the limits of your power. You will often have responsibility without authority. Urge management to align them. In any event, do your best, take responsibility for your mistakes, and let others be responsible for their share of both success and failure.

I'VE GOT YOUR BACK, UNLESS I DON'T

Have you ever worked for someone who lacked the courage to lead; someone who spent more time hiding behind a desk than rolling up his sleeves and getting the job done? I think the hard-driving and experienced executive working right beside you is far superior to the one who fears leaving the safety of his corner office. Those who start at the bottom and work their way up grow into their success and have no such attributes. Those who attain success overnight are often just a few mistakes away from the exit interview. They have been known to say, "Don't confuse me with the facts. I've made up my mind."

The entertainment business is one where you can go from being a low-level assistant to the most sought-after player (actor, director, writer, even producer) overnight. One well-crafted script or independent feature can mean the difference between $400 a week and millions a year. Unfortunately, neither education nor experience is an absolute prerequisite to success. Therefore, it is not uncommon to find yourself working for someone who lacks the knowledge and experience to properly be in charge.

Fortunately, I have worked for some really terrific people. Many have spent years learning the business before securing high-level positions at studios or networks. Because of their experience as filmmakers, they are fair and reasonable in support of your efforts. When I work for these men and women, I know their demands are realistic: they understand the problems I face, they provide knowledgeable advice, and I can count on their support.

Unfortunately, this is not always the case. Sometimes you have to work for poseurs who make life a living hell. Because they lack experience, they are often insecure. Thus they cover up their deficiencies, unfairly assign blame, avoid rendering decisions, and make unrealistic demands.

I faced this problem a few years back while working on a cable television series. The show centered on the lives of three different families. In order to photograph them in their homes week after week, we needed to build numerous sets on a soundstage, (There is not a neighborhood in the world that would want a film company to become a permanent fixture on its streets. Would you want a hundred tough-looking crew members parked in front of your house at 5:30 A.M. every morning?) Since two of the families were upper middle class, the sets had to reflect their social status—something that was going to cost a lot of money to build and dress.

Contrary to the show's requirements, the company financing the show decided we needed to reduce the budget. They insisted we meet with their in-house executive in charge of production and collaborate on ways to accomplish this goal. Since we felt the budget was already as lean as we could make it, we were concerned about what would be asked of us. Another producer and I made our way to the corporate offices armed with whatever supporting documentation we had. After a quick introduction, the executive made the following suggestion:

"You should construct the sets with only two sides. That way you can substantially cut the construction budget."

What?! What was she talking about? Anyone who understands single-camera cinematography knows this will not work. You need to move the camera to film both sides of the same scene for it to cut together. This requires three or four walls depending on the scene's blocking. (Blocking is the way the actors are positioned and move through the scene.) When I tried to explain that this would limit our ability to move the camera and to properly photograph the show, she insisted that she had done it before and we would have to do it her way.

I wanted to ask, "Have you ever actually been on a film set before?" But I suspected this might be a tad injudicious and would only make things worse, so I refrained. I tried to explain to the executive the problems she was creating, but she was unwilling to listen. I even drew a diagram which she refused to consider. Since she could not speak intelligently about the issue or refute our concerns, she used her power over us to insist we follow her directions without contradiction.

The more she was challenged, the more insecure and insistent she became. Instead of trying to educate herself, she became increasingly defensive. Eventually, she changed the subject by sharing with us her numerous screen credits.

One of the shows she had "produced" took me by surprise since I had personally production managed it myself. Having been on set fourteen hours a day, five days a week for eight months, I was intimately familiar with everyone involved. I had never seen her, met her, or heard her name associated with the project. She could sense my confusion and was surprised when I told her of my involvement. Rather quickly, she clarified that she was an in-house attorney at the time and had never actually made it to location.

Terrific! We were answering to someone who cared more about her own reputation than the welfare of the project. This presented a huge problem. On the one hand, our show's creator expected well-constructed sets that could be properly photographed. On the other, we were being forced to build unusable sets to save money. I knew if I built the sets as instructed, I would be the laughingstock of the company. I also suspected that if I did as I was told and the proverbial s--t hit the fan, the executive would abandon me, leaving me holding the bag. In frustration, I turned to one of my mentors for guidance.

He agreed that she was making a ridiculous request that could not be followed. He also agreed that I could not ignore her instructions. And he believed, as I did, that she would sell me down the river if the need arose. His solution was to build the sets the way they should be built, find savings in other areas, and exclude her from as much of the process as possible. His solution worked well.

Another example of this hubristic style of leadership occurred when I was dealing with a very difficult actress on another television series. The actress refused to arrive on time, spent more time on her cell phone than in hair and makeup, failed to show for wardrobe fittings, and was impossible to get to the set when the camera was ready. Because of these constant interruptions, we were often behind schedule.

As we tried alternate solutions, the studio executive decided to take matters into her own hands. She gave us the following instructions. First, make note of all the actress's late arrivals on the production report and thus shame her into timeliness. Second, have an assistant director wait impatiently by her side whenever she is on the cell phone. Third, schedule her call time earlier than needed to ensure she arrives on time. To the inexperienced, these might seem like reasonable solutions. To the experienced—we were doomed!

Foolishly, we followed the executive's instructions, and within a few days, the actress declared war. Now, not only was she late, she did everything she could to punish us with vituperation, condescension, and, but for the criminal laws, vivisection. If that was not bad enough, she contacted the head of the studio—someone with whom she had a personal relationship—to complain about being mistreated. It did not take long before we were reprimanded and instructed to show our lead actress the respect she deserved.

By following ill-conceived demands, our team's reputation was tarnished. But did the executive who instructed us to initiate the harassment step forward and share in the blame? Not on your life. She jumped on the blame bandwagon and pointed a finger our way. It was a miracle we did not lose our jobs. To paraphrase a former general, "I would rather have an hysterical actress in front of me, than this executive behind me."

As I was trying to reconcile the contradictions in this fateful turn of events, a good friend offered some advice. He said, "Never assume the company will back you. They only want you to do what they are requesting if it has a positive outcome. If things go south, it's as if they never knew you. And remember, if someone's got to go, it won't be the actor." I knew he was right. This is, after all, a star-driven business.

I did learn that I had to be more selective about the instructions I was willing to follow. Even if demands were being made from above, I needed to assess whether they were in the best interest of the show and, ultimately, in my best interest. If they were not, I needed to find an alternate way to satisfy my superior(s) or refuse to comply.

When you work for someone who is inexperienced and unrealistic, you must recognize you are at risk. You must weigh obeying a potentially damaging order against disobeying it altogether. If you cannot find an alternate way to satisfy all parties, hold fast to your integrity and seasoned instincts.

Do not assume you must automatically follow any and all orders from above. Following through on unrealistic or improper demands can be more damaging than refusing them. Trust your instincts, be creative, rely on your experience, and choose the path that will result in the best outcome.

WELL, WE HAVE TO BLAME SOMEOME

Why is it that blame is assumed by so few and passed on by so many? Over the years, I have seen people do almost anything to avoid taking responsibility. They take the path of least resistance, avoid making decisions, and point fingers at others to cover their own mistakes. So what happens when you are blamed unfairly, when you are left twisting slowly, slowly in the wind?

The location of a film shoot is one of the most important decisions that has to be made on a film project. Just because a story takes place in Aspen, New Orleans, or Key West does not necessarily mean you want to film there. Some locales refuse to be inconvenienced by filmmaking and will impose impossible restrictions. Others may not have adequate crew living in town, which means the company has extra costs in housing and travel. Some locations are inaccessible or the site fees are too high. Even weather can play a part. You do not want to be filming in Chicago in the winter if your script calls for sunny skies.

The decision on where to shoot is often made collaboratively among the studio, the producers, and, sometimes, the actors. (Some actors are unwilling to work far from home.) And if this decision is made unwisely, it can pose insurmountable problems.

Such was the case on one of my most difficult shows. Before I was hired, the location had been settled. We were to film for eight months at a remote locale that lacked many of the most basic infrastructure resources. Since the show was otherworldly, the scripts called for unusual props, set dressing, wardrobe, and makeup, none of which was readily available.

Each new script seemed to call for increasingly hard-to-obtain resources. We needed a professional football game to be played in a stadium full of fans, a trained dolphin that would dance with an actor, a devil-like creature, period wardrobe, prosthetic makeup, a futuristic set dressing, a downtown city park, specialty equipment, and even a unicorn. Unfortunately, most everything we needed had to be brought in from LA. When you need to fly in a trained monkey for a scene that shoots the next day, it costs a lot of money.

So do stupendous traffic jams such as the one that occurred when we set dressed a clearing—down a narrow dirt road in the boonies—to look like a surreal city plaza (of course none existed at our locale), and then had half a day to shoot the necessary scenes and move to the next location. Chaos theory was proven beyond doubt when the outgoing crew piled into the incoming set strikers causing complete deadlock. I looked for a toilet down which to flush more money.

Now, most "production" executives are primarily interested in the bottom line. Once a budget is set, they want you to hold firm to it. In contrast, while the "creative" executives care about money, they do not want fiscal concerns to be the driving force in deciding what is best for a show. What is the point of shortchanging a project if it makes the show a flop? Saving money on a show that fails is a lot more expensive than spending a little extra on a show that succeeds.

So there is a delicate balance to be achieved between the business and creative policies of a studio. If the policies jibe, then you, as a producer, are in fat city. But sometimes the creative and business factions are working at cross-purposes, and it is your job to somehow walk the tightrope between them. On this show, the two factions were unwilling to compromise. In fact, most of the time they refused to talk to each other at all.

With little studio support and unwillingness by the show runners to rewrite scripts, we needed to provide what each script called for (despite increased costs) or risk shutting down. We tried to keep everyone at the studio apprised of the overages and waited for feedback. None came.

Despite our best efforts, the show performed poorly and was quickly cancelled. Suddenly, everyone was deeply concerned about the cost overruns. It was as if these overages caught everyone at the studio by surprise. But, *we had been telling them all along!*

About two years later, I received a phone call from a high-level executive inquiring about my availability for a new show. I should mention these calls never come when you are calm and relaxed, seated in your home office, prepared to be articulate and self-assured. No, this call came while my infant was in the bathtub, I was helping my significant other pack for five months on the road, and we were in the midst of a heated debate. (Actually, you could probably call it a fight.) I answered the phone in the midst of a tumult. I quickly retreated into the garage and tried to compose myself for the call.

"We are really interested in considering you for an upcoming pilot," he said.

I wanted to tell him how thrilled I was but he continued without pause. "But I need to know how you let the '_____ show' get so out of control."

My mind was racing. How could that dreadful show still be haunting me? Had I not suffered enough!?

Before I could formulate a response, he went on. "In our experience, you have always been fiscally responsible. Is there any reason we should be concerned?" He waited patiently for my explanation.

I was taken aback, but I knew I had to answer. I wanted to shout, "*It was not my fault! No one would listen!*" But I knew that answer would not achieve my goal of gainful employment. I thought through my options as quickly as I could. I finally told him how disappointed I was with the financial outcome of the show. That was most definitely true. I went on to explain what an amazing learning experience it had been for me; how difficult it was to reconcile both the creative and business side of production; and how I believed in the importance of picking the right location to help control costs. I assured him that I was as concerned about the bottom line as he was—as I had always been.

When the conversation ended, he invited me to Los Angeles to meet with the other producers and subsequently offered me the job. Despite my success, part of me felt I had sold out by not defending my previous actions. But none of that mattered to him. He wanted an assurance, not excuses, and I knew that whining and complaining about the unfairness of the previous situation would not serve me well.

Most importantly, I knew the truth. Given the circumstances, I had done the best I could. I knew that the career path I had chosen was a difficult one, and I was not going to change the way Hollywood worked. It would only be a matter of time before I found myself in an equally difficult situation, and I needed to accept that.

None of us wants to be blamed unfairly. When you are, evaluate your involvement, assume responsibility for your mistakes, learn from it, and then face the challenges ahead.

> There will be times when you are blamed unfairly.
> When it happens, do not make excuses or
> desperately defend your position. It will fall on
> deaf ears. Take responsibility for your part,
> communicate the positive lessons learned,
> and face your next challenge.

MAINTAINING YOUR INTEGRITY

BARTENDER, POUR ME ANOTHER

I hate it when people fail to listen to me! It makes me feel as though my lips are moving but nothing is coming out. Almost daily, I tell my daughter to pick up her clothes, yet they remain on the floor. I tell my mother I have never worn a size two, not even at birth, yet she continues to put Barbie-size underwear in my Christmas stocking. But nothing, and I mean nothing, is as frustrating as having both employees and supervisors refuse to listen. Maybe the blender was too loud.

I would say one of the low points in my career resulted from having my advice ignored. I had been asked to take over a very successful television series in its third season. Taking over for someone else is exceedingly difficult. It is like being the new kid on the block when everyone else has grown up together. I tried hard to integrate successfully, confident I could bring positive changes to an already well-run machine. Unfortunately, not everyone shared my views.

The program was a network prime-time drama that featured action sequences, numerous stunts, and complicated special effects on an almost daily basis. The show had a large cast, an enormous crew, and two units shooting simultaneously most of the time. It required everyone to be at the top of their game.

Shortly after my arrival, I noticed that everyone became more relaxed as the day wore on. This struck me as odd since, after twelve hours on your feet, you frequently become tired and agitated. Additionally, everyone seemed a bit more thirsty around five o'clock. And I began to notice an unusual number of red cups floating around the set. Being optimistic, I convinced myself that this was a craft service coincidence.

As time wore on, the red cups kept making an appearance at precisely the same time each day, and I noticed that the drinks were not coming from craft service but rather from the assistant directors' trailer. I learned to my surprise that in addition to maintaining a copier, a fax machine, various computers, and mounds of paperwork, the assistant directors were maintaining and operating a fully stocked bar.

Now, despite what most people think of Hollywood, there is zero tolerance when it comes to drugs or alcohol on a film set. When you are working with heavy equipment, high voltages, fast cars, gun shots, explosives, breaking glass, stunt falls, pyrotechnics, helicopters, and the like, you cannot afford to have people's faculties impaired. The danger is far too great.

Everyone in the industry understands this, which was why the situation was so surprising. What was even more disconcerting was that part of the assistant directors' duties included assuring crew safety. Yet they were the ones compromising it.

The potential liability was tremendous. Moreover, should an accident occur on set, the assistant directors would be the first to be investigated and held accountable along with me, the production manager. Should their negligence be confirmed, we could all be held personally liable. Can you imagine how you would feel if someone under your supervision was hurt or, even worse, killed as a result of irresponsible behavior? I refused to be a party to it.

I immediately ordered the drinking to stop. But no one seemed to care. The red cups kept coming. I tried to impress upon all involved the extent of the risk they were taking personally and professionally. But no one was listening. Next, I tried to enlist the help of some of the executives running the show but to no avail.

Finally, I went to the studio. It backed me completely and gave me the authority to make whatever changes I felt were necessary. The changes I initiated were quickly halted when the lead actor, who sincerely cared about the crew members, made it abundantly clear that no one would lose his or her job for any reason, what-so-ever, period. The crew had become a "family" to him, and he was not going to lose his family! Nor did he seem to view the drinking as a particularly difficult problem.

It was clear to me we were at a standstill. After careful consideration, I decided to resign. In an eighteen-year career, it was only one of two times I did so from a show in production. Not only did I have grave concerns about the safety of our employees, I was not willing to carry responsibility for their safety without the authority to ensure it. I was not willing to work in a hazardous environment where my authority was not supported and respected and my warnings were all but ignored.

Now, in fairness to the studio, the executives and the lead actor, they had a far broader perspective than I did of the show's requirements, and they may have had very sound reasons for not implementing changes at that time. But at my level, the problem was irremediable, so I left.

There are times when we feel we are swimming upstream, that we are all alone in our efforts to do what is right. When you find yourself in this situation, when you have done everything you can do to be accommodating, stand firm in your convictions. Your moral compass will guide you to do what is right and just.

**Do not allow your values and moral standards
to be compromised at work. Stand firm in your
convictions; they are the core of your character.
Then, no matter the outcome, you can take pride
in having done the right thing.**

GEE, IT'S DARK OUT HERE

You are only as good as your word. If you are like me, you value your commitments and will go to great lengths to ensure a promise made is a promise kept. Even better, "Promise only what you can deliver. Then deliver more than you promise." If you fail to keep your promise, you not only disappoint others but you tarnish your good name and hard-won reputation. Especially when the lights come up.

Unfortunately, there are people who make promises they never intend to keep just to get what they want. This situation confronted me on a television pilot. The executive producer was certain his pilot was the next *CSI*. His arrogance and lack of integrity allowed him to ask for handouts while believing he was doing everyone a favor by letting them be part of his "ground breaking" show. Acting like a used car salesman, he would tell anyone in the town where we were filming, "This show is going to put your town on the map."

Since money was tight, he insisted we meet with every city and government agency to see if we could "squeeze" them. We met with the film commission, the mayor's office, the local police, even the tourist bureau asking for various concessions. This was especially embarrassing since I had a prior working relationship with many of these people.

It pained me to be associated with someone who acted in this manner. I was even embarrassed to be in the same room with him. But since I had a prior relationship with the studio and the locals, I felt obliged to see the project through and so I stayed and tried to mitigate the damage.

While most of our contacts were too sophisticated to fall for his Hollywood line, they were still eager to have the business and were willing to help in any way they could. So as preproduction gave way to production and our budget ballooned, the tourist bureau stepped forward and offered some relief. Since they needed promotional material, and we needed additional funds, it was decided that the tourist bureau would pay to light one of the city's most popular tourist attractions for our night shoot, and we would film additional footage for their tourist campaign. It was a win-win situation for everyone involved, and I was pleased to have helped broker it.

On the night of the shoot, we were all under considerable pressure. We were filming on a street lined on both sides with popular restaurants, nightclubs, and an eclectic mix of shops. On most nights, the place was so crowded with tourists it was difficult to cross the street. Most of the revelers were disinterested in being rerouted or having to be quiet to accommodate our filming. So, to successfully shoot the scene, we were given permission to close off the area and control the street for a very short period of time.

Between the extensive lighting setup, the time restrictions, the crowd control, and the multiple camera setups, things were extremely stressful for everyone involved. I was relieved to find most everyone doing what was expected of them and pleased that we were right on schedule. As we waited for the actors to come out of hair and makeup, I noticed our B camera crew sitting around doing nothing. Everything about this night had been planned right down to the last detail. We had instructed the B camera crew to film the tourist bureau footage at precisely this time, but for some reason, they were not following the plan.

Assuming the camera crew had forgotten, I hurried over to remind them of our obligation and to reiterate what needed to be done. The camera operator gave me an apologetic look and told me he had received specific instructions from the executive producer (i.e., the used car salesman) not to shoot anything for the city until all our work was complete. I explained that if we waited, we would not have the time to shoot the footage we had promised. Besides, the B camera crew was not doing anything anyway. We had scheduled the night this way for a reason. Now was the perfect time. The camera operator agreed but what could he do. He had received his instructions from someone whose authority superceded mine. He was stuck.

I rushed over to the executive producer and pleaded my case. Surely, he would not want to risk disappointing a city that had worked so hard for us.

"Hey," he annoyingly responded, "if we get it, we get it; if we don't, we don't."

What! These people had given us half their annual tourist budget. They had taken a big risk on us. We had made a promise. *I* had made a promise!

I reminded him again of our commitment. A commitment he had personally guaranteed. A commitment that needed to be done now or never.

"All I care about is getting what I need to make my show," he responded.

I told him that was not good enough for me. I had made a promise I intended to keep. He reminded me that I worked for him and would do whatever he believed was in the best interest of the show. I told him I could not and would not be party to such duplicity and walked away. I went back to my car, found my phone book, and called the studio. After explaining my situation, the head of production allowed me to resign from the pilot without prejudice provided I did so in an orderly fashion. Before I flew home, I called all the city officials I had let down and apologized for what I considered to be a breach of faith. It was the second and last resignation of my career.

As I tell this story, I am again outraged by what transpired. The sad truth is that but for this man's arrogance, all our needs would have been met. But honoring a commitment was not important to him. He thought nothing of using others for his personal gain.

It happens, however, that life is not without some poetic justice. Years later, when chatting with the studio head of production who graciously allowed me to resign, I learned he felt the television pilot was the worst he had ever seen. The writing, the acting, and directing were spectacularly awful, and the pilot was not picked up. I quietly turned away, looked blissfully to heaven, and whispered, "Thank you."

Taking advantage of others to get what you want is a contemptuous way to conduct business. No one wants to be associated with someone who is untrustworthy. For yourself, be honest, committed, and concerned. When others believe in you and trust you, they will extend themselves, and you will prosper.

> **If you make a promise, keep it. If someone else prevents that without justification, rethink your association. Your word and integrity are two of your most prized assets. Protect them at all costs.**

KNOWING WHEN TO SAY NO

IF HE GOES, I GO

Whenever I am morally confused about a course of action, I consider the golden rule: "Do unto others as you would have them do unto you" (a philosophy you will find repeated in one form or another throughout this book). I ask myself, would I want to be treated the same way if the roles were reversed? Often, the answer forces me to reconsider my approach. Would we yell at our kids, grow impatient with a store clerk, or neglect a friend if we honored this rule? Probably not. Would it change the way we treat people who work for us? Probably so. Even to protect the innocent.

A producer friend of mine recently confided to me that he voluntarily withdrew from a very successful television series many years ago. I wondered why he had left. He had been instrumental in producing the pilot and first season of the show, and it had changed television, gained tremendous popularity, and resulted in a number of related spin-offs. Had he stayed with it, he would have been a very wealthy man. Instead, he chose to sever ties with both the show and its maker. When asked his reason, he told me that he had been directed on more than one occasion to fire employees without cause. Part of the corporate culture was to maintain fear and unrest among the workforce by frequently terminating staff. This was a "motivation" practice he could not condone.

It gave me comfort to hear his story because I had been asked to do something similar and did not care for it one bit. Shortly after starting preproduction on a pilot for an action show, the executive producer came to my office and asked how difficult it would be to fire a teamster.

I explained that we had the right to terminate anyone's employment as long as we could show cause, despite their union affiliation. I noted, however, that unions often fight hard to protect members from unlawful termination, so it was important to make sure we had good reason for acting.

"Has someone done something I don't know about?" I asked him.

"No," he assured me. "I just wish Ted [not real name] was not a teamster."

"Ted's not a teamster," I foolishly (with hindsight) corrected him.

The executive producer's face brightened. "Great!" he exclaimed. "Fire him and bring on someone new."

I was shocked by what he said. This was my fourth show with Ted. He was smart, reliable, creative, friendly, and experienced and had a great working relationship with the entire film community. He knew everyone in city government and was a huge asset to the show.

"Why do you want to get rid of him?" I quickly asked. "He's great at his job."

"Yeah," he arrogantly replied, "there is just something . . . I can't quite put my finger on . . . I just don't like the guy. Maybe he reminds me of someone else I don't like . . . Anyway, get rid of him and get someone new." He departed, pleased that the matter had been so easily resolved.

In retrospect, I wish I had told him off right then and there. I was enraged by the unfairness of the situation. He was asking me to fire someone without cause. And for what? We were talking about jeopardizing a man's livelihood based on ambiguous feelings. Besides, Ted had already turned down other employment opportunities to do this show as a favor to me. I had made a commitment to him in return.

Even if I was willing to compromise my own integrity and fire him without cause, what reason would I give? "Sorry, but the executive producer thinks you might remind him of someone he doesn't like but can't remember who." It would make for great evidence if we were sued. So, I considered my choices.

On the one hand, I felt obliged to carry out the executive producer's instructions. After all, this was his show, and he had the right to hire and fire anyone he wanted. I knew he could technically get away with a termination without cause because our employment contract only guaranteed a week's worth of work. I also knew Ted would never contest the decision as he would not want to cause trouble for me.

On the other hand, I knew Ted's loyalty to me was the result of a relationship built on mutual trust and respect. I needed to preserve that trust and respect by refusing to be party to something so unfair and distasteful. But could I afford to lose my job knowing there might not be anything out there for me for months?

Fortunately, the decision became easier as each day passed. What I eventually learned was that this was not an isolated incident. This executive producer lacked moral integrity, and it affected all of his business dealings. He thought nothing of using people for his own gain, and I subsequently noticed him making promises he had no intention of keeping. (Yes, this is the same executive producer and the same show I quit in the section "Gee, It's Dark Out Here").

As I previously related, I could not continue to be associated with someone I did not trust or respect and so I graciously said no to his unreasonable and unethical demands at the time I resigned. I did, however, stay on until a competent replacement was found and did everything I could to make for a smooth transition.

In the end, I lost months' worth of work and income. But no matter, it was a small price to pay for maintaining my self-respect. The executive producer probably lost more. His selection of the small community where he purchased a home and strutted and preened as Mr. Hollywood Big Shot was Ted's home as well, and Ted was extremely well connected and respected there. Delicious turns of the screw were in Ted's future if he wished. The executive producer earned high marks for once again making the worst possible decision in the circumstances.

There are times when we are asked to do things that we do not approve on moral or ethical grounds. When this happens, we need to weigh the cost of compromising our integrity versus the financial loss we may suffer. When the cost of compromise is too high, we must say no. To determine when the cost of compromise is too high, it helps to apply the golden rule.

> **Never agree to do something you find morally reprehensible. There will be times in your business life when you must say no and accept the consequences. The golden rule provides an exceptionally useful guide in such circumstances.**

DON'T WIPE YOUR FEET ON MY FACE

A tyrant is defined as a cruel and oppressive ruler; someone for whom you definitely do not want to work. The character of

Lucinda in *The Devil Wears Prada* was a perfect example of this. Everything that came out of her mouth was designed to intimidate, deflate, offend, and control the people who worked for her. Her entire staff lived in constant fear of her. Have you lived in fear at work? Could your boss be classified as a tyrant? One of mine could.

Only once in my career have I had to answer to a tyrant. More often than not, I have been associated with decent, level-headed, hard-working people who valued their employees. This might seem surprising since conventional wisdom would have us believe that most high-level executives in the entertainment industry are oppressive. Films like *Swimming with Sharks* depict abusive behavior as a normal part of the Hollywood style. I would disagree with that. But even one tyrant is one too many, and I think their type of abuse is worth comment.

I have friends who have worked for people who have thrown things at them, yelled at them, blamed them for things they had not done, and even threatened them. Sadly, the more successful the abuser, the more willing people are to put up with such treatment because sometimes the opportunities exceed the pain and suffering. But at what cost?

In my case, a producer to whom I was reporting on an hour-long drama was a real hothead. He acted like your best friend one minute and discredited you the next. You never knew what would set him off, but you did everything you could to avoid it. Everyone tiptoed around him and did whatever they could to placate him. Sadly, it was a useless proposition. No matter how cautiously we conducted ourselves, he always found reason to attack.

His style was not as overt as you might expect. Instead of yelling and screaming, he chose a more controlled, surgical-like approach. He would call you into his office and grill you about some error he felt you had made. (He would have been an asset on any police interrogation squad.) No matter what you might or might not have done, by the time you left his office, you were groveling and apologizing for anything and everything in sight.

Then, as added punishment, for a week or two following the verbal beating, he would punish you by refusing to include you in meetings, questioning your every move, giving you degrading tasks to perform, or using you as an example of ridicule.

A favorite ploy of his was to walk into a meeting, point a stern finger at someone, point to his office, and leave expecting them to follow like sheep. I wish I had had the audacity to point back at him with my forefinger and salute him with my middle finger.

Far worse than the abusive way he treated us, however, was the long-lasting effect it had on our psyches. As time passed, I realized I was feeling anxious all the time. I was constantly afraid of what he might say or do. To protect myself, I withdrew, having as little contact with him as possible. Instead of being optimistic, engaged, and motivated (something I try to be on every job), I became overly cautious, self-critical, and easily intimidated. Somehow, I had abandoned the qualities I most admired in myself. I realized this show would be our last together.

When he asked me to return for the next season, I declined. When he asked me to work with him a few years later, I declined again, as have many others. The price of association was too high, the experience too crippling.

Some people are tyrants. They taunt us in the playground, haze us in the fraternity, and intimidate us in the workplace. How we deal with them is critical to both our success and sense of well-being. If your strength and self-confidence are being diminished by someone in authority, speak up. Their behavior is not only harmful, it is possibly unlawful. If the situation does not improve, you may need to simply say "no more" and walk away.

Be aware that abusive behavior in the workplace is debilitating. It will sap your confidence and sense of self-worth and impair your performance. Confront it, overcome it, or end it.

DÓNDE ESTÁ EL PESO?

When the demands of a boss are fanciful, should we as employees be allowed to define for ourselves what is and is not realistic? How much license have we to declare, "You've got to be kidding!?" Would it be intemperate to exclaim, "Are you out of your mind!?" Perhaps so, but not if pesos are involved.

Many years ago I was sent to Mexico to work as a production executive on a television movie. Because of my financial background, my duties were to include oversight of the accounting department. I was to approve all contracts, sign off on all financial expenditures, approve crew and actor payroll, review petty cash expenses, negotiate and manage the local union agreements, and temporarily invest unused funds. All financial transactions were within my jurisdiction.

This movie was unusual because we subcontracted with a Mexican production company to handle all aspects of principal photography. While their employees were gifted filmmakers, they were about twenty years behind the times in technological terms. Modern conveniences to which we were accustomed were unavailable. Computers were rare. Cell phones, if available, were large and cumbersome. Walkie-talkies had limited range. And the locations lacked cellular service. It was a real adjustment for us.

This lack of technology also had a significant impact on the work of the accounting department. In the past, I had always relied on computers to track the thousands of financial transactions involved in making a film. Despite the use of computers in our LA offices, the accountants in Mexico continued to handle all bookkeeping by hand.

Every single transaction was inscribed in a ledger by hand and then transferred to spreadsheets, which were recapped at the end of each day. Hundreds of thousands of numbers that accumulated over time were then reconciled into useable reports. This was exhausting work for a department comprised of two principal accountants and two assistants.

For those unfamiliar with production, films work on a cost-reporting basis. This means that actual costs are compared to a preapproved budget on a weekly basis. All overages or underages are reported so that we can determine whether the show is in financial trouble or if there is additional money available. This financial information is vital as it allows us to make fiscally prudent decisions.

Thus, we might ask: Can we afford a specific location? Is there enough of a surplus to cover more overtime? Are additional background performers affordable? Each decision is made not only on its creative merit but on the financial impact it will have on the show. Without accurate and timely information, we are throwing darts in the dark, and we will almost certainly miss our target. So the accounting department worked assiduously to enter all transactions and update the information submitted.

This movie involved the further complication that all payroll had to be paid in cash. At the time, the Mexican unions required production companies to pay its members in pesos. So every Wednesday, the two primary accountants and I would go to a local bank accompanied by an armed bodyguard (think machine gun) to compile payroll and pick up duffle bags filled with cash. The tellers could not have been more stunned if we were the Hole in the Wall Gang. Indeed, the Hole in the Wall Gang segued into the Keystone Cops when we misplaced a duffle bag full off cash (about U.S. $15,000) in the back of the car taking us to and from the bank and did not discover it until all the chickens had lost their heads and the sky had fallen.

In the locked basement of the bank, we would take half a day to manually count a floor-to-ceiling pile of bills. On any given payday, we counted out roughly three million pesos in small denominations. Once the cash was counted, we returned to the office and separated out each employee's compensation. The entire day was spent preparing payroll. Then on Thursday, we would set up a table in the production office, and a line of one hundred and fifty crew and cast members would collect their pay.

This process went on for six weeks of prep, four weeks of shoot, and two weeks of wrap. Through every phase of production, disbursements were made for food, clothing, hotels, airfare, equipment, trucks, cameras, lights, film, catering, set dressing, locations, fuel, props, vehicles, picture cars, and background extras. And every transaction had to be manually entered and tracked day in and day out.

This was without a doubt the most labor-intensive financial project in my film experience. Not only did we have to report to the local production company in pesos, our parent company also wanted all financial reports converted to dollars. Spreadsheets a mile long covered every surface of the accounting office. Somehow, the local accountants were able to stay on top of this cumbersome task. I was confident they were providing us with accurate, up-to-the-minute information.

When the show finally ended, and wrap was almost complete, we were asked to prepare a final accounting for the studio. For two days, we analyzed, reviewed, and verified the numbers, then compiled reports that summarized the total cost of the show. As we raced to completion, we spent the last twenty-four sleepless hours making our final tallies. As we tracked and verified the final totals, we realized we were off about U.S. $200. *Only $200!* I was giddy with delight. Despite thousands and thousands of entries tracked over the course of three months, our accountants had only miscalculated a couple of hundred dollars. It was a miracle.

When the sun came up, I phoned a studio representative to let him know the reports were enroute via fax. I boasted that we had come within $200 of accounting for all of the $3.5 million expended.

"Don't you think you should try to find it?" he inquired.

I realized he had no grasp of reality. At least not ours. He probably had never worked without computers; had never reviewed lists of numbers compiled by hand; and had never put in the hours we did on a similar project.

Without a moment's hesitation I said, "I'll gladly send you the two hundred bucks!" We laughed, and he agreed to let it go. His request was completely unrealistic, and I suspected he sensed it. It would have taken weeks to go back over every single entry to try and find a few measly dollars, and for what?

Sometimes you are asked to accomplish something you know to be unrealistic. Perhaps the person asking is not completely informed. Perhaps only you are familiar with the limitations involved. Whatever the case may be, if you cannot do something that is requested of you, share your concerns and deliver what you can.

**Do not be afraid to decline an unrealistic request.
Fully explain your reasons. Even the most demanding
boss will appreciate your candor and practicality.
Deliver what you can.**

SUMMARY OF RULES

KNOWING YOUR POWER

RULE 1 Recognize the limits of your power. You will often have responsibility without authority. Urge management to align them. In any event, do your best, take responsibility for your mistakes, and let others be responsible for their share of both success and failure.

RULE 2 Do not assume you must automatically follow any and all orders from above. Following through on unrealistic or improper demands can be more damaging than refusing them. Trust your instincts, be creative, rely on your experience, and choose the path that will result in the best outcome.

RULE 3 There will be times when you are blamed unfairly. When it happens, do not make excuses or desperately defend your position. It will fall on deaf ears. Take responsibility for your part, communicate the positive lessons learned, and face your next challenge.

MAINTAINING YOUR INTEGRITY

RULE 1 Do not allow your values and moral standards to be compromised at work. Stand firm in your convictions; they are the core of your character. Then, no matter the outcome, you can take pride in having done the right thing.

RULE 2 If you make a promise, keep it. If someone else prevents that without justification, rethink your association. Your word and integrity are two of your most prized assets. Protect them at all costs.

KNOWING WHEN TO SAY NO

RULE 1 Never agree to do something you find morally repre-
hensible. There will be times in your business life when you
must say no and accept the consequences. The golden rule
provides an exceptionally useful guide in such circumstances.

RULE 2 Be aware that abusive behavior in the workplace is debilitating. It will sap your confidence and sense of self-worth
and impair your performance. Confront it, overcome it, or
end it.

RULE 3 Do not be afraid to decline an unrealistic request.
Fully explain your reasons. Even the most demanding boss
will appreciate your candor and practicality. Deliver what
you can.

6

Male/Female Interaction

SEX IN THE WORKPLACE

YOU'RE SCREWING ON MY SET?!

Why is it the man you thought you adored is often less compelling after your first night together? Come on, admit it. We have all fallen head over heels; forgetting to keep one foot on the floor. We get swept away by a night of passion only to be awakened by incessant snoring. Breakfast together becomes a painful reminder to think and not just look before we leap. And what happens when the man shares an office next to yours, much less an entire film set?

For anyone who has read the tabloids, it seems common for actors who play love interests on film to become intimate outside work. I suppose this is one of the things that makes Hollywood fascinating. Let's face it, who would not become weak in the knees after kissing Brad Pitt? But what happens if the love affair fizzles before the curtain falls?

While filming a particular television series, I had the unpleasant experience of watching two actors apparently fall in love, consummate their relationship, fall out of love, and participate in a seriously ugly breakup. We suspected involvement soon after the first on-screen kiss. Instead of complaining about trailers and wardrobe and catering and long hours, they were blissfully happy. We often found them laughing affectionately together.

Then one afternoon, we were filming in and around a luxury hotel. We had paid for the use of the lobby and two of the hotel suites. In addition, we purchased most of the sixteenth floor so we would have excess space to film, an area for people to work, and a place to store equipment. We also wanted control of the floor to minimize our impact on other guests. To make good use of the space, I set up a temporary office in one of the rooms. It became a quiet retreat where I could make phone calls, handle paperwork, and try to manage the unending stream of problems.

Around lunch time I made my way down to catering to get something to eat. Since I can consume a three-course meal in under five minutes (a downside of the trade), I finished my lunch and headed back to my office, leaving cast and crew behind. As I reached our floor, the set decorator intercepted me and asked if I would sign off on (inspect and approve) our next set—an elegant hotel suite where we would be filming the rest of the day. It is a common practice to have a director and producer sign off on a set before it is filmed to avoid any last-minute problems.

When we got to the suite, the set decorator put the key in the lock, and we briskly entered, unannounced. There, on the new silk sheets, were our two actors in various stages of undress, carnally making a mess of the set. As quickly as we entered, we split. Out in the hall, the set decorator turned to me in a panic. "The crew will be setting up in twenty minutes. What if they've ruined the sheets? It's the only pair I have. I don't have the money to buy another pair! I don't even know where to get another set!" She was aggrieved. I started to laugh. The whole thing was ridiculous. Of all the places available, they decided to screw on our set! I considered what to do. Should I knock? Should I noisily let myself back in? Should I demand they dress and leave? Should I depart and forget what I saw? The set decorator turned to me for a solution. "OK," I finally said. "I'll ask them to leave and then we can assess the damage."

As I was about to knock, they casually exited as if nothing had happened. Reluctantly, we entered the scene of the assignation, afraid of what we might find. In typical star fashion they did not even bother to make the bed! We stripped (and possibly burned) the sheets and made do with linens from the hotel. By the time the crew arrived, we were back in business, or so we thought.

As it turned out, the actress was looking for something long-term while the actor was looking to burn off lunch. Within a few days, he was arriving on set with fungible groupies. Things went from bad to worse. In an effort to make him pay for his sins, the actress went out of her way to ruin most of his coverage (his close-ups). She refused to rehearse with him, touch him, kiss him, or even look at him. You can imagine how hard it became to portray a loving couple when they refused to be in the same room. So for the rest of the season, we stumbled along. He complained about her, she about him. In the end, we all suffered through the breakup.

In my opinion, relationships are hard enough to sustain without throwing work into the mix. Just look at the tabloids: the vast majority of relationships in the film business that start at work end in disaster. When a relationship fails, we all know that someone is going to get hurt. Remember, there is a fifty-fifty chance that someone will be you.

**It is immature and unseemly to become
sexually active with someone with whom you work.
If the relationship fails, working together will be
agony. Your reputation may suffer permanent
damage as word gets around, which it will.**

LOCATION DOESN'T COUNT

Why do we behave differently far from home? Think back to college when spring break was spent in south Florida or Puerto Vallarta and we did things we would never mention in good company. These trips gave us license to let our hair down and be seemingly unaccountable for our actions. Nowadays, many of us use business trips to relive those youthful days. How many of us too soon forget that photos last while memory fades?

We know the tourist industry capitalizes on sexual impulses. "What Happens in Vegas, Stays in Vegas" is a multimillion dollar ad campaign designed around our need to rebel. New Orleans has thrived as a tourist destination ever since it billed itself as an all-night adult playground. Even Florida has captured the convention market by providing some of the best adult entertainment in the country.

Life in the film business has introduced me to it all. While working in Florida, I had the opportunity to scout a number of strip clubs for our show. After a long morning of nothing but "tits and ass," we stopped to have lunch at one of the better clubs. While the food and service were great, it was hard to ignore our waitress in her rubberband-sized G-string. Oddly, the men did not seem to mind. Anyway, when I paid the bill, I noticed the payee was not the club itself but some executive country club. When I inquired, our waitress laughed at my naïveté. "If we used our real name," she explained, "our clients would not be able to disguise it on their credit cards or expense accounts, and their wives or bosses would be furious." Good point!

I realized then that a lot of people were using business trips as a reason to party, and the film business was no exception. The problem was that film people had more time to get into trouble. While most business trips last only a few days, film crews can be on location for months at a time. Large feature films can last an entire year. Imagine being away from your significant other for that long. It is no wonder people think "location doesn't count."

To illustrate further, let me share a story from one of my shows. I was staying in a hotel with eighty other crew members. Each morning the halls turned into musical chairs as people found their way home after a night of lascivious bliss. Since I was young and single, I thought nothing of it. I had much to learn.

Near the end of the show, we threw a pool party for the cast and crew. One of my co-workers took the opportunity to photograph the event. When the show ended and everyone returned home, she graciously sent copies of her pictures to all of us, letting us know how much she had enjoyed working with us. Pretty sweet, huh? Well, not for some.

The executive producer's wife opened the envelope, looked through the pictures, and stumbled upon a photo of her husband fondling a bikini-clad girl perched on his lap. He had one hand down her pants and the other waving to the camera. I am certain his debauched smile did not help. Needless to say, he was in the doghouse, and my co-worker lost a valued contact.

Now, some would say that the real crime was in getting caught, but I disagree. While I firmly believe adults need to let loose from time to time, I think there is a time and place for it. By all means go out and play, live a little, have your fun. But be careful not to mix work with this type of pleasure. When you are surrounded by good friends, you are free to do and say things without fear of repercussion. But your friends will not judge you the way a co-worker or supervisor might.

When you are at work or away on business, be aware that you are constantly being evaluated. Your standing in the organization as well as your advancement will be directly related to your behavior. Whether you notice it or not, people are keeping a watchful eye, even after the whistle blows.

**Behavior that may be acceptable in your
personal life may not be appropriate at work.
Take care to present yourself in a professional and
dignified manner. Always assume you are being
monitored and evaluated, because you are.**

SEXUAL DISCRIMINATION/HARASSMENT

MY, AREN'T YOU LIMBER

Can men be sexually harassed? Most of the ones I know are flattered when a woman, any woman, offers to leap into the proverbial sack with them. Unlike women, they are less discerning about who, what, when, or how. They are just happy "if." But what if someone's advances makes them feel uncomfortable? What happens when men become prey?

While I am not certain actors are generally more promiscuous than other people, there are some whose actions would shock and amaze you. I suppose it takes a certain type of person to take off his or her clothes in front of strangers on set and kiss someone he or she hardly knows, allowing the whole thing to be captured on film. Even if I could lose the requisite ten pounds, I would not have the courage to do it.

That, of course, brings me to my story. While shooting in a rural part of the country, I had an opportunity to work with two lead actresses starring in a television movie. One was married, had children, was a bit overweight, and was relatively indifferent to the members of the crew. The second was in her late thirties, single, and quite good-looking. It was obvious she had gone to great lengths to maintain her youthful appearance. From the first day on location, she made it clear she was interested in one of our crew members.

The man she desired was a driver on the show. He was single, personable, attractive, and not easily intimidated. It was no secret that she found him desirable and wanted to know him better. Anytime she needed a ride somewhere, he was the one she called. Whenever she needed her trailer moved, he was the one she asked. Whenever she needed something picked up and brought to her, he was the one she summoned. And every night, when the show was wrapped, he was the one she asked out for a drink.

Fortunately, his immediate boss, the transportation coordinator, had strict rules about fraternizing with actors. Under no circumstances was it allowed! So time and time again, he politely declined her social invitations.

At first, I believe he was flattered by all the attention. Frequently, she would bring him little gifts just to say thanks for all his hard work. Certainly being recognized and rewarded had its satisfactions. But as time wore on, it became clear he was feeling uncomfortable. In addition, there was the constant ribbing from his co-workers: twenty or so guys who found the whole thing hilarious. What started out as childish banter, "Oooh, she likes you," soon became, "If you were a real man, you'd just do her." And that was something he clearly did not want to do. The more upset he became, the more they teased him.

I suppose he could have gone to management to complain and ask for help, but at what cost? He believed it was something he should be able to handle on his own, so he kept silent. Of course, had the roles been reversed, the company would have offered to talk to the harasser and demand a change in behavior. But since he was a young single man, no one really saw it as a problem.

Finally, one afternoon, she summoned him to her trailer. Afraid to say no, he went to see what she needed. When he knocked on the door, she seductively asked him in. He opened the door, stepped inside, and found her butt naked and smiling. "I thought you might like to see something special," she said. (As if there was anything left to see.) Then, she bent down, kicked up into a handstand, and spread her legs in an inverted split. Pretty darned impressive, but not for him. He promptly left the trailer and refused to have any further contact with her.

I learned about these allegations through the grapevine and realized that anyone, male or female, can be made to feel sexually harassed. If it could happen to him, it could happen to anyone. While it might happen more often to women, men can be victims too. We all need to be sensitive to the thoughts and feelings of others: what may be flattering to one may be unbearable to another.

**Sexual harassment can happen to anyone,
male or female. Make certain that you are sensitive to
the feelings and concerns of all your employees no
matter their gender, and do what is necessary
to correct inappropriate behavior.**

BUT YOU'RE DRESSED LIKE A STRIPPER!

We all know women who dress provocatively and behave flirtatiously then complain that men only want one thing from them. Well, duh! What you show the world is often what you get back in return. On the other hand, if you present yourself as competent and professional, that is precisely how the world will see and treat you. But what if someone exploits their position for monetary or other gain? Someone who willingly agreed to take it all off.

From time to time we have to deal with sexual harassment complaints in the entertainment business. In this day and age of litigation and liability, we take such complaints very seriously. Sexual harassment is no longer tolerated. When someone behaves badly, corrective action is taken immediately. To make our position clear, we hold sexual harassment seminars to educate our employees as to what is and is not appropriate behavior.

Such two-hour workshops can be especially uncomfortable for some. Many of the men on a film crew—the grips, the drivers, and the carpenters, for example—are particularly masculine. They are strong, gruff, and unlikely to be in touch with their feminine side. For them, open discussion of the subtleties of male/female relationships is often confusing and unpleasant. But no matter, we hold the seminars anyway, and we all promise not to say or do anything to offend each other. Usually, people take this to heart and are respectful, but from time to time mistakes do happen.

As examples, I have had an assistant complain about an overly touchy-feely executive, a homosexual costumer complain about fag jokes, a wardrobe assistant who was reduced to tears when asked to zip the fly of a male actor, and a female carpenter who was offended by a nudie calendar. When these problems occur, I make a concerted effort to eliminate the offensive behavior and reestablish a respectful workplace.

Sometimes I am successful, and sometimes not. On one occasion, we were filming a scene in a strip club, and we hired an actress to play the part of the stripper. Throughout the casting process, we repeatedly asked the candidates if they were comfortable with the role. The woman who accepted the part had played similar characters before, had pole-dance training, was comfortable with nudity, and assured us that she was ready and eager to work on our show.

On the day of the shoot, we went out of our way to ensure that everyone was comfortable with the setting, the nudity, and the scene. We held a miniharassment meeting to remind everyone how to behave. We made arrangements with wardrobe to have someone standing by at all times to cover the actress as soon as the camera stopped. We even cautioned our extras director to remove any background personnel who were disrespectful in any way. And finally, I spoke directly to the actress to let her know I was there for her if she needed me. As a woman, I too had been in situations that made me uncomfortable, and I wanted to make sure it did not happen on my set.

The shooting proceeded smoothly. The actress was fantastic. The extras hooted and hollered and waved money as scripted but adopted a respectful manner when the cameras were turned off. Wardrobe kept the actress covered at all times except when necessary, and not a single joke or extraneous comment was heard. Before wrap, I made it a point to check with the actress to make certain she was happy with the day's work. She assured me that she was, and I left feeling good about the benign environment we had created.

Until early the next morning, that is, when her agent phoned threatening to file a sexual harassment suit. I was floored. What could possibly have happened? Had I missed something? I immediately involved the studio. Together, we discussed all the precautionary steps we had taken with the agent. We even reviewed the conversations I had had with the actress in which she confirmed her satisfaction with the shoot. Regardless, he kept insisting that she had been harassed because, "People were staring at her." Was I hearing this right?! She was playing a *stripper*!

No matter how much I wanted to believe her, I realized that we were being played for suckers. Should we pay off a struggling actress to make this go away? Should she be allowed to make a few bucks by playing out this hand? No. We told them to file the suit, and they quickly suggested a few thousand dollars would make the problem go away. We told them to take a hike.

I lost all respect for the woman that day. Her actions not only made her look foolish but also hurt other women who might actually have a valid claim. I learned that in this area I could no longer take someone at his or her word. In the future, I would have to dig deeper and question values as well as motives.

Doing your job is hard enough without having to feel embarrassed, oppressed, offended, or sexually harassed. There is no room for such activity in the workplace. But for people to be respected, they must also act in an honest and dignified manner. Then and only then will we know when someone is really in need of help.

> **Sexual harassment should never be tolerated in the workplace. Do everything you can to protect your employees, but take special care in evaluating the values and motives behind each claim to ensure fairness and balance in the proceedings.**

WHO PUT THE HOOKER IN THE SCENE?

We have all heard stories about the "casting couch": a place where women can earn extra credit for services rendered and hopefully further their careers. While most women work hard and earn what they have, the casting couch mentality sometimes creates a bias when women succeed. People often ask, "Did she sleep her way to the top?" And while this mentality offends me, I am afraid it is sometimes all too real. But what of the person who supplies the couch?

Let me share an experience I had shooting a network series a few years back. The director was hired by the studio to direct one episode of a thirteen-episode order. He was scheduled to travel to our location, spend seven days preparing, eight days shooting, and a few days editing in Los Angeles. It is important to understand that unlike features, television directors are hired guns who usually spend a short period of time on a project. While their contribution is key, they wield less power than feature directors. In television, the real power is with the executive producer who is usually the one who creates and writes the show. Directors, therefore, are usually eager to please so that they will be invited back. This fosters a collaborative relationship between the director and all parties involved. On the rare occasion when you wind up with a dud, you can take comfort from knowing you only have to work together for a brief period of time.

Well, nothing could have been brief enough with this particular director. He was arrogant, disrespectful, and, above all, completely ill-prepared. During most of prep, he would disappear for hours at a time, without any indication when he might be back. Since we were shooting in a desirable location, I think he saw it as an opportunity for a free vacation. Since he was rarely available for consultation, no one knew what to prepare or what he might want when filming began. Everyone was forced to make assumptions in his absence; something we do not do casually. Then, things got worse once the cameras rolled. Without warning, he would leave the set around 6 P.M. regardless of whether the day's work had been completed. On more than one occasion a producer had to jump in and cover for him. But even that did not prepare us for the coup de grâce.

On the last night of his shoot, we were filming in a trendy

restaurant/lounge. The scene took place between two of our lead actors as they were seated at a bar engaged in intimate conversation. Production had done wonders in setting the stage. Dozens of extras had been individually dressed to create a sense of elegance. The props department had taken great care to prepare the perfect food for the patrons to eat. The lighting and design were flawless, and our director actually decided to show up; fortunately, we thought. All was going splendidly until the director of photography (DP) tapped me on the shoulder to ask, "Who is she?" He pointed to a horribly dressed, disheveled-looking woman seated right next to one of the actors. As we had only completed half the scene, the cameras were still rolling.

"I have no idea," I answered. "Where did she come from?"

"I don't know," he responded, "but she wasn't in any of the earlier coverage."

By now the room was abuzz: everyone wondering who she was; everyone knowing her presence was creating a real problem.

"We have to pull her out or reshoot the whole scene," the DP continued.

What he was trying to say was that continuity had been broken. That happens when, for example, a car is clearly visible in a scene, but after you cut right back to the same scene using the same angle, it mysteriously disappears. Well, that is what we had here. If we kept her in the scene now, when she had been absent before, she would appear out of thin air. We could not let this continue.

I walked over to the director and asked if we could stop the cameras until we resolved the problem. He became annoyed and told me he had put her in himself and he wanted her to stay. I tried to explain that if she stayed, we would need to start from scratch and reshoot everything. Since we had only secured the bar for a certain number of hours, we would not have the time necessary for a full reshoot. Becoming increasingly frustrated, he told me to leave her in, and he would cut around her. I could not imagine how this was possible, so I consulted with our script supervisor. She assured me that what he was suggesting could not be done.

I was not sure what to do. Why would he intentionally sabotage his own show? As I looked back at her, I noticed her smiling and winking at the director. Clearly, they had something going on. Their relationship was compromising our show. I needed some leverage. I looked around for some of the guys he had been partying with after hours. A few were off-camera setting up lights. I went over to them and asked point-blank if she was his girlfriend. One of the guys laughed and said, "Yeah, for a hundred bucks an hour, she'd be your girlfriend, too."

That was it. He had finally crossed the line. I walked over to the first assistant director and told him to cut the camera and politely removed her from the set. Of course, the director was furious, but when I reminded him that the studio might frown on his use of local hookers, he stormed off in a huff.

I could have allowed him to dig his own grave that day but at what cost? He had been disrespectful of everyone, including his paid companion. He deserved to be singled out and forced to clean up his act. By refusing to sit idly by, I sent a clear message to the cast and crew that such behavior would not be tolerated, even from someone at the top.

Do not tolerate offensive sexual behavior. If you have the power to stop it, act swiftly and decisively.

SEXUAL CONTENT

IF YOU CAN'T STAND THE HEAT, GET OUT OF THE WRITERS' ROOM

It seems we all have friends who like to share their sexual exploits: people who feel completely comfortable discussing the most intimate details of their sex lives no matter how unusual or embarrassing. Are you comfortable with this kind of sharing? I know I am not. Of course, there is no way to gauge how someone will react to sex talk until they are confronted with it. But what if the confrontation takes place with people paid to talk about sex?

In the entertainment business, writers are paid huge sums of money to tell stories that center around the wonderful world of sex. Imagine the writers on *Friends*. They created and sustained a successful show that analyzed every aspect of human relationships. The show tackled stories about one-night stands, marriage, homosexuality, good sex, bad sex, breakups, single parenting, surrogate parenting, and the like. And where do you think many of these stories came from? They came from personal experiences that the writers were willing to share.

How about *Sex and the City*? Can you imagine the discussions that went on in that writers' room? They took sexuality to a new level. Every time two people had sex on the show, a writer had to define in detail what was going to happen, a director had to choreograph it for the camera, and actors had to execute it. Could you have comfortably participated in that process?

I remember on one series, the writers were struggling with a particular story line about a married couple with two children who had been together for over ten years. Their sex life had become monotonous, and they were looking for a variety of ways to spice things up. The episode in question showed them trying a series of activities to bring passion back into their marriage. They tried having sex in the backseat of a car, on a sand-swept beach, even in front of the refrigerator with food as foreplay. Each attempt failed more miserably than the last. Finally, the episode was to end with them back in their own bed doing something amusing. The writers wanted the wife to surprise her husband by doing something shocking but funny. But what could that be?

There was considerable discussion about it between the writers and some of the staff. Various people offered suggestions from personal experience to enhance the story. Prior to this discussion, I thought of myself as being fairly open-minded, but I realized that I was not at all comfortable discussing my personal circumstances with my work associates. There was very little that could offend me, but also very little I was willing to share. I quickly realized I had no business in the writers' room.

Just so you know, the story was finally completed with the wife putting her thumb in a new and exciting place that completely freaked out her husband, sending him flying out of bed to cower in the corner. In the end, the characters decided they were pretty content with their "boring and monotonous" sex life. And I decided I was happy keeping my love life private.

I learned from this experience that there was a limit to what I was willing to share. I realized that if I felt this way, others would as well. We all have our limits; we all have our boundaries. As employers, we must be sensitive to what our fellow employees deem appropriate and within the bounds of propriety.

> **Everyone has different limits regarding the appropriateness of sex talk. We should be highly sensitive to the feelings of our employees and co-workers in this delicate and difficult area to assure a pleasant and positive working environment.**

NASTY PROPS AND TOYS—GIGGLE, GIGGLE

Have you ever spent any time in an adult sex shop? Yeah, right, me neither. But I have been told there is a wondrous world of toys and games there that most of us never knew existed. I think we would all agree such things are completely inappropriate in the workplace. But what if your job requires you to shop for them?

On certain television shows it is not uncommon for the prop-master to have to buy sex props and toys and instruct others on how to use them. Here are two examples where this occurred:

On one show, there was a scene about a single mother who has not had sex in years. Needing satisfaction, she resorts to the help of a vibrator only to find the batteries are dying. First, she swaps out the batteries from a toy, then the television remote, then the batteries from the fire detector. Eventually, she gives up in frustration and slams the vibrator against the bed frame. To accommodate this scene, someone needed to obtain the device, and since we were taking creative license by swapping out different-sized batteries, we needed to modify it as well. In addition, we needed to make sure the actress was comfortable with the selection made on her behalf. And we needed to buy at least five identical vibrators in case one or more broke during filming. A lot of time, effort, and discussion went into picking the right vibrator.

The second example centered on a story line where a wife wakes up to find her husband fast asleep beside her. As she looks at him, she notices he is sporting a morning erection that pushes up from beneath the covers. Fascinated, she pokes at it until he starts to wake. Again, a great deal of thought went into making this scene work. How do you create a erection, especially one that can be poked at and spring back to life? What would the actor be comfortable using? What would the actress be comfortable poking?

We talked at length about this, trying to design something that would work efficiently. Finally, the propmaster opined that the only solution was a strap-on. We agreed to give it a try, and she went out to purchase a few. The propmaster had to assist the actor in wearing the device, and we needed to provide the actors some private rehearsal time to make sure they were comfortable using it. Fortunately, it worked like a charm, and we proceeded to film the scene.

These examples point up certain factors that need to be considered. With a large group of men and women standing around watching scenes like these, someone is going to feel uncomfortable, especially if others are making offhanded comments. The best we can do to maintain a level of professionalism is to allow anyone who feels embarrassed to leave the set. But what about the propmaster? What if he or she is uncomfortable with the environment and with having to purchase and work with sex toys?

The larger question really is how do we satisfy the requirements of the job when the job description requires us to participate in things we deem inappropriate? In the case of the propmaster and the strap-on, she viewed her job responsibilities as being the same whether she was working with food or sex toys. Neither one affected her more or less than the other. Neither was inappropriate. They were both simply tools of the trade, and she was able to work comfortably with them. After all, certain jobs require sexual content to exist.

While an employer should be sensitive to the needs of his or her employees and maintain a sexually appropriate workplace, so must an employee take responsibility for meeting the requirements of the job and declining those jobs he or she finds offensive.

> **Make sure you hire the right person for the job. While you have a responsibility to protect your employees from a sexually hostile environment, so too should the consenting employee be capable of fulfilling a job that has sexual content without concern or objection.**

YOUR REPUTATION

SORRY TO WAKE YOU, IS DANIELLE THERE?

Have you ever done something you were ashamed of, something you wish had never occurred? Perhaps you deflowered the copy boy on the Xerox machine. Or became drunk at the company picnic and went skinny-dipping in the fountain. Let us be honest. We have all done embarrassing things we wish we had not; things we would just as soon forget. So how do we move past these unfortunate events and regain our dignity and rebuild our reputation? Especially from a strange bed.

To give you guidance, I will share a terribly embarrassing story of my own. Many years ago I was on location working on a miniseries. I had been hired as a production executive to oversee filming and monitor the finances of the show. I took my job very seriously and made it a point to behave in a professional manner at all times. In addition to my daily duties, I asked our executive producer to let me assume additional responsibility as the assistant director of a splinter unit.

A splinter unit is made up of a separate camera crew, a few grips, drivers, a location representative, production assistants, an assistant director, a director, and a few background actors. On this particular show, the unit was to photograph aerial and ground footage as transition shots for the primary film. This required us to visit numerous locations all over town in a very short period of time. Since we could only afford one splinter unit day, we needed to maintain a very tight schedule.

To ensure success, I prepared the shooting schedule in minute detail, assembled the appropriate crew, and secured the proper equipment well in advance of filming. I left nothing to chance. After carefully analyzing the coming day's work, the crew and I agreed to meet in the hotel lobby by 6 A.M. the next morning to get an early start.

As I closed my office that night, I was confident that I was ready for the challenge ahead. I made my way from my office to my hotel room, anxious to get some sleep. (The offices were located in the hotel we were staying in.) As I passed through the lobby, our transportation coordinator stopped me with a few last-minute questions. We decided to discuss them over a quick nightcap in the hotel bar.

Exactly what happened next is private: the important point is where the story leads. Sound asleep and hungover, I woke the next morning in a strange room to the annoying sound of a ringing telephone. As I tried to bury my head deeper in the pillow, I heard a man's voice say "Hold on, she's right here." My eyes popped open. Right where? *Oh, no!* Then, someone handed me a phone, and I heard my producer asking where I was. Of course, he already knew. He had just found me in some guy's hotel suite. Aaaagh! To make matters worse, the clock read 6:35 A.M. *I was thirty-five minutes late!* I immediately jumped out of bed, spent three seconds in the shower, put on yesterday's clothes, and ran to the lobby.

What had I done!? I had let everyone down. I left my crew waiting for thirty-five minutes and jeopardized the entire day's shoot. Dressed and disheveled, I entered the lobby to the glaring faces of my fellow workers. Some were mad, some were embarrassed, and some could not contain their mirth. I, of course, was discombobulated. I wondered how many people knew. How many people had they called before they found me? I was utterly humiliated.

Well, what could I do? I had made a dreadful mistake, and I knew that the only way out was to own up to it. I apologized for my unprofessional behavior, apologized for wasting everyone's valuable time, and asked for forgiveness. And I was surprised how quickly people were willing to forgive and forget. Well, not entirely forget. The jokes took awhile to die down. But I do believe people were forgiving because I was willing to take responsibility for my actions and because what I had done was so out of character for me. They knew that this was a one-time thing, never to be repeated.

Having lived through it, I firmly believe that everyone is entitled to one "get out of jail free" card. As humans, we are allowed to make mistakes. If you fall down, my advice is to get up, brush yourself off, make amends, and never ever do it again.

Should you behave in an embarrassing fashion, own up to your error, forgive yourself, and carry on. Everyone is entitled to make a mistake. Your reputation can be salvaged if you act with honesty and integrity.

BUT YOU PROMISED TO DO IT IN THE NUDE!

What is the key to maintaining a good reputation? Is it working hard? Behaving a certain way? Or is it keeping your word, particularly in a man's world? I believe keeping your word is the most important regardless of the circumstances. So what happens when you promise to do something that makes you uncomfortable? Especially before millions.

This happens to actors all the time. Actors are asked to do a variety of things the average person would not or could not do. Often they must say and do things that make them uneasy; things they would never say or do in real life.

I would like to give you three examples of this with very different outcomes. In the first example, I remember holding a casting session on the side of a remote country road. The part we were casting called for a sickly old man to breath his dying breath. The man we originally hired fell ill, and we were forced to recast overnight. Since we were filming on location, we had to bring the candidates to us. So there we were: me, a producer, a country road, and five men in their mid-to-late eighties ready and willing to play dead.

This may seem like an easy part to cast, but acting dead is incredibly difficult. Seriously, try lying absolutely still barely breathing for an extended period of time. Not so easy. In any event, we had no place to hold the audition. Finally, I politely asked the gentlemen to lie down in the road. (Just a note: We had a police blockade so there were no passing vehicles.) I soon learned that people in their eighties have a hard time lowering themselves to the ground. With great effort, we eventually got them into a horizontal position.

Each man took his turn giving his best performance. Some did better than others. One of them could not help laughing; two kept moving or breathing loudly; one decided he did not want to participate; and one was so convincing that I was concerned he might have actually passed away. When we confirmed that he was still with us, we gladly gave him the part. As for the man who chose not to participate, I admired him the most for withdrawing from the audition. Rather than promise to do something he might not be able to do, he politely bowed out. So often that is not the case.

That is not the case because actors are often desperate to be cast in a part, any part, and they commit without thinking. And when they commit, we expect them to perform the part as described. But this can turn out to be a huge problem, especially when nudity is concerned. You might think that in this day and age nudity would hardly matter. Well, think again.

As my second example, we frequently audition women to act in nude scenes. When this happens, we take painstaking measures to ensure everyone is comfortable with the work. We make certain the candidate knows the requirements of the scene and is willing and able to perform them. We repeatedly ask the woman if she can work under such conditions. Yet, something seems to happen between the casting session and the film set that baffles me. About 60 percent of the time women who agree to play a part in the nude refuse to do it when the camera starts to roll. I do not know why, but it is a constant problem and one I find incredibly frustrating. How can you shoot a nude love scene with clothes on? How can someone skinny dip with clothes on? How can someone take a shower with clothes on? *It cannot be done!*

Now mind you, I have total respect for a woman's right to remain clothed. No one should have to reveal more of herself then she is comfortable with, and certainly not on network television where her minister might see her. But for heaven's sake, if you are not comfortable with nudity, do not promise to do it. Even in this situation, a commitment is a commitment. I suppose we need to ask ourselves: Is someone's reputation more likely to be harmed from being viewed in the nude or from failing to keep their word?

I was able to answer that question on my last show. We hired a young actress to perform a rather provocative sex scene on camera. With unbelievable courage, she disrobed, assumed the position, and acted out one of the funniest sex scenes I have ever seen. She took risks personally and professionally that few could do. And she did it in front of the entire cast and crew. As I watched the scene play out, I realized how much I admired and respected her. The fact that she was nude with her legs in the air was irrelevant. I was profoundly impressed that under such challenging circumstances she delivered what she had promised, with dignity. She did it with courage and skill, and she impressed every last one of us.

In the end, your reputation is primarily based on delivering what you have promised, on keeping your word.

Being true to your word is the best way to enhance your reputation for reliability and dependability. Do not offer or revoke lightly.

YOU'VE GOT 15 MINUTES, LET'S GET THIS OVER WITH

Have you ever worked for someone who was a little too touchy-feely? Not enough to allege sexual harassment, but enough to make you uncomfortable: a pat on the knee, a shoulder squeeze, a lingering eye. The truth is most woman have dealt with unwanted male attention throughout their lives. The question is: How do we deal with it at work? Shock therapy perhaps.

As I have noted, we all react differently to different situations. What is offensive to some is considered funny to others. Some women thrive on any kind of male attention, while others are offended by a polite compliment. The key is to know how you feel and then to express those feelings to others.

In my opinion, these issues between men and women are all part of a normal learning curve. To define boundaries, someone often needs to push limits (whether inadvertently or consciously) until another draws the line. Only then can we ascertain what is acceptable and what is not. If someone at work flirts with you and you go along to be "nice," what message are you sending? You cannot fault them for continuing to flirt because your behavior is telling them it is acceptable. However, if you thank them for the initial compliment then ask them to stop, you have clearly set your boundaries for any future interaction. More often than not, the unwanted behavior will change. (If it does not, the situation may constitute sexual harassment and outside assistance may be required.)

To avoid these uncomfortable situations, I encourage women to speak up at the first sign of trouble. It is far less embarrassing for all concerned. If you wait too long, you run the risk of sending the wrong message. As humans, we read each other's signals to know how to act and react. If they are not clear, we become confused.

To illustrate, let me share a mistake I made years ago. I was working at my first job, having recently graduated from college. My boss was about ten years older than me. He was good-looking, successful, kind—and appeared to be happily married. The problem was he enjoyed flirting with me. At first I was flattered by his attention, but as time wore on I became increasingly uncomfortable. He never touched me or forced me to do anything inappropriate, but he often joked about sharing a "quickie."

I wanted to tell him how I felt but was afraid to offend him or jeopardize my standing with the company. I tried convincing myself that his compliments were harmless, and I was reading too much into them. I feared that if I confronted him, he would laugh at me or tell me I had misread his cues. I felt stuck. Over time, my personality changed from outgoing and confident to closed off and unsure, especially when I was around him. Since I avoided him, I was no longer getting noticed for the work I was doing.

Finally, the problem came to a head. Late one night after my co-workers had gone home, I found myself working alone with him in his office. Anxious and irritable, I waited for the joking to begin, knowing I had reached my breaking point. I was ready to stand up for myself having decided that no job was worth feeling the way I was feeling. And then it happened.

"Think we have time for a quickie?" he joked.

"Why the hell not," I replied, jumping onto his couch.

His eyes went wide.

"You have fifteen minutes and then I never *ever* want to hear another word about it."

He stood motionless.

"Come on," I chided. "What are you waiting for?" I was on a roll. "It's all you've talked about since I got here. Let's *do it!*"

He suddenly looked scared. Who was this insane woman on his couch and how was he going to get rid of her? He retreated into the corner.

"I apologize," he stuttered. "I thought it was our little joke. I never thought you'd take me seriously!"

I could now see he was not, and never had been, a threat. I started to laugh. All that worrying for nothing. But had I not addressed the issue, I never would have known.

"Really, I'm sorry," he continued. "Why didn't you speak up sooner?"

Why indeed?! I jumped off his couch and left his office feeling renewed. I realized that to be true myself I had to clearly set my boundaries right from the start. All women do. Fortunately, he was a good guy and decided to overlook my psychotic episode. His joking subsided, and we were able to work well together until the project ended.

The lesson I learned is that you should not be afraid to speak up and let people know how you feel. Perhaps you might want to try something a tad less radical than my example, but if someone says or does something that makes you uncomfortable, fix it right then and there. You have a right to work in a safe and respectful environment.

Set clear boundaries so that people you work with know what is and is not acceptable concerning sexual innuendo, swearing, offensive touching, and the like. Everyone deserves to be treated with respect, especially you.

SUMMARY OF RULES

SEX IN THE WORKPLACE

RULE 1   It is immature and unseemly to become sexually active with someone with whom you work. If the relationship fails, working together will be agony. Your reputation may suffer permanent damage as word gets around, which it will.

RULE 2   Behavior that may be acceptable in your personal life may not be appropriate at work. Take care to present yourself in a professional and dignified manner. Always assume you are being monitored and evaluated, because you are.

SEXUAL DISCRIMINATION/HARASSMENT

RULE 1   Sexual harassment can happen to anyone, male or female. Make certain that you are sensitive to the feelings and concerns of all your employees no matter their gender, and do what is necessary to correct inappropriate behavior.

RULE 2   Sexual harassment should never be tolerated in the workplace. Do everything you can to protect your employees, but take special care in evaluating the values and motives behind each claim to ensure fairness and balance in the proceedings.

RULE 3   Do not tolerate offensive sexual behavior. If you have the power to stop it, act swiftly and decisively.

SEXUAL CONTENT

RULE 1   Everyone has different limits regarding the appropriateness of sex talk. We should be highly sensitive to the feelings of our employees and co-workers in this delicate and difficult area to assure a pleasant and positive working environment.

RULE 2   Make sure you hire the right person for the job. While you have a responsibility to protect your employees from a sexually hostile environment, so too should the consenting employee be capable of fulfilling a job that has sexual content without concern or objection.

YOUR REPUTATION

RULE 1   Should you behave in an embarrassing fashion, own up to your error, forgive yourself, and carry on. Everyone is entitled to make a mistake. Your reputation can be salvaged if you act with honesty and integrity.

RULE 2   Being true to your word is the best way to enhance your reputation for reliability and dependability. Do not offer or revoke lightly.

RULE 3   Set clear boundaries so that people you work with know what is and is not acceptable concerning sexual innuendo, swearing, offensive touching, and the like. Everyone deserves to be treated with respect, especially you.

7

Dealing with Difficult People

UNREASONABLE PEOPLE AND DEMANDS

WHEN ONLY COUTURE WILL DO

What is it that makes people think they need certain tangible goods to be happy? Do they think expensive things define who they are? Do they think that by acquiring certain items the world will perceive them differently, increasing their importance and making them feel better about themselves? Whatever their reasons, their insatiable appetite for material goods makes it difficult for those of us who have to satisfy them. Unless, of course, we slip in counterfeits.

During one of my earlier shows, I paid a visit to the wardrobe department where the crew was anxiously preparing for a fitting with the lead actress. The wardrobe department is usually set up with a few offices, a storage room with floor-to-ceiling racks of clothes, a seamstress room with various sewing machines, and a fitting area in which the actors try on clothes. Based on the script, a specific look for each character is predetermined by the director, designer, and producers. The costume designer then goes out and purchases an assortment of costumes for the actors to try. Then, they all decide what clothing will best support the character and make the actor happy. Costume designers have a very difficult job.

To illustrate, think how difficult it normally is to find that perfect evening gown for a special night out. Now imagine that you will be filmed in it for hundreds of thousands of people to see. Also consider that you might have put on a few extra pounds and are self-conscious about your appearance. Magnify this by ten, and you begin to appreciate the minefield costume designers walk through.

On this particular day, I was looking through racks of clothes while waiting to speak with the designer. I noticed the seamstress removing all the sewn-in tags from a handful of outfits. I was concerned because I knew that 80 percent of the items would not be used and eventually would be returned to the stores from which they came for a full refund. The show only required fifteen costume changes for this particular character, and we had numerous options to choose from. I watched the seamstress for a moment longer but could not imagine what she was doing.

When the designer finally arrived, I asked for an explanation. She winked at me and said, "I have no idea what you're talking about." The conversation moved on to more pressing issues. About fifteen minutes later, our lead actress arrived for her fitting and immediately began selecting the clothes she liked. After careful inspection she made her choices, which turned out to be the items the seamstress had worked on earlier. It all began to make perfect sense when I realized that these clothes now had designer labels sewn into them.

The costume designer, an older woman who had been around the block a time or two, knew the actress would only be willing to wear named designers. As a film star, she had grown accustomed to being provided with very expensive clothes. This being a television show, our paltry budget could not accommodate her demands. The costume designer's solution was to pick the clothes she felt were most appropriate, change the labels, and let the actress feel she was getting exactly what she wanted. The result was that the costumes were great, the actress was happy, and the department stayed on budget.

Now, not all actors think this way. There are those that will wear anything you hand them even if they look awful in it. There are those who are so into their character that only absolute authenticity will do. And there are those who would show up naked if you told them to. The challenge is in understanding the psychology of each individual actor and making him or her happy.

On one show, the script was about a woman who was in serious financial trouble and was no longer able to maintain her upper-class lifestyle. As part of the story, she was reduced to purchasing knock-off handbags. It was a major story point that helped to define the character's economic situation. In keeping with the story, the propmaster went out and bought an assortment of knock-off handbags for the actress to choose from. The propmaster's selections were rejected, and the actress insisted on carrying an authentic and very expensive designer bag. When the propmaster tried to reason with her, explaining that the story was about a knock-off, the actress refused to listen. Her response was simply, "I'll act that it's a knock-off." How can you argue with that?

As you can see, some of these demands can be ridiculous, even illogical. But are they any crazier than insisting on driving a luxury automobile or wearing a Rolex watch? Ours is a culture that defines us by the things we acquire, the things we think we need. We all have our personal list of "must haves." Who is to say when one of us has gone too far? But more importantly, how do we deal with these requests at work?

At one time or another, all of us will be forced to deal with difficult people who make unreasonable demands. I have learned that simply dismissing their needs as ludicrous is most unwise. By shutting them down, you make it impossible to work together effectively in the future and risk permanently damaging your relationship. But what if you cannot accommodate their needs? What if they want things that you simply cannot afford or are not in a position to give?

The best place to begin is to listen, really listen. What they may be asking for is not necessarily what they want but may be symbolic of something else entirely. For instance, in our business actors may be concerned about their appearance because they were not happy with the way they looked on a previous show. They may want to be compensated in other ways if they are unhappy with their deal. They may be nervous about the upcoming work and need some positive reinforcement.

Whatever the situation, as a professional you are best served if you engage them. Respect them, listen closely to them, try to fully understand them, acknowledge their needs, and then support them as best as you can without compromising yourself in the process. You will find that by doing so you can maintain a good working relationship with even the most difficult people.

Actively listen to what difficult people are asking for, make an effort to understand their needs, and avoid making negative assumptions about their motives. There may be alternative ways to satisfy them.

I WANT WHAT SHE IS HAVING ... AND THEN SOME

As children we learn early on how to get along with others. Perhaps it is all that time in the sandbox, having to share our shovels and not throw sand. We learn to treat others the way we want to be treated—with care and respect. Hopefully, we see that everyone is the same. But what happens when someone failed to pay attention in kindergarten when the concept of fair play was discussed?

Unfortunately, I have had the unpleasant experience of working with some very self-absorbed, egocentric, and narcissistic people who I was unable to placate despite my best efforts and understanding. They are few and far between in Hollywood, but they do exist, and it is virtually impossible to deal with them alone. In my experience, they are immune to the laws of social intercourse that the rest of us must follow. They believe their needs are paramount, and it is up to the universe to make sure those needs are met.

I had such an experience on a television movie shot up north. We were filming a show that required us to be outside in the snow and rain for hours on end. Since most of us were from southern California, we were ill-prepared for the weather and quickly rushed out to purchase cold-weather gear.

Regrettably, our lead actress was high maintenance. She had a personal assistant who followed her from show to show. It was this girl's job to take care of all the actress's personal needs: to set up her apartment, to keep her kitchen stocked, to do all her shopping, and to be her constant companion. The girl worked diligently from five in the morning to midnight most days and gave up her weekends whenever her boss needed her—all for almost no recognition and a lousy $350 per week in pay. What a glamorous business!

On the first Saturday after our arrival, the assistant went shopping to buy herself a coat. She had spent the week freezing like the rest of us and finally had time to rectify the situation. She took her meager salary and spent a third of it on a beautiful red coat she found on sale at Nordstrom's. The coat was lined and trimmed in a faux fur, which made it especially warm. She looked great in it and was delighted to have found something she could afford.

Monday morning she reported to the set at 5 A.M. when her boss was scheduled to be in hair and makeup. She arrived on time, rushed to catering to get her boss some breakfast, and made her way to the hair and makeup trailer to deliver it. As soon as she stepped inside, the actress took one look at the coat and had to have it. Without batting an eye, she exclaimed that the assistant did not look good in red and that she would look better in it. The assistant did not know what to say or do. She did not want to lose her job over a mere coat. Reluctantly, she handed over the garment. To add insult to injury, the actress did not offer to pay for it. Instead, she insisted that the assistant refrain from purchasing an identical replacement. Apparently, she did not want to be seen wearing the same coat as her personal slave.

Well, you can imagine how angry this made everyone who heard the story. But what could we do? The studio would not get involved in such a personal matter. Everyone continued to stew.

A few days later I was summoned to the set. Apparently, the actress was enraged and demanded to speak to someone from production. Upon my arrival and much to my surprise, every woman on the set was wearing the exact same red coat. The costume supervisor had gone out and purchased every identical coat she could find and shipped them to location. What a statement!

That sea of red said something to me. There is strength in numbers. The assistant could not stand up to someone so powerful. But with the help of other women, she could stand united and make her voice heard. Perhaps it would help in the future.

In business, you may find yourself in a situation in which you feel helpless. During those times, reach out to others. If you are struggling, there may be others struggling, too. And perhaps with their help, you can find a solution together.

Sometimes strength in numbers will solve a seemingly intractable problem in dealing with unreasonable but powerful people.

A TRUE ARTIST DOES NOT AN ASS MAKE

Could you be the character attacked on that pinball machine, or the ranger captain storming Omaha Beach? There is a reason actors are so well paid and their contributions are so valued. They entertain us, teach us, and allow us to experience feelings and emotions we might not otherwise have. But how they behave on the screen is sadly not always indicative of how they behave in the real world. I mean really not indicative.

One of the more difficult aspects of my job is to deal with actors. Do not get me wrong—I have a great deal of respect and admiration for them and their abilities. As someone who got a D in Acting 101, I know they do something I lack the courage to do and that they take unbelievable risks. They expose themselves both physically and emotionally for the world to see.

But in my experience, talent can be extraordinarily difficult. I have had stars refuse to take a certain airline if the boarding gate was not close enough to a Starbucks. One actor actually deboarded a plane when he realized there were no footrests in first class. Some actors will only wear couture or authentic Rolex and Patek Philippe watches (it helps them stay in character). Other actors insist that they get to keep any object they touch on screen even though they are millionaires many times over. Some demand that crew members never make eye contact with them. One particular actor insists that a basketball court be erected wherever he films even if the production company has to dig up a two-hundred-year-old plantation to pour the cement pad to meet his needs.

On occasion, actors refuse to come out of their trailers or even show up for work. Others have to be the last one called to set so that no one can keep them waiting. One actress could not be touched by the sun, so we had to employ a production assistant to run around holding an umbrella over her head. Another actor had to have someone follow him around after work so that he would not get drunk and engage in bar fights that could damage his on-camera good looks.

The list goes on. I am sure every show has someone whose behavior is undeniably boorish. I often feel the entertainment industry itself creates such folks by its methods. No other business would put up with such improper behavior. But, in truth, such behavior is unnecessary. There are actors who do not lose perspective, men and women who remain unchanged by fame and fortune.

Happily, these are consummate professionals. One well-known actor made it a practice to have regular meetings with the rest of the cast on his television show. By setting a good example for the cast and demanding they follow suit, he made it almost impossible for bad behavior to exist. This enabled the company to maintain a pleasant work environment for years. Others have been known to go out of their way to recognize members of their team. Some actors make it a point to know every crew member's name by heart, which is not an easy task when you have so many workers on each production. And some exhibit great generosity toward their co-workers by purchasing wonderful "wrap" gifts for everyone involved on a show when it ends.

What is of interest to me is that there is no correlation between the way one behaves and the amount of talent one possesses. Success does not seem to turn the heads of those who are well adjusted and grounded in reality. Some of the most successful and talented people I know are also the most professional and courteous. Some of the worst behaved are one box office failure away from the oblivion they deserve.

I am sure if you look at your own work situation, you too will be able to separate the doers from the divas, the compatible from the asses and self-absorbed. In dealing with the latter, it is important to remember that bad behavior is a discrete phenomenon. It does not necessarily relate to, or comprise the source of, someone's level of skill or value. It just means that they never learned how to play well with others.

Do not be intimidated or discouraged by bad behavior. Though you may have to tolerate it, distinguish it from ability and support and respect the courteous and talented.

BRIDGING THE COMMUNICATIONS GAP

I'M FLUENT IN ALIEN SPEAK

The book *Men Are from Mars, Women Are from Venus* highlighted an interesting and somewhat obvious phenomenon: We do not all communicate the same way. Because we generally look the same and act the same, we often make the mistake of assuming we should communicate the same. I am here to tell you that we do not. Especially with someone from outer space.

As with most people in business, I enjoy learning from others. I seek advice from those I most admire and respect. I find it saves a lot of time and trouble learning from the mistakes of others rather than committing them myself. One of the questions I often ask my co-workers is how to get the best out of those who are the most difficult. In my business, that person is often the star of the show. The feedback I have received has varied, but there is one consistent piece of advice worth sharing. When working with one of my favorite producers, I asked how he dealt with difficult talent and he responded, "Treat them like aliens."

Huh!? I did not expect that. But it makes perfect sense. Just as couples are encouraged to be sensitive to differences in each other's style of communication, so all of us should realize that certain people communicate in a way that seems alien. In business, I often cannot apply my sense of logic or values to what I hear. The way some people interact is completely foreign to me.

I remember on one occasion I had been summoned to an actor's side because he wanted to discuss the next day's shoot. He was upset by his work schedule. Based on our plan, he would have to show up for work at 7:30 A.M. the next day, work until about 10 a.m., leave for a few hours, and then return to work from 7 to 9 P.M. Since he was the lead in the show, he felt we should be more accommodating in scheduling his time. Having him work at the top and bottom of the day was not in his best interest.

Normally, we would not straddle a lead's schedule like this, and he knew it. But in this particular instance, there were other is-sues to consider. First, we were shooting in two separate locations: a hotel lobby and a coffee shop, both requiring his presence. Sec-ond, we were dealing with a child actor in one of the scenes who, by law, was only allowed to work a specific number of hours. And lastly, the final scene of the day was a night exterior requiring us to wait for darkness.

I approached him with the utmost confidence that we had cre-ated the very best schedule we could. I was certain I could success-fully explain our position and that he would agree with it knowing we had been reasonable in our approach. I presented my case.

When I finished I assumed we were in full agreement. He looked at me, obviously annoyed, and said, "I don't know what you're talking about. I just want to know why you're making me wait all day to finish my work. It's unacceptable!"

Had he not been listening? Had I not answered his question in detail? What more did he want? In my mind he should have un-derstood completely and agreed. He kept staring at me waiting for a suitable explanation. I stared back. Finally, my amazing assis-tant director noticed I was in a bind and came over to rescue me. "May I steal her for just a second?" he asked the actor. "I prom-ise to bring her right back." I quickly walked away, relieved by the diversion.

When we were at a safe distance, the assistant director turned to me and said, "He can't process that much information. You're talking to a man whose whole life is orchestrated for him. They tell him where to be, what to wear, what to say, what to eat, how to live. You're talking in a language he can't possibly understand."

"So how do I answer his question?" I asked.

"You need to speak his language."

I thought for a few minutes then went back to the actor's side. "We need to straddle your schedule so that we can shoot two lo-cations today and give you Friday off."

He smiled, "Excellent plan."

Not everyone communicates the way you do. What you hear coming out of your mouth may not be heard the same way by the recipient. We all process information differently by filtering it through our database of personal experiences. Do not assume that you and the person you are speaking to are hearing and understanding the same thing.

**When conflict arises, be aware that
everyone communicates differently, and
remember that when designing a compromise.**

TALKING TO THE TOT

As parents we learn that patience and positive reinforcement are important in successfully raising kids. By focusing on their small successes and overlooking frequent failures, we help teach and guide them as they grow. Can you imagine rolling your eyes or yelling at your one-year-old as he struggles to navigate his first step? Of course not! So wouldn't it be nice if we could adopt those useful parenting skills when dealing in a nonpatronizing way with other adults rather than becoming annoyed and angry when they initially fail to live up to our expectations? Even when they ask, "Who am I?"

In our business, one particular person has found a way to do just that: the director. Somehow these talented artists can motivate people to do what they want, when they want and make them feel good about it in the process. The most skillful can instill confidence in the insecure, enthusiasm in the indifferent, and focus in the distracted. With an adept hand, they guide the cast and crew in the direction the show must go. How exactly do they connect so readily with such a wide variety of personalities? I believe they do it as a parent would do it, without judgment. Just as we approach our children with complete acceptance, so a good director approaches his charges the same way. There are numerous examples of how this works, but I will cite just one.

On one particular comedy series, we were filming in an upper-middle-class home. As is usually the case, we were running late and were behind schedule. We were lighting our last scene of the day in which a group of kids return home interrupting their parents discussion. I was anxious to finish the day's work as I was keenly aware of how much the overtime was costing. Finally, the director of photography finished lighting and turned the set over to the director. We rehearsed a few times and were ready to shoot when one of the actors stepped off his mark and approached the director who happened to be seated next to me.

"Where am I coming from?" the young actor asked.

I rolled my eyes and before I could stop myself said, "The front door, of course." As soon as it came out of my mouth, I knew it was the wrong thing to say. He was not asking literally, he was asking metaphorically.

Thankfully, the director intervened. "Good question," he said. And while I impatiently watched the clock, the two discussed the actor's understanding of the scene. They agreed on his back story and state of mind, and eventually he returned to his mark and nailed the performance.

What seemed unimportant to me was vitally important to this actor. The director understood and respected him enough to engage in a nonjudgmental conversation, which resulted in all parties feeling satisfied. Had the actor not presented his question and reconciled his concerns, we could still be sitting there waiting for him to deliver a good performance.

Very often directors must get actors to say words they do not want to say and do things they do not want to do. On some shows, actors disagree with writers on the direction the show is taking. On others, actors are unhappy with the way a script is written or the direction in which their character is going. Usually when this happens there is great resistance and what should be easy becomes impossibly difficult to accomplish. It takes a skilled negotiator to get people to cooperate under these circumstances.

As is the case in any business, we all have to work with difficult personalities, with people who disagree with each other, and with people who are unhappy about the way things are being accomplished. When you find yourself in such a situation, try to adopt a nonjudgmental, open-minded attitude and communicate with the same type of acceptance you would afford your four-year-old who is learning to swim.

> **Approach others with an accepting and non-judgmental attitude, and you will almost always foster a spirit of cooperation and accomplish your goals.**

WHEN THE DIFFICULT PERSON IS YOUR BOSS

THE CIGAR-SMOKING, KARATE-CHOPPING FAT BOY

One of my favorite commercials on television is for Career Maker.com. The spot features an executive who is working for a group of chimpanzees. While the chimps go crazy, this poor guy tries to maintain a professional demeanor. I am sure many of us can identify and empathize with his dilemma. If only we could choose our own bosses. How happy we would be if we worked only for people we respected and admired; the kind of people who bring out the very best in us. Sadly, the world does not always work that way. Sometimes you just have to answer to a chimp.

A few years back I was asked to manage a pilot to be shot in the South. While I had performed a lot of work in the past for the studio involved, I was unfamiliar with the producer and director it had hired. Upon meeting them, I knew almost immediately that this was going to be a difficult project.

In my opinion, there are essentially two types of people in business: those that are passionate about, and dedicated to, their work and are willing to labor steadfastly toward their goals, and those who are more interested in appearance than substance. I equate the second group to the popular kids in high school who did not care who they hurt as they built up their rep.

In any event, on this pilot I knew I was working with the kind of people who give Hollywood a bad name. They thumb their noses at members of the local community, certain they are more sophisticated and successful than anyone they meet. Yet even as they insult the people they came in contact with, they expect to be given what they want on a silver platter.

Shortly after arriving on the job, I joined the producer and director in a scout van to look at possible shooting locations that the location manager had preselected for us. The script called for a bar, a few middle-class homes, and an airport. Our location manager was from this part of the country and had established a stellar reputation in the community. Having worked with him before, I considered him to be one of the best at his job. As always, he had chosen a number of places that were visually interesting and clearly supported the script.

His task had already proven to be a challenge. The script called for a lot of gunfire and explosions making it difficult for him to persuade property owners to allow us to film on their properties. Some people were just not interested in us possibly blowing up their homes. Imagine! Anyway, because these owners were already skittish, I knew we would have to be on our best behavior to persuade them to cooperate: I assumed everyone in our group understood this.

Our first stop was a small one-story home in a modest neighborhood. We pulled up to the curb, exited the van, and waited for the location manager to gain access. As we were waiting to go inside, our director lit up a stogy. Since smoking is common on most film sets, I did not give it a second thought until he arrogantly carried his lit cigar into the house. What type of person has the unmitigated gall to enter a complete stranger's home and blow cigar smoke all over the place? The location manager and I were stunned. We kept exchanging looks trying to decide what to do. Finally, sick of the stink and embarrassed by the director's behavior, I quietly asked if he would put it out. Of course, the elderly woman who owned the house was star struck and quickly jumped to his defense, assuring him she did not mind. He gave me a "mind your own business" look and puffed away. Needless to say, while the owner was happy to appease him in person, she refused to let us back in to film. My apology did little to persuade her.

We stopped next at a number of bars. The script we were working on simply called for a scene to be shot in a bar. It did not specify whether it should be a sports bar, Caribbean bar, smoky Irish pub, or something similar. When this happens, we look to the director, producer, and production designer to determine what type of bar it should be. Sometimes we view a number of locations before we get a clear idea of what we want. On some shows, the location manager will find something so wonderful that the writer actually writes to it. My point is this: finding a place to film is a collaborative process that requires a great deal of searching. We proceeded with that in mind.

I started to relax a little at this point, knowing that even if the director insisted on smoking, it would be far less noticeable in a bar. My sense of calm was short-lived. As soon as we entered the first bar, the director and producer began to criticize every last detail about the place. The layout was all wrong, the décor was ugly, the place stunk, the staff was funny-looking. On and on they went—all in the presence of the owner who had been kind enough to show us around. I was mortified. What kind of example were we setting? What must these people think of us? I waited until everyone else returned to the van to express my heartfelt apology. Again, we were asked not to return.

The remainder of the day continued in the same vein: insult, apology, insult, apology. My only consolation was that the two men grew tired of taking the time to tear each place apart. Instead they would enter a location, look at one another, loudly proclaim "caca," and then walk out without thanking the owner for his or her time. I could not apologize enough to all the people our group offended.

The last stop of the day was the local airport. Airports have become increasingly difficult to film as security has become tighter. Most airports do not want to be distracted by a shooting crew and simply refuse to accommodate one. Fortunately, this airport was willing (reluctantly) to consider our request for a film permit, but it was going to require a great deal of negotiating to make it happen. Knowing how poorly the day had gone thus far, I tried to delicately explain to our team our fragile relationship with the airport authority. I asked everyone to remain on their best behavior. Naturally, my admonition fell on deaf ears. Instead, I got a five-minute lecture on how I needed to work on my negativity. Apparently I needed to be more of a "can do" person. By the time we arrived, I was ready to throw myself in front of a 747.

As we toured the airport, respectfully asking questions to help better assess the feasibility of shooting our script, I began to feel I had gotten through to the producer and director. So far things were going well: no cigar smoking, no insults flying. I could feel the hair on the back of my neck start to flatten for the first time all day. Then, without warning, the airport representative turned to me and asked, "What on earth is he doing?" To my horror, our director, standing six feet two inches and weighing easily 240 pounds, was kicking his foot in the air like Chuck Norris. As he continued moving through the airport, he would karate chop the air with both his hands and feet. We stood speechless. Finally, when all eyes were on him, he stopped for a second, smiled, and announced "I'm a black belt in karate," as if this were explanation enough.

That was it. Based on such poor behavior, no one would allow us to film on their properties. Now we had nowhere to shoot. The location manger and I had spent the entire day cleaning up after the producer and director, apologizing profusely on their behalf.

We did everything we could to salvage our chances. We carried the burden of keeping things afloat, while the men who had the most to lose were sabotaging our every effort. And what was most astonishing is that they took no responsibility for it. In fact, they blamed us for not getting them what they wanted.

The question we needed to ask ourselves was why we were accepting responsibility for a problem we did not create. Why take responsibility for someone else's actions? Why did we need to make amends to anyone who would listen? And why did we feel the need to fix everything and make things right?

I believe the answer is simple. There are those who take personal responsibility very seriously and those that do not. Those in the first category will go to great lengths to ensure the success of any project with which they are associated. Those in the second category will let others jump in and save them rather than doing the hard work themselves, taking advantage of the people who care the most. Having made a commitment to the success of the show, the location manager and I felt morally obligated to give it our all—but only to a point.

As I said earlier, we rarely get to decide for whom we will work. I certainly would not have chosen this experience. But in retrospect, it taught me a valuable lesson. Sometimes we are forced to work for people we neither admire nor respect. Sometimes we have to work for people we truly do not like. But we always have a right to protect ourselves and our reputation. There will always be people who will try to take advantage. Do not let them. By valuing yourself enough to set clear boundaries and by refusing to let others walk all over you, you send a message of strength and conviction that others will be forced to respect.

Refuse to let others take advantage of you.
Cooperate and be courteous and respectful,
but draw the line when unjustly faulted or exploited.

MY FIRST BIG BREAK WENT BUST

It has been my experience that while things often work out in the end, they never seem to work out exactly the way you expect them to. In fact, if you add Murphy's law into the mix, you are usually in for a bumpy ride. But take heart, even the toughest times often turn out for the best. Even when dealing with the Wicked Witch of the West.

Early in my career, I knew I wanted to produce. My path was pretty clear: use my experience as an accountant, parlay that into management, and eventually become a producer. Seemed so clear and easy. The only hitch was that at each juncture, I needed to have people willing to take a chance on me. I also needed to make the most of any rare opportunities that came my way.

A couple of years after I had worked on my first film, I decided that I had been a production accountant long enough and that I was ready to make the big step to management. I was young, unencumbered by bills, and completely optimistic. Up to this point, any difficulties I had encountered were quickly overcome. I had no doubt that the right project would come my way, and all I had to do was shine.

A few weeks after I made my decision, the company I had been working with offered me a dream job. I had been a production supervisor on a show it had just finished in Mexico, and the company was about to start another television movie stateside. I was offered the job of production manager. This was it—my big break. My future was looking bright. I was certain that this was the beginning of something big.

Anxious to get started, I spent the entire weekend making lists, planning my approach, picking out just the right outfit. I needed to impress. Then on Monday morning, I arrived at the office at 5 A.M. and got to work. I began by breaking down the script and working on a board. For those unfamiliar with this process, it meant I dissected the script into scenes, identified which actors were needed, and specified where the scenes would be shot. Then, I analyzed all the special needs of the project: props, automobiles, visual effects, stunts, and so on. Finally, I laid out the scenes in shooting order, creating a plan of attack. By the time the office came alive at 9 A.M. I was feeling confident I had everything under control.

I should mention that the company had hired me without consulting the creative producer, something that happens from time to time. As soon as she arrived in her office, I went in to introduce myself and to let her know what I was doing and how much progress I had made. In retrospect, I probably came across as too eager to please, but this really was my big break. We engaged in a few minutes of small talk, but then she dismissed me rather quickly. The rest of the day she kept to herself, and I innocently went about my tasks.

As I left that evening, I popped my head into the office of the studio executive who had hired me to wish him a good night. Reluctantly, he told me the creative producer was put off by the studio "forcing" me on her and that she was concerned about my lack of experience. The truth was that she had her own production manager who she had hoped to bring on the show and was not happy about working with someone new. He assured me that he was behind me 100 percent and was certain that once she saw how competent I was, all would be fine.

I left his office feeling rather deflated. My enthusiasm and confidence were replaced with self-doubt and concern. I began to worry about what she might do.

In retrospect, I think she had decided almost immediately that if she could not get rid of me on her own, she would make my life so miserable I would choose to leave. Her strategy was simple: find my weakness and exploit it. Knowing I was new to the position, she homed in on my lack of confidence by continually questioning my every decision. She made it a point to correct me in front of others and find fault whenever she could. The more we worked together, the weaker I became. I no longer felt self-assured and eager to press forward. I began to doubt my every move.

Things that I would normally tackle with ease started to throw me. And there she was, a constant witness to my failure. A week together felt like an eternity. It seemed as if I was getting smaller by the day.

The final straw came two weeks into preproduction. We were scouting a popular bar in a downtown location. As soon as we entered the premises, we knew it was not right for our show. We quickly turned to leave. It was getting late, and we had a few more stops to make. We were all hungry and tired. As we left, I commented to no one in particular that I needed to use the restroom, and I would meet the group in the van.

When I returned, they were gone. They had left me behind. Since my purse was in the van, I had no money and no cell phone. I was completely stranded. I had been forgotten by a group of people I was supposed to be managing, and I had made myself so small they did not even notice I was missing. Utterly humiliated, I asked the bartender if I could use the phone and called the office. After being put on hold for a good fifteen minutes, the office coordinator came back on the line to inform me that she could send someone to pick me up in an hour but if I did not mind walking a couple of miles, I could catch up with the crew, who were dining at a restaurant up the road. So there I was, hiking through downtown, alone.

I entered the restaurant to the shock and surprise of my crew. They began laughing. "Oh, my God!" they shouted. "I can't believe we forgot you." They turned to each other, "Did you even notice she was gone?" I took my seat and strained to keep from crying.

The next day the studio executive called me into his office and asked if I wanted to quit. I told him no, the creative producer would have to fire me. He told me he could not protect me any longer. We both knew I had not performed under pressure. I had let the creative producer take away my voice, my confidence. Completely wounded, I made my way to her office with trepidation. She took her time explaining to me why she had to let me go and then told me why I would never make a good producer. I smiled back and assured her she was wrong. I wished her luck and left.

Obviously, this did not turn out the way I had planned. The truth was that my big break went bust. But I did walk away with something. I learned that there is a reason the strong survive and the weak do not. There are those in business who will always look for your weakness, sometimes unconsciously, and try to exploit it. The key is not to let them. Find your strength and hold on dearly. No one can make you feel small but yourself.

Lack or loss of confidence is internally generated.
No one can make you feel small if you do not let them.
Mentally resist your fault finders
and always believe in yourself.

DANCING ON EGGSHELLS

Who out there has had to work for a jerk? I am sure all of us can recount stories of nasty people to whom we have answered. But what is it that makes them so bad? And why is it that what one person considers intolerable, others do not seem to mind? Does our own behavior contribute to these adversarial relationships? Do we make these Princes of Darkness larger than life?

Personally, I have learned from the worst and I have learned from the best. I have talked about the best elsewhere, but here I will relive my most difficult relationship, which I touched on in "Don't Wipe Your Feet on My Face." Fortunately for those of us in the freelance world, even if we are subject to the management of a tyrant, we know that the vile relationship will be short-lived. If we can find the strength to muddle through, the end is always near. For those of you who feel you see an eternity of pain and oppression ahead, these thoughts might be of some help to you.

Not long ago, I had the opportunity to work on a one-hour prime-time drama where I was to report directly to a man a few years my senior. He had a great deal of experience, and I was looking forward to working with and learning from him. It seemed like the perfect opportunity.

Soon after my arrival, I realized that we were completely incompatible. My first indication that there was a problem was when I was summoned to his office like a child called to the principal's office. Much to my surprise, he reprimanded me at length for talking creatively about a script with one of the writers. I had made the inexcusable mistake of reaching out to another employee without his permission. On other shows this strengthening of relationships is encouraged, so I was utterly floored by his reaction. During my debriefing, I was told in no uncertain terms that all future communications would have to go through him, without exception.

Our next disagreement occurred at one of our weekly production meetings. These meetings are traditionally a time for all department heads to come together and discuss the script with the director. Usually, it is an opportunity for the free flow of ideas and a great deal of laughter. This meeting had none of that. Almost no one spoke and the few that did, did so with trepidation. When we left the meeting, I asked a fellow employee what was up. Apparently, our boss only wanted people to speak when spoken to. I could not believe that people were working under such oppressive conditions.

This paragon of virtue further infuriated me by his unwillingness to let people make time for their families. Children were not allowed to visit. Families were not allowed to spend lunch together. People who work on movies or in television sacrifice a great deal of their personal lives to do the job. It is not uncommon for us to work fourteen-hour days, leaving little time for friends or family. Indeed, it is an unwritten rule in our industry that we all must squeeze in family time when and where we can so as not to miss important events in our spouse's or children's lives. As a working mother, I greatly value co-workers who understand the importance of family. My boss did not. In his opinion, nothing mattered more than the show. Period.

The most difficult aspect of dealing with this boss was in never knowing where you stood. It was virtually impossible to anticipate his many mood swings. When you would have to interact with him, you never knew if you would be greeted with a warm hug or chastised for making a mistake of which you were completely unaware. You could be dressed down or praised without even knowing what was coming. I spent the season walking on eggshells. It was an utterly miserable experience.

No matter how I tried, I could not reconcile my management style with his. I strongly disagreed with almost everything he did, and I was not alone. Almost everyone I worked with disliked the way he operated; but I began to notice that almost everyone else was better able to deal with him. While I would obsess over the way he did things and criticize his every move, others chose to accept him for what he was and went about their business doing the best they could. Finally, one day I got it. The proverbial lightbulb went on in my head. I was never going to change him. He was who he was. And more importantly, he was the boss; I was not.

Eventually, life became a whole lot easier for me. I realized I only had two choices. I could accept him the way he was and do my best under the circumstances, or I could choose to work elsewhere. Fortunately for me, the show ended and I was able to move on. The point is: Do not waste time and mental energy on people you do not like, even those you have to work for.

**Difficult and unpleasant bosses are not likely
to reform. Do not personalize their behavior.
Accept the things you cannot change,
change the things you can, and move if you must.**

PROBLEMS WITH SUBORDINATES

THE BEST WAY TO DEAL WITH WOMEN IS TO COMPLIMENT THEIR SHOES

Sad as it is, there will always be people who do not like working for you. It is hard to accept, but it is true. Some people might have issues working for a woman. Others may not like reporting to someone younger than themselves. Some may be prejudiced against you because you are too old, too fat, too tall, too short, or too tan. You get the picture. And on occasion, you may just re-mind them of their ex-spouse who is suing them for the stereo, the boat, the car, the house, and the purebred dachshund. My point is, sometimes you just cannot win them over. Even with a stunning pair of shoes.

Normally, I pride myself on getting along well with my crew but on one occasion all the charm in the world could not save me. The show I was working on had been picked up for twelve episodes. We decided to produce it in a converted warehouse in Los Angeles. We were taking over a facility used by a popular show that had been in production for four years and was now cancelled. Both shows were produced by the same studio, which seemed anxious to keep the current crew employed. We agreed that utilizing an existing crew had merit. It would greatly reduce the learning curve since these people already worked well to-gether. We set out interviewing everyone on the former staff in hopes they could carry over to our show.

The interviews went well, at first. Everyone was grateful for the opportunity of continued employment. As freelancers, work is work. You are happy to have it. However, one of our potential employees wanted more than just a job. As part of his employ-ment arrangement, he wanted every other Friday off to pursue one of his hobbies. Apparently, the previous show was able to ac-commodate him in its final season.

We, on the other hand, were just getting started and did not feel it was in our best interest to make special concessions for anyone. I strongly believe that whenever possible, people should be treated equally: what you do for one you do for all. If we allowed the employee special time off, we would have to juggle the schedule for everyone else. After mulling it over, we decided that if he wanted to work on our show, he would have to work the same hours as everyone else. He agreed to our terms and accepted the job.

A few weeks after filming began, he approached me and much to my surprise asked if he could take the next Friday off. I should point out that this gentleman was considerably older than me and had been in the business twice as long. I politely declined his request. I reminded him that we had a deal and that if I did it for him I would have to do it for everyone else. He disagreed. It was his opinion that he warranted special treatment since he was a recognized expert in his field. We continued around and around getting nowhere. The more we talked, the angrier he got. Finally, he threatened to go over my head; a move I strongly encouraged. Much to his dismay, our senior producer insisted he accept my decision. I assumed the issue had been put to rest.

The next day as I went about my business, I was visited on set by a studio representative. It seemed my disgruntled employee had taken his dispute a step further. At 1:30 A.M. the previous morning, he had placed an anonymous call to the head of the studio. Among other things, his message complained of the abuse he and others endured at the hands of the production manager (that would be me). Now I was under investigation. Even though the studio knew about our unresolved issue, the problem had made its way too far up the chain to be ignored. A formal investigation was underway. The rest of the day I watched in concern as the studio representative interviewed every member of my crew. Fortunately, by the end of the day I was in the clear. In fact, most of the crew rallied around me showing their support. Many were enraged by what the disgruntled employee had done. Foolishly, I again thought the matter had been put to rest.

A few weeks later, he came to me again. Only this time he did not ask me; he told me he was taking the next Friday off. I had had enough. But if I fired him now, I would probably be subject to accusations of age discrimination on top of wrongful termination. This was not a fight I could win on my own. I turned to the studio for advice. The senior executive at the time was an amazing man who was fair and decent to a fault. With years of experience under his belt, he completely understood the situation.

Unfortunately, by having to enlist his help, I felt as though I had failed him. How had I let this get so out of control? Why could I not resolve it on my own? After explaining the most recent turn of events, he told me to give the employee one more chance and to tell him that his job was on the line if he did not show up for work as scheduled. I delivered the message.

The next Friday the employee was a no-show. He sent someone else to replace him. I notified the studio executive who promptly called him at home and fired him on the spot. Then things got ugly. Our disgruntled ex-employee immediately phoned his crew on set and told them to walk. Out of loyalty to him, they quietly wrapped up his equipment and left. The entire shoot came to a screeching halt. Without his crew and equipment in place, we could not continue working unless we wanted to make the first silent film in years. We scrambled to find replacements, but when all was said and done, the company lost hours of work and thousands of dollars.

But, alas, it did not end there. A month or so later, we received a formal union grievance seeking damages. The union wanted us to absolve the crew of any wrongdoing, thus allowing them to work for the studio again. Additionally—and you'll love this—they sought back pay for the gentleman who had been fired. They also wanted him to be paid his remaining salary plus benefits for the entire season.

As you can imagine, a number of meetings followed. Most of these meetings would consist of me, our lawyer, the studio executive, the terminated employee, and his union representative. At one such meeting, the union representative, a man in his late six-ties, decided to take charge. He began by explaining that not all employees can find a way to communicate effectively with their supervisors—a point we were all willing to accept. He said that this was no one's fault, but that in his experience if people wanted to iron out a real problem, they needed to sit down and talk "man to man." At first I gave him the benefit of the doubt. Surely, he was using a catch phrase just to illustrate a point.

He went on: "I tell my members, if you need to get down to business, go find a man." There was that "man" word again. I looked around the room to see if anyone was reacting as I was. My two confidants looked mildly amused. He continued, "I tell my members, the best way to deal with women is to compliment their shoes." My jaw hit the floor. Had he really said that? I im-mediately looked down at my feet as did everyone else in the room. To my horror, I was wearing a pair of bright red, faux snakeskin, high-heeled sling backs. Crap!

He pointed to my feet. "Those are real nice," he said.

I jumped out of my seat utterly offended. No one else moved. I stood alone while everyone tried to decide what to do. Finally, the studio executive rose and agreed that the discussion was not appropriate, and we were getting nowhere. We would reconvene at a later date.

As I left that day I tried to comprehend what had happened. I knew I was on the right side of the conflict. I knew the employee and his union were wrong. I knew what was said was blatant sex dis-crimination. But none of that mattered. I could not change the cir-cumstances, and I certainly was not going to change the way these men felt about me. What I could control was how I reacted to it.

We tried to meet a few more times with dismal results. Finally, we came together for what would be our final negotiation. After a great deal of struggling, we agreed on a resolution. As we all got up to leave, it was suggested by the mediator that the opposing sides shake hands in a gesture of goodwill. The room went still. No one was willing to make the first move. There was too much bad blood. I kept thinking of what these men had said. I had been undermined, personally attacked, and discriminated against as a woman. The last thing I wanted to do was shake their hands, much less be in the same room with them. So I had a choice to make: I could let them get the better of me, or I could be the bigger person. Finally, I reached out across the table. Relieved, everyone else followed. I could not change the way they behaved, but perhaps I could change the way they saw women by the way I chose to act.

In any business, you will be forced to deal with people who do not like you for any number of reasons unrelated to the person you are. Some will undermine your authority; others will try to sabotage your efforts. Your only weapon is to be as consistently professional, courteous, and fair as possible in your dealings with them. Never give them ammunition against you. No one can fault you for taking the high road.

Diminish discrimination and attenuate bias in your co-workers and subordinates by setting a praiseworthy example. Be consistently professional, courteous, and fair. No one can ever fault you for taking the high road.

YOU DON'T SCARE ME

Intimidate: 1. To make afraid, to make timid. 2. To force or deter with threats or violence.

Some may find intimidation a persuasive tool when conducting business. I am sure if you work for the Mafia or some other criminal organization, you have found it useful in the extreme.

It happens that I am not very good at it. My five foot three inch frame and youthful appearance do not lend themselves to this tactic. In fact, most people laugh at me when I try. And since I have failed to refine my intimidation skills, I am usually at a loss to defend myself against them. Especially in a remote parking lot late at night.

Many of you may not know this, but the Teamsters Union in certain parts of the country has a reputation for being very intimidating. Rumor has it that those who fail to do business their way have regretted it. Scary! So, when I was sent to a particular locale to manage a new series, I knew I would have my hands full. The teamsters on my show were assigned to me by their union. I had no input as to the workers I could employ. I was simply told who I would have the pleasure of working with and quickly found myself in charge of a very tough-looking bunch of men.

It is important to understand that the teamsters are the backbone of every show. They support each and every department. Since they are responsible for transporting the company, they work the longest hours. The transportation department rents, runs, maintains, and moves all the heavy equipment for the various departments, including wardrobe, hair/makeup, props, set decoration, grip, electric, cast, power, camera, craft service, and catering. Everyone on a film crew works out of a truck that needs to be properly serviced and maintained. The teamsters are responsible for making sure everything is in the right place at the right time. It may sound easy, but when you are filming three locations in a day, try loading, moving, parking, setting up, and powering twenty pieces of equipment in under an hour—three times. It takes real skill and an eye for logistics. And if it is not done properly, it can bring a production to a swift halt.

In order for the show to run smoothly, I had to find a way to get these guys on my side. I knew if they sensed weakness, they would have me for lunch (figuratively, of course). I also knew that if I came in with strong demands, I would really piss them off. I was not sure what to do.

I decided to ignore their reputation in this particular locale and to approach them the same way I would approach crew on any other show. I figured that if I could get to know them, and they me, we could find a way to work well together. I started to think my idea might actually work until I was cornered in a dark parking lot by one of the men. I was walking to my car after we had completed shooting for the day, and one of the teamsters stepped in my path and said we had to talk. I looked around and realized I was alone. It was no accident that he had approached me like this. I pretended nothing was wrong and waited for him to speak. He told me that on his shows, his crew clocked in at first call and clocked out at last. What he was telling me was that no matter how many hours any of the men actually worked, they would all be paid for as many hours as he wanted them to be paid.

This was the first time someone had tried to intimidate me this way. Normally, on a film set, people start their day at varying times. For example, one driver might come in at 3:30 A.M. to warm up the makeup trailer if an actor has a 4 A.M. call. The prop driver may not start until 7 A.M. if the shooting call is not until 8 A.M. Everyone is called in when and only when they are needed. Each day the production manager goes to great lengths to decide when each person will start. Since most shooting days are already fourteen hours long, it is important to minimize any extra overtime.

What this man was suggesting would not only be unfair to everyone else, but it would cost the company dearly over the season. What could I do? I asked if this is what all the other shows did. He said, "Yes, in fact it was." I said, "Wow, that's a sweet deal!" And I wished him a good night.

I knew complaining to the company would do me no good. They were not in the trenches with these guys, and reciting company policy was not going to keep me safe. I knew if I simply refused and paid them for the hours they really worked, they would find other ways to cash in or retaliate, such as submitting fake receipts, showing up late with equipment, or having unexpected breakdowns that could stop filming. I was in a bind.

I decided to contact other producers who had recently filmed in this locale. Some had been intimidated into paying, others had not. Not much help there. I asked around until I knew who had loyalty to whom, who owed whom, and ultimately who had the real power. I used my relationships with other teamsters around the country to help me with my situation. I asked those that could to put in a good word for me with men they knew in our locale. I even compiled a list of the teamsters who rumor had it were trustworthy and dealt with them the most. All the while, I tried to get to know the guys personally. I tried to establish a relationship based on mutual respect and appreciation. As the days wore on, I made no mention of the threat.

When time cards were finally turned in, I immediately flipped to those of the drivers. I needed to see if the men I had gotten to know were going to rip-off the company and ultimately me. I was relieved to find that not one of them had padded their time. Even the man who had cornered me in the parking lot had been honest about the hours he worked. And in return for their honesty, I made it a point to respect their contribution. I paid them fairly for the work they did, and I went out of my way to make sure they felt appreciated. In the end I got to know some pretty amazing men. They worked hard for me because I had earned their respect.

You cannot demand respect from your subordinates. You have to earn it by giving it. It is something you need to think about and affirmatively act upon.

I GUESS THE WARDEN WON'T LET YOU IN

Not every profession requires you to work with criminals. Usually those that do require special training, as in the case of policemen, psychologists, and social workers. But sometimes life puts us in the path of some unsavory characters. Some call them felons; others call them jailbirds. I, on occasion, have had to call them employees.

This occurred on a television series whose story took place in a prison. Fortunately, our location manager located a high-security prison that would let us shoot its interiors.

Once any location is selected, the location manager takes the director, first assistant director, producers, production designer, set decorator, director of photography, stunt coordinator, effects coordinator, and representatives from the grip/electric and transportation departments to see it. Each person assesses the location's feasibility based on his or her department's needs. The director will talk the group through his shot list: a list that explains where each camera will be positioned and how a scene will be photographed. The production designer will work with the art department to determine what changes need to be made to the set (paint, flooring, dressing, and so on). The director of photography will decide how to light the scenes and will help the director construct his shot list. The transportation coordinator will check to see that the work trucks can be placed close enough to the location to support the crew. And the producer will oversee the entire process. We call this a tech scout.

As we made our way through the halls of the prison, the warden stopped us to say hello. Even before introductions began, he asked me to urgently come to his office. I had the sinking feeling you get when you see a cop following in your rearview mirror. Something was wrong. Once we were settled in his office, he turned to me and said, "As I already have mentioned, I would be happy to make our facility available to you and your show." I thanked him. He continued, "But you must know, a convicted felon who has done time here is not allowed back on the premises. No exceptions."

What? Why is he telling me this?

He continued. "Your men will have to leave immediately."

My men? What men? He could sense my confusion.

"A couple of your employees have done time here. As I've said, they cannot be on the property, not even in the parking lot. Please ask them to leave."

I was shocked. The men I had just seen behind bars were hardened criminals. They were in solitary; they had big ugly tattoos; they threw food. How could my crew be part of that? How could I work with ex-cons who had engaged in criminal acts?

He waited for my reply. "OK," I finally said. "I will make sure they leave promptly and do not return."

He nodded and escorted me back to my party.

"Is everything all right?" our director asked.

What was I going to say? Everyone waited for an explanation. My mind raced. Who were the ex-cons and what had they done? I looked my crew over with trepidation and suspicion. Then, I realized I needed to get control of the situation. I needed to remind myself that on the ride over, I actually liked all these people. We had laughed together and worked well together. They had treated me respectfully and worked hard for or with me. Was I going to ignore all of that?

So I smiled and jokingly said "Anyone who feels overly familiar with this place or unusually uncomfortable here for any reason should probably leave now and wait in the van. Oh, and could you park off the property."

It took a few seconds for my pronouncement to register, then two of my staff left the prison. On the day of filming, we made other arrangements so that all the convicted felons working for me had the day off. It seemed like the only reasonable thing to do.

This occurrence partially changed my view of the two employees. But I knew in order for us to continue working together, I had to focus on who they were now not who they were then. I had to concentrate on current facts rather than get caught up in rumors or gossip or history. I needed to deal with them as the persons I knew them to be. Anything beyond that was none of my business. In the end, they did a great job for me.

**Give your subordinates the benefit
of the doubt regarding difficulties they may
have had in the past. Evaluate them based on
your experience of them and treat them
with the respect they have thus far earned.**

SUMMARY OF RULES

UNREASONABLE PEOPLE AND DEMANDS

RULE 1   Actively listen to what difficult people are asking for, make an effort to understand their needs, and avoid making negative assumptions about their motives. There may be alternative ways to satisfy them.

RULE 2   Sometimes strength in numbers will solve a seemingly intractable problem in dealing with unreasonable but powerful people.

RULE 3   Do not be intimidated or discouraged by bad behavior. Though you may have to tolerate it, distinguish it from ability and support and respect the courteous and talented.

BRIDGING THE COMMUNICATIONS GAP

RULE 1   When conflict arises, be aware that everyone communicates differently, and remember that when designing a compromise.

RULE 2   Approach others with an accepting and nonjudgmental attitude, and you will almost always foster a spirit of cooperation and accomplish your goals.

WHEN THE DIFFICULT PERSON IS YOUR BOSS

RULE 1   Refuse to let others take advantage of you. Cooperate and be courteous and respectful, but draw the line when unjustly faulted or exploited.

RULE 2   Lack or loss of confidence is internally generated. No one can make you feel small if you do not let them. Mentally resist your fault finders and always believe in yourself.

RULE 3 Difficult and unpleasant bosses are not likely to reform. Do not personalize their behavior. Accept the things you cannot change, change the things you can, and move if you must.

PROBLEMS WITH SUBORDINATES

RULE 1 Diminish discrimination and attenuate bias in your co-workers and subordinates by setting a praiseworthy example. Be consistently professional, courteous, and fair. No one can ever fault you for taking the high road.

RULE 2 You cannot demand respect from your subordinates. You have to earn it by giving it. It is something you need to think about and affirmatively act upon.

RULE 3 Give your subordinates the benefit of the doubt regarding difficulties they may have had in the past. Evaluate them based on your experience of them and treat them with the respect they have thus far earned.

8

Balancing Work and Family

HIRING FRIENDS OR FAMILY MEMBERS

YOU'RE NOT THE BOSS OF ME

Have you ever allowed personal feelings for someone to cloud your better judgment? Have you ever hired someone just because they played a significant role in your personal life? Working with a boyfriend, girlfriend, husband, wife, sister, brother, even a best friend can create unexpected and unhappy consequences. Even as respects the Daily Double.

As I have said, it is immature and unseemly to become sexually active with someone with whom you work. But in the film business, it is not uncommon for friends or family members or lovers to work on the same project. Because of the long hours, some people see it as the only way to spend quality time together. I know a production designer who consistently hires her boyfriend as her lead scenic painter. I have worked with a producer who uses his brother as his art director. I know a unit production manager whose husband is almost always her first assistant director. All these pairings worked out well to a greater or lesser degree, but none were without difficulty and conflict. Here are a couple of examples that did not work out so well.

On one of our television shows, I was forced to investigate a physical abuse claim between two employees. The injured party claimed that a co-worker had repeatedly kicked and thrown things at him. I spent hours interviewing all parties involved. It became clear that the accused worker had an anger management problem and had had altercations with other employees. When I tried discussing this with his immediate supervisor, she seemed resistant to acknowledge the problem. When she continued to make excuses for his inappropriate behavior, I became suspicious. Finally, I realized what was going on. She was intimately involved with him, and their relationship was clouding her ability to assess him objectively and manage him properly.

On another show about fourteen years ago, I was working in the Midwest with another production executive who had unwisely started dating one of her employees. One afternoon he failed to show up for a very important meeting. Concerned, she contacted him on his cell phone. He apologized for his absence and assured her that he was, at that very moment, looking for a picture car she needed. (A picture car is any vehicle photographed during filmmaking.) As she was about to hang up, she heard the undeniable sound of a horse race in the background. (Cue hoof beat: "Da data da data da data da.")

"That lying son of a b . . . !" she exclaimed, as she banged down the phone. While the rest of us were working our tails off, he was betting on the ponies. But she could not confront him nor express her dissatisfaction. They had just started dating, and she wanted him to care for her. So, she chose to look the other way knowing she was acting improperly. She let her personal feelings get in the way of her professional judgment.

As the relationship continued, she tried to level the playing field by applying the same business principles to him that she would apply to any other employee. She told him he would be treated the same as anyone else in his position, and she expected him to treat her the same way he would any other supervisor. Things worked out, the job ended well, and they subsequently moved in together. Awhile later they found themselves working on the same television movie. At first, she was encouraged by how smoothly things were going, both at work and at home. They had it all. Then, one evening, she came home after a very hard day. As she entered the house, she asked him to help her with a minor chore. Before she could finish her request, he declined asserting, "If you get to be the boss at work, I get to be the boss at home!"

Whoa!? Was he kidding? So much for successfully finding a way to work side by side with a significant other. While she was living in a fantasy world thinking everything between them was great, he was having problems with the power structure—i.e., *her*! This time, she had no idea how to solve the problem. She could not help the fact that she was his boss at work, nor was she willing to relinquish her rights at home. Perhaps the only solution was for them to work apart.

Combining a work relationship with a personal one can be tricky. How do you tell a lover, friend, or brother he is doing a poor job? How do you discipline someone at work then expect them to cuddle you at home? How do you defend the actions of a subordinate if your boss knows he is a family member? When you mix personal relationships with professional ones, you run the risk of showing favoritism or being overly demanding; you avoid conflict altogether or become too harsh in your criticism. Your business relationship completely alters your personal relationship and vice versa.

Despite all these potential problems, it is possible to have a healthy happy professional relationship with someone close to you. The trick is for both parties to remove personal feelings from the equation and to see it as a business arrangement. By treating everyone the same and always being fair, you minimize the risk of preferential treatment, good or bad.

**When employing intimates, friends, or family, take
great care to (1) give notice to management,
(2) avoid preferential treatment regardless of the
personal relationship, and (3) manage all
employees fairly and consistently.**

FAMILIES SHOULD BE SEEN AND NOT HEARD

"Behind every successful man," the saying goes "is a good woman." Hmmm . . . I would have to agree with that just as I would say, "Behind every successful woman is a good man." The point is we need not discriminate. Both men and woman can provide great support to their family members and help them succeed. But to what extent may family members interfere in their spouse's or relative's work life? When do they become officious intermeddlers instead of enablers? Especially if public sex is involved.

Not long ago, I was working with a lead actress whose character was scripted as something of a hussy. Throughout the season, she was asked to participate in a number of raunchy sex scenes. Since the show was produced for cable television, network standards and practices (what is deemed acceptable for general viewing) did not apply. We were free to be as racy as we wanted to be, and the show runner wrote the scenes accordingly.

As we were preparing to shoot the first sex scene on a particular show, the lead actress came over and introduced me to her husband. I had not met him before, but he was on set and I could certainly understand why. Who would not be concerned if their spouse was "getting it on" in front of a huge audience? I know if the roles were reversed, I would not be eager to watch my husband rub up against a sexy starlet even though it might result in my own weight loss or a visit to Victoria's Secret. Certainly, I was curious to see what role the husband would play. But he just sat quietly out of the way and watched.

A few weeks later another sex scene was scheduled, and again her husband was right by her side. This pattern continued. Each and every time she as much as kissed another man on set, her husband was there to watch her back—or possibly front.

I had mixed feelings about his involvement. On the one hand, I understood why he would want to protect his wife. On the other, he had no right to be there, no reason to be involved. After all, he was not working on the project. I worried about what he was trying to accomplish. Our directors were concerned that his presence might be distracting his wife, making it impossible for them to film the scene the way they wanted. Would he refuse to allow her to do certain things? Would he try to direct her himself? Would he ask for a scene to be rewritten? Would his presence make her self-conscious and negatively affect her performance? We all watched and waited.

As the lead actress was asked to remove articles of clothing, embrace her costar, and whimper lustful sounds show after show, I felt for the poor guy as he sat stoically on the sidelines. I kept waiting for him to jump in and demand changes. But to my surprise, he did not interfere. He respected the process.

In fact, his presence was so unobtrusive, it actually helped us. Whenever the director yelled cut, the actress returned to her husband's side. There, he would listen to her, calm her fears, praise her work, make a few suggestions, and simply show his support. He exerted his influence in a subtle yet positive way without interfering in our business. His participation was "behind the scenes," so to speak, not overt or pushy. Because of his style, we were all pleased to have him with us.

Family members can provide great support, advice, and guidance to us in our careers. But there is a time and place for everything. Make sure your spouse or relative does not become so involved in your work that he or she oversteps the boundaries of unobtrusiveness, common sense, and good practice.

**To prevent inappropriate involvement of family members
at work, it is essential to establish ground rules upfront.
Set boundaries, emphasize noninterference,
and limit improper access.**

BEING THERE FOR YOUR KIDS

WE DIDN'T KNOW SHE HAD A MOM

Am I the only mother who forgets to pack a lunch, pick up the requisite toy for the holiday toy drive, or dress my daughter in the right color for her choir debut? While most of the other mothers at school bake cookies, help in the classroom, and put Martha Stewart to shame with their crafty ideas, I am thankful when we arrive at school before the bell rings. For any working mother, the balance between work and family is a tightrope we nervously walk, afraid that at any moment we will fall helplessly into the abyss of ineffectiveness. Until, out of the mouths of babes.

As anyone in the film business can attest, a twelve-to-fourteen-hour day is normal. Then, there is the ever-changing work schedule: one day starts at 6 A.M. the next at 3 P.M. Then, there are the all-nighters. Remember those college days when we would consume gallons of coffee to stay awake and cram until sunrise? In the film business some of us still do it! Add to that the demands of motherhood, and you start to appreciate the dilemma.

During the first few years of my daughter's education, I would meet with her teachers at mandatory back-to-school nights. I would smile ruefully while trying to explain my unusual situation and assure them that while I would not always be present in body, I would certainly be there in spirit. This information was not received with unbridled enthusiasm.

I was concerned that I was being perceived as a less-than-fit mother and that my absences were causing other mothers to grow increasingly concerned for my daughter's well-being. In my night-

mares, the judge declared me unworthy and unqualified to rear
the issue of my body. To rationalize these fears, I opened my
checkbook wide for my daughter, trying to make up for my absences with money. I kept reminding myself that I had to work
and that someone had to pay the bills. But no matter what I did
or said, feelings of guilt followed me everywhere.

Then, one day I received a flash of insight from an unlikely
source. My daughter's voice broke through. Excited by her ability
to write, she came home with a letter, which she proudly displayed
on the fridge. The note read as follows:

> "Dear momy,
> I am so eksidid wine you are oof wrke. I luv you.
> luv ERICA"

Oh, God! Talk about a hit to the guilt button! Talk about a
pluck of the remorse string!

At the time, I had just finished an especially difficult show and
was looking forward to a few months off to slow down and un-
wind. I had no idea how much my daughter needed this time to
reconnect. She was looking forward to having her mother back, if
only for a while. Since she had never complained before about my
being away at work, I had assumed (in error) that she was fine
with my absence and understood its necessity. I misread the signs.

I resolved to take a long, hard look at the way I was living my
life and decided to make a change. I decided to rely less on child-
care and to take a more active role in my daughter's day-to-day
life. I decided to reach out and get to know her friends and their
families. I decided to participate more by volunteering my time at
her school. And most importantly, I decided to be the kind of
mommy she wanted me to be. But how was I going to make these
changes and still pursue a career that was so demanding?

In this, I know I am not alone. Making time for children is one
of the most difficult adjustments career women have to make. For
any woman who values her career and its progress, taking time to
accommodate family can be a very difficult proposition. Many

feel they must give up long-cherished goals. But I found that this was not really the case. I simply had to set limits that were appropriate for me while still respecting the job and its requirements.

First, I decided to work less. I began selecting projects that were shorter in duration. I focused more on half-hour comedies that took five days to shoot per episode rather than hourlong dramas that took eight. I turned down jobs that required commutes of over an hour and scaled back my lifestyle to accommodate my reduced income. I brought my daughter to work more often so that we could have special time together. I even set up video conferencing on our computers so we could see each other when we were apart. And, for the first time in my career, I let my employers know in advance that I was a single mother with responsibilities and would be grateful for whatever support they could give me.

To my surprise, almost all my bosses were incredibly supportive. Many have families of their own and understand the importance of striking a balance between work and family. And since I always satisfactorily complete my work, I continue to find employment and strive toward my goals.

Now, in addition to progress in my career, I have something equally as valuable. I have wonderful memories of time spent with my daughter. I have enjoyed classroom field trips, sleepovers, mothers' day brunches, naps, visits to the manicurist, holiday performances, flu bugs, runny noses, temper tantrums, books read, movies watched, and all the wonderful moments that pass all too quickly.

To any mother struggling to balance work and child-rearing, I say strike a balance. You do not have to give up one to gain the other. Ask that you be supported at work so you can be the kind of mother you want to be. Admit you have a life outside the office. Most everyone else does! Why not you? And in my experience, the better balanced your life, the better you perform the job. There is a whole list of choices that can be just right for you in striking the balance that works best. Examine and embrace them.

**Motherhood and career are not mutually exclusive.
Strike a balance so that both aspects of your life
can be successful and rewarding. Be imaginative in
scheduling your time and ask your boss for help.**

MOMMY HAS TO GO NOW

Have you ever worked with someone who is always dealing with a personal crisis? Her son was just suspended for peeing in the toy chest at school, and she had to leave work to retrieve him. His fourth nanny just quit, and he needed a few days off to arrange day care. His teenager just got caught playing doctor with the science teacher and required immediate enrollment in boarding school. Her newborn just threw up on the babysitter, and she could not get to work on time. We all have problems, but where do you draw the line between family obligations and work? When do you skip that diaper change?

As a working mother, I have great empathy for those trying to balance work and family. I pride myself on being understanding and supportive. But as a supervisor, I have had to put my foot down when someone's home life makes it impossible for him or her to do the job. An example of this occurred with a location manager I often hired. For many years, she was the first person I called when a new project came up. She was gifted, hard-working, and reliable. I always knew I could count on her to do a first-rate job no matter the show or the players involved.

Shortly after we began preproduction on a new television series, I scheduled an appointment for her to come in to meet the producers and give them a show and tell. During this process we look at photographs of potential locations and decide which ones meet our visual and written criteria. When the location manager finally arrived for the meeting, I was beside myself with frustration. First, she arrived forty minutes late, without an explanation or apology. Second, she had her toddler attached to her hip with the attitude that this was perfectly acceptable.

As we tried to discuss the photos in detail, I watched in amazement as her son commandeered every object within his reach. It happened that the producer whose office we were using did not have children of his own and did not find her son's antics endearing in the least. Over and over again, he would leap from his chair to salvage some expensive treasure from destruction.

It became impossible to carry on any in-depth conversation as she kept interrupting us to tell her son, "No touch, no touch," which, of course, he ignored. The final straw was when she pulled his pants down to smell for "poopy." Confirming it's arrival, she left us speechless as she exited the meeting to rectify (no pun intended) the problem. Her future with me slipped away.

Another situation that comes to mind involved a wardrobe supervisor with whom I also enjoyed working. After her son was born, she became increasing unreliable. I would hire her only to have her repeatedly withdraw days before a shoot because she could not find reliable child care. While I knew how difficult her situation was, I was not willing to be continuously inconvenienced by it. Unfortunately for her, there were other people who could do the job as well and were far more reliable. I needed to have people who knew how to keep family and work in balance.

To all parents juggling kids and work, I say be organized and plan ahead. For example, do not take a job until you have reliable child care. Waiting until the last minute to obtain it may seem like a smart cost-saving measure, but you could be left stranded. Also, be prepared for the unexpected. Have backup child care for unanticipated occurrences such as: "Johnny came home sick from school," or "The babysitter did not show," or "It's a half day for teacher conferences," or "I need to work late." The list goes on and so can you.

The need for balance is clear: On the one hand, we do not want to be so committed to our careers that we neglect our families. On the other hand, we are being paid to work and we need to recognize that with that comes a certain amount of commitment. The answer lies somewhere in the middle. When at work, be at work. When at home, give undivided attention to your loved ones. Easy to say, hard to do. No one wants an employee who always has one foot out the door so plan ahead.

Do not let problems at home compromise your commitments at work. By making arrangements in advance, you will be better prepared to deal with the unexpected without neglecting your duties as either a mother or an employee.

SUMMARY OF RULES

HIRING FRIENDS OR FAMILY MEMBERS

RULE 1   To prevent inappropriate involvement of family members at work, it is essential to establish ground rules upfront. Set boundaries, emphasize noninterference, and dampen expectations of favoritism.

RULE 2   When employing intimates, friends, or family, take great care to (1) give notice to management, (2) avoid preferential treatment regardless of the personal relationship, and (3) manage all employees fairly and consistently.

BEING THERE FOR YOUR KIDS

RULE 1   Motherhood and career are not mutually exclusive. Strike a balance so that both aspects of your life can be successful and rewarding. Be imaginative in scheduling your time and ask your boss for help.

RULE 2   Do not let problems at home compromise your commitments at work. By making arrangements in advance, you will be better prepared to deal with the unexpected without neglecting your duties as either a mother or an employee.

9
Exit Strategy

KNOWING WHEN IT'S THE WRONG JOB

SUNDAY EVENING BLUES

I love Sundays. It is the one day of the week I feel no pressure; no need to run around checking things off my "to do" list. I can stay in my pj's until late afternoon, reading the Sunday paper and sipping warm cups of coffee. I can play games and color with my daughter. It is a day with no plans, no have-tos, no obligations. A day to live moment by moment unless, of course, the sunsets turn blue.

Sweet Sundays were not always so. There was a time in my life when I was working on a particular show in the Southwest and began to dread Sundays. Instead of it being a full day of rest, it became a day ending with anxiety. Around 5 P.M. on Sunday afternoons, I would begin to feel out-of-sorts. I became easily irritated by small annoyances that normally would not have mattered. A feeling of doom and gloom would wash over me, but I could not identify its source. I would feel unnaturally tired and downcast despite having had a wonderful day.

As the problem persisted, I began to experience insomnia. In the wee hours, I would lie awake holding "committee meetings" in my head. I would think about the week ahead and obsess over problems yet to occur. Even in sleep, my dreams were invaded by thoughts of work. My knight in shining armor had no chance to steal in and sweep me off my feet, whoever he was. My inauguration as president was stillborn. My walk on the moon, kaput!

By the time I made it to the office on Monday, I was tired and stressed, and this feeling would persist until Friday afternoon, when the gray cloud lifted and life would brighten. It took months for me to acknowledge this cycle.

I suspected at first I was experiencing "Sunday evening blues"—a recurring phenomenon among workers. The high stress and extremely long hours involved in film production were taking their toll. The transition between my weekend life and work life was jarring and unsettling.

On the weekends, I had the luxury of sleeping as late as I wanted. During the work week, I had to rise by five in the morning to be on set by call. On the weekends, I drove infrequently. During the work week, my commute took hours. On the weekends, I had only a few decisions to make. During the work week, I was forced to make hundreds of rapid-fire decisions in rapid-fire succession.

I became concerned that I was experiencing complete burnout and would need to find a new calling. I kept thinking, "Now what?! What else am I qualified to do? How would I do it? How would I make money?"

I decided instead to tough it out. I tried combating my Sunday depression with various techniques and distractions. When disturbing thoughts would invade my peaceful Sunday afternoons, I would write them down promising to reflect on them come Monday. I scheduled diverting and interesting activities to keep my mind occupied on Sunday evenings. I chatted with friends and shared my concerns. But no matter what I tried, by Sunday evening, you could color me blue.

Then, I started to take a closer look at specific elements of my work. Was there any way to make the job more enjoyable? Could I reframe my thinking to better appreciate and enjoy the experience? I tried to look for things to celebrate each day. I tried to focus on small accomplishments. I tried taking extra time to be more sociable, more relaxed, and more personable. While my attitude improved, my Sunday evening blues did not.

Next, I took a hard look at the show itself. How did it differ from the shows I previously enjoyed? Why did it cause me greater stress and concern? Upon reflection, the differences were substantial. The problems we were encountering seemed endless. This was, in fact, a star-crossed show. The production Gods were after me.

Weather, which is usually a minimal consideration, frequently caused work to come to a complete halt. Torrential downpours washed away our only access to a remote homestead located miles from town. Manpower and heavy equipment were needed day after day to rebuild roads. The crew became tired and irritated at having to work so often in the rain, cold, and mud. And our limited resources were draining away.

Accidents occurred much more frequently, forcing us to send a number of people to local emergency rooms. Shooting locations that had been locked down for weeks became unavailable, sending our sweet and unassuming location manager to the brink of a nervous breakdown. One of our main actors, a seasoned veteran in his early eighties, was struggling to remember his lines, causing everyone concern and frustration. Picture cars that worked beautifully during rehearsal would fail to start once the cameras rolled. Even livestock refused to cooperate.

At the insistence of our lead actor, we even called in a shaman to bless our show, hopeful he could remove the dark cloud that hung over us. Unfortunately, the shaman discovered we were filming on an ancient burial ground and could only offer limited assurances.

I realized that exhaustion, frustration, and dread had replaced my usual enthusiasm, certainty, and confidence. But what could I do?

Despite my best efforts, I wielded only so much power. Was I really expected to change the immutable? Of course not. The best I could hope for was to offer solutions, provide support, comfort those in need, and hope the sun would soon shine. In short, I once again had to accept the things I could not change, change the things I could, and not beat myself up day after day.

Upon accepting my limitations, upon remembering that I could look for something else when the season ended, my Sunday evening blues started to dissipate. I was able to enjoy every bit of my weekend and was able to use the time to rest up for the challenges that lay ahead. More importantly, I began to grasp the underlying meaning of Sunday evening blues.

Sometimes you are in such a stressful or unrewarding situation that your anxiety takes over, affecting your outlook and even your health. When this happens, identify the source of your problem. If you are continuing to suffer, make changes to improve your situation.

> **Problems at work can have a serious effect on your mental and physical well-being. Such effects are hard to recognize. "Sunday evening blues" can let you know when it is time to create or seek a more positive work environment.**

YOU HAVEN'T GROWN AN INCH

Can you do your job with one hand tied behind your back? Are you so familiar with your responsibilities that you can perform them in your sleep? Are you able to do the work of two people in half the time? If the answer to these questions is a resounding, yes, maybe it is time to quit.

Many years ago I had two production offers in hand. First, I was offered a popular teen soap opera shooting in Los Angeles. The show was an hour drama that followed the lives of a group of high school friends. The show was shot almost entirely on a soundstage with little location work. The cast was small, and there were no name actors needing special attention. The "action" consisted almost entirely of talking heads. In addition, the show was in its second season, so most of the sets were built, the contracts negotiated, and the crew hired and well trained. Overall, the show was well run. They just needed someone to keep the momentum going.

At the same time, I was offered a new series that was to shoot far from home. The show needed everything. It needed to find an abandoned warehouse and convert it into a soundstage. It needed to design and build numerous sets. It needed to find and hire an entire crew. And it needed to have all equipment deals, union contracts, and travel accommodations negotiated. The show was also extremely complicated. It presented a huge financial risk. It had a large permanent cast with numerous day players. There were special effects, stunts, and computer-generated images. The locations were treacherous and difficult to shoot—as I later confirmed to my dismay when I humped thirty pounds of camera equipment up a mountain to facilitate a panoramic ocean background shot and asked myself the time-honored question: "What the hell am I doing here?"

All in all, I knew it would be a far greater challenge to produce the second show than the teen drama, and so I accepted it. I knew the hours would be longer, the stress higher, and the problems more severe. But I believed I would be a far better producer with the experience it offered. As I made my decision, I wondered if others followed a similar philosophy.

Then, a few years ago, I attended a women's conference where Anne Sweeney was one of the speakers. Ms. Sweeney is the co-chair of Disney Media Networks and the president of Disney-ABC Television Group. She has been referred to as the "Most Powerful Woman in Entertainment" and was listed in Forbes as one of the "World's 100 Most Powerful Women." During her speech, she talked about her requirements for accepting a job. She explained that she would always choose the position for which she felt least qualified. She would choose the greater challenge. I admired her approach and would say it certainly has served her well. Her philosophy ratified my own way of thinking.

Now, some people find comfort in familiarity. Not everyone needs to be constantly challenged. Some people value the reassurance of knowing what is expected of them and the confident feeling they can deliver. They are not looking to move up or on. They want to stay where they are for as long as they can. I say good for them! Personal work styles deserve respect.

Others do not have the luxury of choice. My grandmother was one of them. When her husband died unexpectedly, she was forced to care for three small children and went to work as a piecework seamstress in a Hathaway clothing mill. The work required her to sew the same type of fabric over and over, day in and day out. Each worker was responsible for a different part of the shirt: some sewed button holes, some zippers, some collars, and some shirt sleeves. Since they were paid by the piece, the more familiar they were with the process, the faster they sewed and the more money they made. In effect, they could not change jobs if they wanted to.

I tried envisioning myself in her shoes: the same repetitive motion, every minute of every day, year after year. The mere thought was simply horrifying. I realized that I had been given a gift: the opportunity to take risks and to challenge myself. Unlike my grandmother, I could try new things. I knew I needed to make the most of it.

I have done so at every turn. Very recently I was offered a children's television series scheduled to begin its second season. It offered shorter hours and fewer headaches. I thought how nice work could be without potential disasters at every turn. No more standing on a street corner waiting for the rain to pass. No more praying that the car will flip properly and no one will get hurt. No more panic when a location is lost, and there is nowhere else to film. But as I considered taking the offer, something strange happened: I noticed I was not nervous. I did not have butterflies in my stomach. I did not feel anxious or the least bit uneasy. Clearly, this was not the show for me.

I needed to feel out of my element, just a little. You know, the old "fish out of water" plot line. Feelings of uneasiness confirmed that I was stretching, that I was challenging myself to learn more and to accomplish more. I did not want a show I could do with my eyes closed. I wanted a show that required me to be on tiptoes.

Without being properly challenged, we can become lethargic, unmotivated, passive, and disinterested. When you find that your job no longer challenges you, it might be time for a change. Ask for more responsibility. Try a new position in the company. If absolutely necessary, put feelers out and start looking for new opportunities. By continuing to reach, we stay engaged and focused and that makes work far more rewarding.

**Work should be challenging and stimulating.
Reach beyond your grasp. Seek positions that allow for
learning and growth. Let apprehension be your guide.**

HAVING THE FREEDOM TO WALK

MONEY MAKES MY WORLD GO WHEREVER I WANT IT TO

Are you prepared for a rainy day? I am not talking about raincoats and galoshes. I am taking about savings as in money in the bank. Anyone working freelance knows you should have six to nine months worth of savings to cover you in case of emergency (i.e., unemployment). I suppose the same is true for those holding regular jobs. Unfortunately, many of the people I know in the film business do not have enough to cover a pizza and a beer. For them, once the boat leaves the dock, they might find themselves up the creek without a kayak.

As I write this, I can think of numerous friends and colleagues who would switch careers tomorrow if money were not a factor. I know a high-powered lawyer who would much rather be teaching high school math but cannot afford to do so. A friend of mine in advertising has spent years dreaming about owning a bed and breakfast, but his overhead requirements keep him plugging away at something he finds entirely unrewarding. Even my dentist laments his choice to follow in his father's footsteps; hoping one day he can follow his dream of becoming an actor.

Techies want to be writers, writers want to be psychologists, psychologists want to be attorneys, and attorneys want to be artists. Maybe we should all just switch places.

In an earlier chapter I mentioned I felt trapped in my original career as an accountant. I knew I was not satisfied with the work but had grown accustomed to the money and lifestyle it provided. I had to ask myself, "Are you willing to compromise your financial security to try something new?" I decided that yes, I was, and proceeded to accept whatever pay cut was necessary. And what a pay cut it was! I went from approximately $1,500 a week (this was years ago) to as little as $300 a week, depending on the project. But it was a cut I could live with. Not only was I doing something I enjoyed, I knew in time my value and compensation would rise. That had only been possible because I had saved for a rainy day. I understood that having enough savings to carry me through the rough times made it possible for me to achieve my goals. Had I been buried under a mountain of financial obligations, I would still be a practicing CPA and not a very happy one.

My view of money changed in another way. While I had expected to mourn the loss of my spending power, the opposite was true. I no longer needed to buy the latest and greatest toy to make myself feel better. I did not need to acquire a new wardrobe to make up for the stuff that was lacking. I was not using money to satisfy some unfulfilled desire. Since I was more satisfied with my life as a whole, the money had less importance to me.

Then I met someone who confirmed my beliefs. I was working in the mountains filming a series of water-related stunts. In addition to the stuntmen, we hired a group of extreme sportsman to provide safety for the cast and crew. Their job was to rig and monitor safety lines to which the crew secured themselves while working in dangerous areas. They also manned safety boats in case an accident occurred. And on the rare occasion a piece of equipment or a clumsy crew member fell into the torrent, they would chase them downstream and rescue them. I watched in awe as they navigated each body of water with skill and ease.

One weekend, the leader of the group offered to fulfill a life-long dream of mine by teaching me to kayak. Let me share my kayaking "fun" for you: rollovers, lost paddles, repeated rescues, coughed-up river water, the surface-reflected image of a drowned rat, a kayak-hefting, exhausting trek uphill from riverbank to road, the deflating absence of a waiting pickup truck, and the one-and-a-half mile Bataan death march back to the put-in point. Where was the limo?! My kingdom for a limo!

After the day of "fun" in the sun, he invited me back to his house to join him and his girlfriend for dinner. I should point out that my host was one of the most recognized and sought-after rafters in the world. Having negotiated his deal, I knew he came with a hefty price tag. Despite all of that, he lived a modest existence.

His home was a small wooden shack he had personally built deep in the woods. The power was provided by a jury-rigged line attached to a city-owned utility pole. Even the plumbing was a recent addition: it made the adjacent outhouse obsolete. That was something I deeply appreciated.

He went on to explain that he was a "squatter" and had obtained rights to the land after living on it unnoticed for a number of years. When I questioned his motives, he shared his life philosophy: "Work only as much as is necessary to sustain a peaceful existence." According to his calculations, he was able to survive on about $5,000 a year. The work he was currently doing on our show would last him for a very long time. As soon as we were finished filming, he planned to divide his time between Canada and Costa Rica doing what he loved best: skiing and white-water rafting.

I must say I was impressed. But I knew I could never follow in his footsteps: heat and running water are far too important to me. But I did admire his frugality and the simplicity it brought to his life. In his mind, a body of water, a loving partner, a pair of skis, a good kayak, and a lot of rice were all he really needed. He taught me that as long as we believe material gain is the primary source of our happiness, we will fail to live fully. If, instead, we view money as a security net, a foundation, a tool to design the life we want, I am convinced we will be more fulfilled.

Therefore, stop spending every dime you have and start saving. Eventually, that little nest egg will grow and afford you new opportunities. Your pot of gold could allow you to continue your education, start a business, say no to an unfulfilling career, or even write a book. All it takes is a little discipline and some smart choices.

Nest eggs are not just for retirement or a luxury treat or an unspecified rainy day. They are the single-most important asset you have to ensure career satisfaction.

IS BURGER KING HIRING?

Have you ever spent time in the unemployment line? I have. For those in the entertainment business, unemployment is never far off. It is almost a lifestyle. The president of the studio is fired, the show's ratings tank, the show runner has a nervous breakdown, the lead actor is back in rehab, or you just need a change and suddenly—bingo!—out of work again. Take heart, you will not only endure, you will prevail. If not, there is a fast-food paper hat waiting for you.

I was recently out of work for ten months. I was also struggling to make a position change. I wanted to make a vertical move upward to full producer and thus provide myself with more challenging work and greater compensation. I decided that to make that happen, I needed to keep myself available for the right job when it came along. Instead of taking a show that did not meet my criteria, I would hold out for exactly what I wanted.

I needed to do this because in network television there are essentially two hiring seasons per year: one is pilot season in the beginning of the year and the other is when new series go into production after the summer. If you are already working on a show when pilot season rolls around, you are not available to accept a better job with a different show without breaking prior commitments. The same holds true if you are working on a regular series after the summer.

The result of my holding out was the rejection of a number of job offers, a lot of quality time with my daughter, and not much money in the bank. I can tell you, it was a very sobering experience. I worried a great deal about my financial security and what the future would hold. From time to time, I wavered in my conviction and considered giving up and going back to doing what I had done before. Several especially difficult decisions faced me during pilot season. I had already been out of work for six months and was distracted with worry. Since pilot season is a very busy time in television, I knew I would receive a number of offers. But would they be the ones I wanted? The calls came in, but I bowed out.

Then a producer friend of mine called. I had not worked with him for many years, but we maintained a solid friendship. He was producing a network series that was touted as one of the next big hits, and he wanted me as a co-producer. The show was well written, the cast top rate, there was travel involved, and it would provide much needed income. I was at a loss to know what to do. The thought of giving up my dream and taking the show because of exigencies was too depressing to contemplate. But what if nothing else came along? Did I believe in myself enough to hold out?

After careful consideration, I decided holding out was the right thing to do and that the risk would eventually pay off. So, I reluctantly turned down the show. I wish I could say I was elated by my decision. The truth was I was a cathedral of ticks.

Another four months passed without work, and I began to lose confidence in my abilities. I began to think I would never work again. To assuage my fears, I reminded myself that I was highly employable and could get a lesser job easily. But self-doubt was my new best friend. It made me suspect I was entirely lacking in critical skills.

Sure, I knew how to stroke egos and placate unjustified fears. I knew how to assure someone that despite their anorexic frame, they did not look fat on camera. I knew how to calm an executive who could not find a parking place for his Ferrari. I even knew how to coax the disgruntled out of a trailer when the door was locked and tears were involved. I also knew how to obtain hot food for two hundred in under an hour, locate a black bear that could dance in circles, build a space capsule in a day or two, get a horse to talk, make someone fly, have objects disappear, and even make it snow. But was I top-drawer producer material?

To make matters worse, I had a friend who was struggling with her own unemployment situation. She had been out of work for a long, long time and was contemplating a career change. Together, we shared our concerns and tried to help build each other's spirits.

Allow me to mention that my friend is a very talented production designer with a blue-chip résumé. She started working in costuming on Broadway, then as a scenic artist in theater, then as a set decorator in films, and finally as a production designer. On some shows, she had a large staff executing her vision. On other projects, she could be found with a hammer and nail putting a set together herself.

Her mettle was really tested when we worked on a show that used a house built on a marsh, and she added a gazebo, an animal compound, a pond, and a pier in the expansive backyard—all of which kept sinking through twenty-two episodes. With Styrofoam, jacks, paint, and perspective, she kept it all "above ground," while wading in knee-high mud from the daily downpour.

As I analyzed her situation, I realized that her experiences had served her well. She was resourceful, creative, artistic, and extremely responsible: all qualities any employer would value. I knew without a doubt that, in time, these skills would again be put to good use.

Why was her worth so clear to me while mine was so cloudy? I needed to look harder at my own experiences. Damn it, I had a lot to offer! I needed to keep the faith that there was a job out there for me. And there was. After ten long months, a full producer's job was offered and accepted.

Despite our varied backgrounds, we all have valuable skills. Do not underestimate your qualifications. Like me, your journey may not be a traditional one, but it has provided you with a bushel basket of worthwhile skills. Do not let fear of unemployment keep you from making changes in your career. We all fear the unknown and often doubt ourselves, but there are always good jobs out there for good people. And you will find one, too. In the meantime, you can always flip burgers.

If unemployed, brace yourself. You will be consumed by doubt and uncertainty. Expect it, receive it, confront it, and overcome it. Trust in your experience and qualifications. You can always find work.

MOM . . . I'M HOME

Are you worried about that empty nest? You should not be. Today, fourteen million adult children in the United States live at home with their parents. Canada is experiencing a similar trend. Perhaps the fact that we have become a downwardly mobile society contributes to this. It is no longer assured that we will create a better life for ourselves than our parents did for themselves, not with escalating housing costs and increasing personal debt. So when does it make sense for a child to return to the nest and announce, "Mom . . . I'm home!"

As I mentioned, after seventeen years in the film business, I decided it was time for a change. I wanted to take the next step in my career and needed to position myself so that I would be available when opportunity knocked. I began as a production accountant, moved up to production executive, then to production manager, and finally to co-producer. Then, it was time to stretch again. My goal was full producer, and I was determined to make it happen.

Prior to this decision, I worked steadily from one job to the next with little downtime. As long as a project interested and challenged me and I liked the people involved, I eagerly accepted attractive offers. Although I always wanted to move up in my career, I never made myself available to do so. As luck would have it, whenever I was offered the perfect job, I was always committed to another project. This had to change. I realized I needed to stop accepting work that did not meet my personal goal. I realized I needed to take a risk, a substantial risk.

To facilitate this, I decided to view the challenge the same way someone would view launching a business. I knew that the start-up would be lean and I needed to position myself so that money would not be a factor in my decision-making process. Previously, I had enjoyed a fairly comfortable lifestyle. As a single mother, I was paying for a four-bedroom home in an expensive part of Los Angeles. I had my daughter in private school, and I employed a full-time, live-in nanny. Something had to give. I had to find a way to eliminate money pressures from the equation.

Then, over dinner one night, my father suggested I move back in with my mother. *What! Are you out of your mind?!* I should mention my mother and father have been divorced for thirty years. While his offer was incredibly generous, he, of course, had no right to make it. Nevertheless, my mother got wind of it and made the same offer. I knew she would welcome me and her granddaughter with open arms.

At first, it was something I would not consider. I was a grown woman, used to having my own home filled with my own things. I could come and go as I please, entertain who I wished, and create an atmosphere that was right for me and my daughter. How could I possibly live under someone else's roof? What would my friends think? How could I have a date pick me up at my mother's house? Aaaaghhh! The horror. The horror.

But as I thought more about it, I had to weigh what was more important to me: continuing in jobs that were leaving me dissatisfied or taking a risk to do something more rewarding. I realized that if I did not take my shot, I would regret not having tried. And so, I "temporarily" took the plunge. After all, the meaning of life is a deathbed without regrets.

I almost cried as the moving truck carried my stuff to storage. Good-bye 600-thread-count California king sheets. Hello lumpy queen in the guest room. My how I had fallen. But I am happy to report it worked out quite well, and the benefits have been many. Now, when I come home at the end of a long day, I have another adult with whom to socialize. My daughter gets to spend quality time with her grandmother. And most importantly, I am able to save money; I'm empowered to turn down unsatisfying work and privileged to accept work I enjoy.

I also clean my plate, keep my elbows off the table, never slurp my soup, carry my dishes to the kitchen, use my indoor voice, play my music softly, pick up my clothes, and never, ever talk with my mouth full.

The payoff? I recently signed a great deal to produce a new television series about a woman trying to make it in Hollywood. Talk about your karma!

Sometimes we need to take two steps back before we can take one step forward. And sometimes we have to make huge compromises to make a dream come true. Hey, maybe that spare bedroom at Mom's is empty and waiting.

When confronting tough career choices, audit your assets to see which will enhance your bargaining position. Family and friends are superb resources in that regard. Engage their help without imposing.

LEAVING WITH DIGNITY

FIREPROOF YOUR BRIDGE

Have you ever wanted to tell your boss to go fly a kite? Or wanted to give that annoying co-worker a piece of your mind? Or craved the freedom to speak honestly about all that is wrong with the organization? As appealing as these outbursts might be, you might want to think twice about doing them. Burning bridges just leaves rubble.

As I discussed in chapter 5, I was forced to withdraw from a show as a result of alcohol abuse on set that I could not eliminate. The decision was difficult for me. First, it meant severing ties, even temporarily, with a studio that had provided me with numerous employment opportunities. Second, it meant giving up long-term employment and substantial compensation on a well-respected show. Third, it meant disappointing people on the project who had come to count on me and did not want me to leave.

Even though I was forced into the decision to resign, I was fearful I would be burning bridges I had worked years to build. In a town that runs on reputation and references, leaving a show like this would be a black mark on my record. At the very least, it would require extensive explanation in all subsequent interviews. I realized the only way I could feel good about my decision, and my departure was to do everything I could to make my withdrawal a positive experience for both me and my co-workers. So this is what I did:

First, I assured the studio that I would assist in any way I could to help find my replacement. I sat in on interviews, spoke privately with candidates, and gave my opinions when asked.

Second, I agreed to stay as long as it would take to make sure my replacement was fully knowledgeable and ready to take over the reins. For two weeks, I continued to come to the office and do my job with a smile on my face. I offered my replacement complete support and did everything I could to communicate any and all necessary information to assure his success.

Third, I made sure I completed every piece of work that was pending on my desk so my replacement could start with a clean slate. I consulted with him and tried to incorporate his wishes in every decision of significance.

Fourth, I made an appointment to meet with the very people who had defied my orders and in doing so caused my departure. I listened to their criticism of me and offered them advice I hoped would serve them well in the future.

Finally, I made it a point to go to all the various producers to thank them for the opportunity they had given me and to wish them well in the future.

The final two weeks were especially difficult. Many people were angry at me for leaving and made a point of letting me know it. Others were openly hostile as they disliked the changes I tried to make. Some were delighted by my departure and spoke openly about it. And many, many others showed their support and sympathy. I was moved to tears when members of the costume, transportation, accounting, and props departments pleaded with me to stay, and deeply touched when the director of photography called a halt to filming to hug me good-bye on set. But despite all the emotions and difficulties, I was and am glad I maintained the same level of commitment at the end of my job as I had at the beginning.

All in all, I can happily report the fallout was minimal. The studio has since rehired me, and all the producers have, to my knowledge, given me positive references. What could have been an ugly and painful departure turned out to be a great learning experience. Instead of harboring negative feelings about what had happened, I took it as an opportunity to broaden my horizons and solidify my reputation.

There will come a time when you will have to say good-bye to the people with whom you are working. Whether it is your choice to leave or the choice is made for you, think long and hard about the legacy you wish to leave behind. Take great care in establishing your departing image. Do not be remembered as someone who behaved badly or was hostile or retaliatory. Give people a chance to be surprised and impressed by your dignity, your commitment, and your professionalism.

> **Appropriate departures are as much a part of career success as judicious job selection and outstanding job performance. Be helpful, dignified, hard working, and cheerful as you head for the exit, whether voluntarily or involuntarily.**

FRIENDS PLUS FEAR EQUALS FOE

Survival of the fittest: the idea that the strong survive and the weak perish. In business, people align themselves with the fittest with alacrity. Perhaps it is our need to associate with success that causes us to do so. But what happens when success slips away? John Kennedy mused after the Bay of Pigs fiasco, "Victory has a thousand fathers, but defeat is an orphan." In film, the orphanages are packed.

You can always tell when a show you are working on is in trouble. An eerie silence descends over the production office. Phones that once rang off the hook become quiescent. Associates who returned calls immediately suddenly take days to respond. You feel like a leper in a massage parlor. No one in the business wants to be near you.

One of the sadder realities of the film business is that people fall out of favor ever so quickly. For those on the creative side in particular, the job can swiftly become a minefield of unfair practices and frequent disappointments. Shows are cancelled after just two airings; actors are recast if they do not test well; directors are blamed for problems beyond their control; and show runners are abandoned even though they created the show.

Imagine originating something worthwhile, getting it made, getting it sold, and then being told you are incapable of managing it further? It is very depressing and disheartening for those who fall from grace.

I remember working on a pilot that was cancelled even before the cameras started rolling. The studio was unhappy with the script and decided with considerable justification not to spend millions on the project. Unfortunately, the decision was not made until we were well into preproduction. We had already set up offices, scouted locations, hired crew, negotiated deals, and flown the head writer/creator in from New York. Nonetheless, I got the "end it" call one morning on my way to the office. Per the studio, all work was to stop immediately, all contracts were to be terminated, and all offices were to be shut down. I promptly went about the business of closing up shop.

The problem was that no one remembered to tell the head writer that his baby had been killed. Assuming he was the first to have been notified, I called him to coordinate his flight arrangements home. He was horribly surprised and extremely upset by my call. It was awful. I became an unwitting executioner nonpareil.

On another occasion, I watched sadly as the show runner of a network thriller was replaced. Apparently his vision no longer conformed to the vision of the creative executive at the studio. This was hard to understand since we were making the very same show that had been successfully sold to a network that appeared to love it. Inexplicably, the creative executive converted a dark, sci-fi thriller for teens into a version of Scooby Doo, and the show was history after a couple of episodes.

Another setback occurred when a director I know delivered a mediocre pilot to the studio. Prior to our association, he had received acclaim for an independent feature he had written and directed. He came to us as the new golden boy. He was adored by the studio during prep and most of the shoot. But his name became mud when for reasons unknown he ultimately delivered a substandard product and could not live up to the reputation that preceded him. Unfortunately, he was never able to recover from this failing and was eventually pushed out.

You can just picture the denouement: The producers receive copies of the director's cut of the pilot for individual review. Then, they meet to discuss it. If it is good, they happily compare notes. If it is not, darkness descends. They hem, they haw, they shuffle, they shift. No one wants to be the first to let the cat out of the bag. A polite reference here, a tentative critique there, some honesty, a bit more candor, then—*bam!* Slash, burn, gouge, rip, pummel, and pound. "What a maroon!" "What treacle!" Devastated and depressed, they trudge slowly toward the editing room with visions of pink slips dancing in their heads.

But in all these instances, the hiring pattern was similar. First, the prodigy was praised, admired, even revered by the people who had hired him. He was thus enabled to make stiff demands, such as a salary of $35,000 an episode, creative control, and an excessive staff. Then, as time wore on, people started to lose confidence, question their hiring decision, fear failure by association, and as quickly as the wind changes direction, they jump ship. The phrase "You're on your own" comes to mind.

How was it manifested? People distanced themselves quickly. Personal relationships took on a cooler tone. Few were available to lend support. Calls went unanswered. After all, once the prodigy became contagious, no one wanted to risk catching his cold.

Having said all that, the good news in Hollywood is that everyone is capable of a comeback. Just look at Maria Carey or John Travolta or Rob Lowe. Hollywood is always ready to give people a second chance; especially if they have something it wants, and that something is talent. Additionally, much of the success of their comebacks was attributable to the exemplary manner in which they conducted themselves when the going got tough.

In the three examples I cited above regarding the head writer, the show runner, and the director, the crestfallen behaved differently. One lashed out by whining and complaining to anyone who would listen. One simply packed up his toys and went home with little fanfare.

And one departed with his head held high and his dignity intact. He acknowledged and accepted what had happened. He tried to focus on the positive aspects of what had occurred. He continued to communicate openly and to treat everyone he spoke to with respect. In doing so, he maintained his reputation and prestige.

It is easy to be confident, cooperative, positive, and respectful when everything is going your way. The true test of character is when things are not in your favor; when you are left to twist slowly in the wind. It is not easy to be civil to those who are trying to diss or diminish you. By maintaining your integrity and always acting in a professional manner, you show your critics that you may be battered and bruised, but you are not beaten.

Despite the way some people are treating you, despite being abandoned by your peers, respond with integrity, dignity, and class. In doing so, you will depart leaving a positive impression on even your severest critics. Here is where "what goes around comes around" really counts.

HAVING A PLAN B

MY PRETEND JOB

"Help! I can't get off the couch!" After all, Martha is on at 10 A.M. followed by the Gilmore Girls at 11, then two solid hours of soaps. After that, Maury at 2, Oprah at 3, and Dr. Phil or Ellen at 4. Luckily, by then, the kids are returning from school and need your attention. If not, you have HGTV to help you remodel on a budget. If you have a DVR, well, the sky's the limit. Just pray that hubby does not ask what you did all day or you might have to back and fill. Instead, let's pretend . . .

I was having dinner recently with a group of girlfriends; all of whom have elementary schoolchildren and have or have had lucrative careers. One owns a tea house; one is a systems analyst; and one was an attorney in a prior life. The attorney gave up the law temporarily to become a stay-at-home mommy. Over dinner, she admitted to us how utterly bored she was with her current "assignment" and how desperately she needed to get back to work. To my surprise, she admitted watching copious amounts of daytime television as a diversion.

Now, I am personally in awe of people who can lounge around with their feet up watching television during the day. Maybe it is because I attended a special church for children of Jewish-Catholic marriages. You know, the Church of Our Lady of Perpetual Guilt. But when I try to do the same, I am filled with shame. I am afraid I will be "outed" and looked down upon for being unproductive. But I know someone must be watching the shows or they would not be on the air.

So, let's 'fess up. Who watches? Hands please!

Yowza! That many!? It is clearly a downtime narcotic. The more you watch, the more you need.

And it can be mighty tempting. We have all been out of work, even for a little while. Perhaps we are taking a few years off to raise our children. Maybe we are in between jobs and trying to decide on our next move. Perhaps we have just been fired and need to heal our wounds. Or perhaps we just need a break from the daily grind. Whatever our reasons, having too much free time on our hands can, in my opinion, be a slippery slope to sloth. But let us not pick on television alone.

Without direction or obligation, we can become lost in our own boredom. It is like slipping into depression; it becomes a vicious cycle that cannot be broken. We lack motivation to accomplish goals, so we do nothing. Without accomplishments to keep us inspired, we flounder. We become trapped in a downward spiral. Television vegging is just one manifestation of the problem.

I have personally had numerous periods of unemployment. A show ends, and another is not scheduled to start for months. A project is unexpectedly cancelled, and everyone is out of work. Pilot season is deferred until the first of the year. Whatever the circumstance, there are always gaps in my employment.

Early in my career, I took advantage of the downtime by attending classes or catching up on my reading. It did not take long before I lamented my freedom. The truth was, I was bored out of my mind. Working in an industry that accomplishes so much in such a short period of time made it impossible for me to find satisfaction in an activity without prompt, tangible results. Somehow, completing my grocery shopping for the week was just not enough. I knew I needed to have a purpose, and so I set out to create one.

It backfired. I set myself up in a friend's office where I had my own phone line and could stay busy away from home. So that callers might assume I was both important and employed, I answered the phone in a falsetto thusly:

"Hello, Cellar Door Productions."

"Is Danielle Weinstock in?"

"One moment, please. May I tell her who's calling?"

"Danielle? . . . Is that you?"

(Sudden panic. Deafening silence.)

"Danielle? Come on, I know it's you!"

(Click.)

Once mortified, twice shy. I concluded there must be a better way. I had to analyze my downtime needs more thoroughly.

For me, the discipline of going to work each day was very important. So in between shows, I started setting up a temporary office where I could go and simulate relevant work. I would force myself to spend a few hours each day being productive. During that time, I would read books about entertainment, analyze classic movies, market myself, send out résumés, read the trades, and keep up with work-related contacts. I even set aside a certain number of hours to write so I could better understand scripts and story construction.

The goal was simple: Stay involved in a pertinent way. Even when I was out of work, I needed to feel the sense of drive that I had on the job. When someone asked what I did for a living, I wanted to give more of an answer than "flipping channels."

We all need to be challenged, to strive for our goals, to feel proud of our successes. We all need projects that inspire us and keep us engaged so that we can continue to develop, learn, and grow. If you are out of work whether temporarily or permanently, create a pretend job to capture and sustain that challenge. Just think, you can even be president!

> **During employment downtime, stay motivated by creating a pretend job. The commitment, discipline, and challenge will keep you focused and will counter both malaise and depression.**

I'M STILL A CONTRIBUTING MEMBER OF SOCIETY

Ours is a culture preoccupied with titles. The more important your title, the more important you must be. After all, what is the first thing someone asks you? "So, what do you do for a living?" And you answer with pride, "I am an advertising executive." "I am a certified public accountant." "I am a landscape architect." But what if what you do does not fit into a respectable category? Indeed, what if you have no title at all?

Titles, or credits as we call them, are very important in the film business. When I started working in film, I refused to get swept up in the title mania. Young and naïve, I believed that it was not what you were called but what you accomplished that mattered. Then my great circular journey to reality began.

Some titles are clearer than others. Animal trainer, for instance, tells you exactly what someone does. The same holds true for costumer, lighting technician, and stuntman. Then, there are titles incomprehensible to the uninitiated. Gang boss, captain, and best boy, for example, mean little to the outside world. You might think these titles mean, respectively, someone in the Mafia, someone directing a vessel, and just a really great guy. Actually, a gang boss runs a construction crew, a captain runs transportation, and a best boy runs the grip or electric department.

There is also a plethora of producer credits: executive producer, co-executive producer, supervising producer, line producer, producer, co-producer, associate producer, and production executive. Not only does each title mean something different, they vary from show to show and from features to television.

Normally, in television, the executive producer is the show's creator and head writer. Then the co-executive producer would be an additional head writer brought in to oversee the direction of the show. The supervising producer could be a high-level writer or a line producer who is being rewarded for exceptional service. A line producer is someone who is responsible for physical production. The producer and co-producer could be just about anyone; even someone's friend. The associate producer is usually in charge of post-production, and the production executive is often a studio executive who is overseeing the show.

Why is all this important, other than to give agents something to negotiate? Because credits affect people in a variety of ways. First, they determine the power structure: who is on top, who has authority, who makes the ultimate decisions. Next, they affect how and to what degree someone is involved. Are they included in creative discussions? Is their advice sought on important matters? What meetings may they attend? And finally, credits have a significant effect on compensation. Obviously, the higher the title, the higher the pay.

I finally had to accept the fact that my title mattered. In my case, a title often means the difference between participating or not participating in casting and post-production—two of my favorite specialties.

In fact, I was once rudely dismissed (with some panache, I must admit) from an editing session when the studio executive asked, "Who are you?'

"I'm the co-producer," I responded with pride, having just delivered the show on budget.

"Could you get me some coffee?" he asked, and then sent me away with a casual wave of his hand. Apparently, my title was insufficient to allow me to participate at his level.

But having a top credit is not enough. Equally important is the type of show on which a credit is earned. Is it a popular prime-time network drama or a children's Saturday morning series? Does it feature name actors, or is it on some obscure cable channel which has no money? And of great significance, who is watching and what kind of ratings does the show command?

Everyone with whom you come in contact in the business is interested in your standing. Whether you are waiting on set, sharing a cup of coffee with colleagues, or networking at a party, you can bet the first question asked of you will be, "So, what are you working on?" The unstated portion of the question is, "What is your title, so I know how powerful you are?"

I have been asked the question and answered it thousands of times. Sometimes, I beam with pride. "Oh, I've been working as a producer on _____." But just as often, I tuck my tail between my legs and answer, "Oh, I've been out of work awhile." Sometimes you're on top, sometimes you're not.

But when questioned this way, you must, of course, defend your honor by continuing on with, "I'm waiting to hear about a show my agent hooked me up with," or "I was supposed to do that Fox comedy but the plug was pulled." Anything to assure yourself and others that, "*I am not a failure! I am a contributing member of society!*"

It seems ridiculous, but most of us overly define ourselves by what we do and what we are called. It is not just peer pressure from outside forces that perpetuates the importance of titles. It is something with which we identify on a very personal level. Perhaps there is a self-justification gene deep inside. We define our value by titles, and when a title is no longer attached to our name, we have to redefine ourselves all over again.

My personal experience with titles caused some curious and unforeseen reactions such as:

- Frustration: when my parents kept introducing me incorrectly to friends as a production assistant (an entry-level gopher), despite my working as a production supervisor;

- Amazement: at the feeding frenzy for titles when a co-worker was promoted and everyone else in the pecking order clamored to move up;

- Embarrassment: when my credit (name and title) at the beginning of a particular show always seemed to be displayed while sexually explicit material from the show's opening sequence played underneath; and

- Delight: when, after my work on a feature film, I learned of my secret promotion from production supervisor to associate producer by watching the credits roll on at the premier.

Since I have lived a lifetime in the freelance world, I understand how fleeting titles can be. They change every few months, time and time again. I therefore have come to terms with my fleeting fame. I realize that I am who I am: a mother, a friend, a sister, a daughter, and sometimes a producer. Very simply, I value myself by the experiences I have, the knowledge I possess, and the values by which I live. I am not what I do.

There will always be another show and another person asking, "So, what have you been working on?" And no matter my response, I will deliver it with the same level of pride as if I were at the top of the pecking order.

So when you find yourself between jobs, when you do not have a title to brandish, remember where you came from and where you are going. Your history and your future are as important to the person you are as a few letters after your name.

**No matter where you are in your career or your life,
you are still a contributing member of society.
Who you are and how you live are what really matters.
Titles and positions are useful to focus ambition but
are siren songs for the credulous.**

SUMMARY OF RULES

KNOWING WHEN IT'S THE WRONG JOB

RULE 1 Problems at work can have a serious effect on your mental and physical well-being. Such effects are hard to recognize. "Sunday evening blues" can let you know when it is time to create or seek a more positive work environment.

RULE 2 Work should be challenging and stimulating. Reach beyond your grasp. Seek positions that allow for learning and growth. Let apprehension be your guide.

HAVING THE FREEDOM TO WALK

RULE 1 Nest eggs are not just for retirement or a luxury treat or an unspecified rainy day. They are the single-most important asset you have to ensure career satisfaction.

RULE 2 If unemployed, brace yourself. You will be consumed by doubt and uncertainty. Expect it, receive it, confront it, and overcome it. Trust in your experience and qualifications. You can always find work.

RULE 3 When confronting tough career choices, audit your assets to see which will enhance your bargaining position. Family and friends are superb resources in that regard. Engage their help without imposing.

LEAVING WITH DIGNITY

RULE 1   Appropriate departures are as much a part of career success as judicious job selection and outstanding job performance. Be helpful, dignified, hard working, and cheerful as you head for the exit, whether voluntarily or involuntarily.

RULE 2   Despite the way some people are treating you, despite being abandoned by your peers, respond with integrity, dignity, and class. In doing so, you will depart leaving a positive impression on even your severest critics. Here is where "what goes around comes around" really counts.

HAVING A PLAN B

RULE 1   During employment downtime, stay motivated by creating a pretend job. The commitment, discipline, and challenge will keep you focused and will counter both malaise and depression.

RULE 2   No matter where you are in your career or your life, you are still a contributing member of society. Who you are and how you live are what really matters. Titles and positions are useful to focus ambition but are siren songs for the credulous.

10
FINAL THOUGHTS

A PATH FOR CONSIDERATION

In reviewing the lessons I learned on a film set to derive an appropriate conclusion for my unsolicited advice, it occurred to me that I was heading toward delivering pompous, predictable, and presumptuous platitudes worthy of Patty Perfect, Goody Two-shoes, Mary Poppins, and the Girl Scouts of America. The saccharin alone would kill you.

But as contemplation turned to reflection to revelation, it also occurred to me that if the platitudes could be harnessed in a meaningful way to a methodology that would yield a beneficial result, the exercise might be worth the effort. I decided therefore to enlist the following paradigm in my analysis:

PLATITUDES

achieved by a

METHODOLOGY

lead to a

BENEFICIAL RESULT

It also became clear that I needed to apply the paradigm to both business and personal affairs because the two are utterly interdependent: they reinforce each other, complement each other, and validate each other. Together they lead to a higher accomplishment. I therefore concluded that:

IN YOUR BUSINESS LIFE, YOU SHOULD BE

Professional
Mature
Dedicated
Committed
Industrious
Creative
Imaginative
Evenhanded
Even-tempered
Flexible
Reasonable
Timely
Dependable
Candid
A team player

IN YOUR PERSONAL LIFE, YOU SHOULD BE

Considerate
Generous
Nonjudgmental
Understanding
Caring
Decent
Unselfish
Respectful
Sincere
Fair
Compassionate
Thoughtful
Cooperative
Charitable
Patient

WHICH IS ACHIEVED BY

Hard work

WHICH IS ACHIEVED BY

Reason

AND RESULTS IN

Success

AND RESULTS IN

Self-respect

Then, to the extent you can combine these characteristics from your business and personal life, your life will be well lived.